Praise For America's Test Kitchen Titles

"If there's room in the budget for one multicooker/Instant Pot cookbook, make it this one."
BOOKLIST ON *MULTICOOKER PERFECTION*

"This book upgrades slow cooking for discriminating, 21st-century palates—that is indeed revolutionary."
THE DALLAS MORNING NEWS ON *SLOW COOKER REVOLUTION*

"This book begins with a detailed buying guide, a critical summary of available sizes and attachments, and a list of clever food processor techniques. Easy and versatile dishes follow . . . Both new and veteran food processor owners will love this practical guide."
LIBRARY JOURNAL ON *FOOD PROCESSOR PERFECTION*

"Another winning cookbook from ATK. . . . The folks at America's Test Kitchen apply their rigorous experiments to determine the facts about these pans."
BOOKLIST ON *COOK IT IN CAST IRON*

"It's all about technique and timing, and the ATK crew delivers their usual clear instructions to ensure success. . . . The thoughtful balance of practicality and imagination will inspire readers of all tastes and skill levels."
PUBLISHERS WEEKLY (STARRED REVIEW) ON *HOW TO ROAST EVERYTHING*

"This encyclopedia of meat cookery would feel completely overwhelming if it weren't so meticulously organized and artfully designed. This is Cook's Illustrated at its finest."
THE KITCHN ON *THE COOK'S ILLUSTRATED MEAT BOOK*

Selected as the Cookbook Award Winner of 2017 in the Baking Category
INTERNATIONAL ASSOCIATION OF CULINARY PROFESSIONALS (IACP) ON *BREAD ILLUSTRATED*

"The book offers an impressive education for curious cake makers, new and experienced alike. A summation of 25 years of cake making at ATK, there are cakes for every taste."
THE WALL STREET JOURNAL ON *THE PERFECT CAKE*

Selected as one of the 10 Best New Cookbooks of 2017
THE LA TIMES ON *THE PERFECT COOKIE*

"The 21st-century *Fannie Farmer Cookbook* or *The Joy of Cooking*. If you had to have one cookbook and that's all you could have, this one would do it."
CBS SAN FRANCISCO ON *THE NEW FAMILY COOKBOOK*

"The go-to gift book for newlyweds, small families, or empty nesters."
ORLANDO SENTINEL ON *THE COMPLETE COOKING FOR TWO COOKBOOK*

"The sum total of exhaustive experimentation . . . anyone interested in gluten-free cookery simply shouldn't be without it."
NIGELLA LAWSON ON *THE HOW CAN IT BE GLUTEN-FREE COOKBOOK*

"A one-volume kitchen seminar, addressing in one smart chapter after another the sometimes surprising whys behind a cook's best practices. . . . You get the myth, the theory, the science, and the proof, all rigorously interrogated as only America's Test Kitchen can do."
NPR ON *THE SCIENCE OF GOOD COOKING*

"The perfect kitchen home companion. . . . The practical side of things is very much on display . . . cook-friendly and kitchen-oriented, illuminating the process of preparing food instead of mystifying it."
THE WALL STREET JOURNAL ON *THE COOK'S ILLUSTRATED COOKBOOK*

SOUS VIDE *for* EVERYBODY

The Easy, Foolproof Cooking Technique
That's Sweeping the World

America's Test Kitchen

Library of Congress Cataloging-in-Publication Data
Names: America's Test Kitchen (Firm), publisher.
Title: Sous vide for everybody : the easy, foolproof cooking technique
    that's sweeping the world / America's Test Kitchen.
Description: Boston, MA : America's Test Kitchen, [2018] | Includes index.
Identifiers: LCCN 2018015574 | ISBN 9781945256493 (pbk.)
Subjects: LCSH: Sous-vide cooking. | LCGFT: Cookbooks.
Classification: LCC TX690.7 .S69 2018 | DDC 641.5/87--dc23
LC record available at https://lccn.loc.gov/2018015574

AMERICA'S TEST KITCHEN

AMERICA'S TEST KITCHEN
21 Drydock Avenue, Boston, MA 02210
Manufactured in the United States of America
10 9 8 7 6 5 4

Distributed by Penguin Random House Publisher Services
Tel: 800.733.3000

Pictured on front cover: Vanilla Bean Ice Cream (page 200),
Peppercorn-Crusted Roast Beef (page 76), White Bean
Hummus (page 175), Hard-Cooked Eggs (page 22), Shredded
Chicken Tacos (Tinga de Pollo) (page 56)
Pictured on back cover: Crème Brûlée (page 203)

Editorial Director, Books ELIZABETH CARDUFF
Executive Food Editor DAN ZUCCARELLO
Executive Editor, Science MOLLY BIRNBAUM
Associate Editor TIM CHIN
Test Cook SASHA MARX
Senior Science Research Editor PAUL ADAMS
Science Tasting Panel ANNE WOLF, STEVE KLISE,
    LEAH COLINS, ANDREW JANJIGIAN, DAN SOUZA,
    LAN LAM, AND KRISTIN SARGIANIS
Editorial Assistants ALYSSA LANGER AND KELLY GAUTHIER
Design Director, Books CAROLE GOODMAN
Deputy Art Directors ALLISON BOALES AND JEN KANAVOS HOFFMAN
Associate Art Director KATIE BARRANGER
Production Designer REINALDO CRUZ
Photography Director JULIE BOZZO COTE
Photography Producers MARY BALL AND MEREDITH MULCAHY
Senior Staff Photographer DANIEL J. VAN ACKERE
Staff Photographers STEVE KLISE AND KEVIN WHITE
Additional Photography KELLER + KELLER AND CARL TREMBLAY
Food Styling CATRINE KELTY, CHANTAL LAMBETH,
    KENDRA MCKNIGHT, ELLE SIMONE SCOTT, AND SALLY STAUB
Photoshoot Kitchen Team
    Photo Team and Social Events Manager TIMOTHY MCQUINN
    Lead Test Cook DANIEL CELLUCCI
    Test Cook JESSICA RUDOLPH
    Assistant Test Cooks SARAH EWALD, ERIC HAESSLER, AND
        MADY NICHAS
Illustration TOBATRON
Production Director GUY ROCHFORD
Senior Production Manager JESSICA LINDHEIMER QUIRK
Production Manager CHRISTINE SPANGER
Imaging Manager LAUREN ROBBINS
Production and Imaging Specialists HEATHER DUBE, DENNIS NOBLE,
    AND JESSICA VOAS
Senior Editor, Tastings and Testings LAUREN SAVOIE
Copy Editor LOUISE EMERICK
Proofreader ANN-MARIE IMBORNONI
Indexer ELIZABETH PARSON

Chief Creative Officer JACK BISHOP
Executive Editorial Directors JULIA COLLIN DAVISON AND
    BRIDGET LANCASTER

CONTENTS

Welcome to America's Test Kitchen

This book has been tested, written, and edited by the folks at America's Test Kitchen. Located in Boston's Seaport District in the historic Innovation and Design Building, it features 15,000 square feet of kitchen space, including multiple photography and video studios. It is the home of *Cook's Illustrated* magazine and *Cook's Country* magazine and is the workday destination for more than 60 test cooks, editors, and cookware specialists. Our mission is to test recipes over and over again until we understand how and why they work and until we arrive at the best version.

We start the process of testing a recipe with a complete lack of preconceptions, which means that we accept no claim, no technique, and no recipe at face value. We simply assemble as many variations as possible, test a half-dozen of the most promising, and taste the results blind. We then construct our own recipe and continue to test it, varying ingredients, techniques, and cooking times until we reach a consensus. As we like to say in the test kitchen, "We make the mistakes so you don't have to." The result, we hope, is the best version of a particular recipe, but we realize that only you can be the final judge of our success (or failure). We use the same rigorous approach when we test equipment and taste ingredients.

All of this would not be possible without a belief that good cooking, much like good music, is based on a foundation of objective technique. Some people like spicy foods and others don't, but there is a right way to sauté, there is a best way to cook a pot roast, and there are measurable scientific principles involved in producing perfectly beaten, stable egg whites. Our ultimate goal is to investigate the fundamental principles of cooking to give you the techniques, tools, and ingredients you need to become a better cook. It is as simple as that.

To see what goes on behind the scenes at America's Test Kitchen, check out our social media channels for kitchen snapshots, exclusive content, video tips, and much more. You can watch us work (in our actual test kitchen) by tuning in to *America's Test Kitchen* or *Cook's Country* on public television or on our websites. Download our award-winning podcast *Proof*, which goes beyond recipes to solve food mysteries (AmericasTestKitchen.com/proof), or listen in to test kitchen experts on public radio (SplendidTable.org) to hear insights that illuminate the truth about real home cooking. Want to hone your cooking skills or finally learn how to bake—with an America's Test Kitchen test cook? Enroll in one of our online cooking classes. And you can engage the next generation of home cooks with kid-tested recipes from America's Test Kitchen Kids.

However you choose to visit us, we welcome you into our kitchen, where you can stand by our side as we test our way to the best recipes in America.

facebook.com/AmericasTestKitchen

twitter.com/TestKitchen

youtube.com/AmericasTestKitchen

instagram.com/TestKitchen

pinterest.com/TestKitchen

AmericasTestKitchen.com

CooksIllustrated.com

CooksCountry.com

OnlineCookingSchool.com

AmericasTestKitchen.com/kids

Listing of Recipes

INTRODUCTION

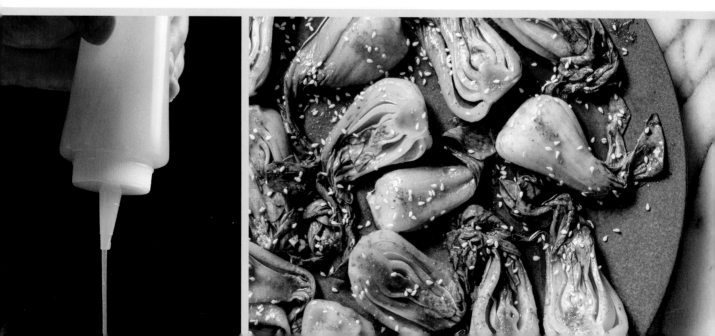

What is sous vide?

Even if you weren't familiar with sous vide before picking up this book, chances are you've eaten food prepared this way. In the past decade, this method—cooking food in a precisely controlled water bath—has trickled its way down from Michelin-star restaurants such as Alinea in Chicago and Per Se in New York to chains including Chipotle, Panera, and Starbucks. And now it has entered the home kitchen.

Here's how it works A sous vide machine (also called an immersion circulator) is used to preheat a water bath to a precise temperature. Food is sealed in plastic bags (though not always; you can also sous vide in glass jars, and eggs can be cooked right in their shells) and immersed in the bath. The food eventually reaches the same temperature as the water, which is often set to the ideal serving temperature of the final dish. For meat, poultry, and fish, there is usually a quick searing step before serving. This differs from conventional stovetop and oven methods, in which the heat used is much higher than the serving temperature of the food, making it imperative to remove the food at just the right moment, when it's done but not overcooked.

But with sous vide there's usually no risk of over-cooking, making it a game-changing technique—especially for temperature-sensitive (and often expensive) foods such as fish or steak. The low cooking temperature ensures meat remains juicy; it's never dry. And dialing in the precise temperature creates exceptionally consistent results that can't be achieved with traditional methods. Long, slow cooking breaks down collagen to render even tough cuts such as chuck or pork shoulder extremely tender. It also eases the daunting task of cooking for a holiday meal or dinner party since large quantities of food can be prepped hours in advance and held at the perfect temperature until serving time.

"The single biggest advantage sous vide has for a person is emotional," says Scott Heimendinger, cofounder of the sous-vide company Sansaire and technical director of the cookbook publishers Modernist Cuisine. "It alleviates anxiety." Whether you're cooking for one on a weeknight or throwing a dinner party for people you want to impress, your anxieties can be alleviated because with the precision of sous vide, a great meal is virtually guaranteed. "Plus you don't have to be stuck in the kitchen," he adds. "You can be with your guests because your food is not going to overcook as it sits in the bath."

Where does sous vide come from?

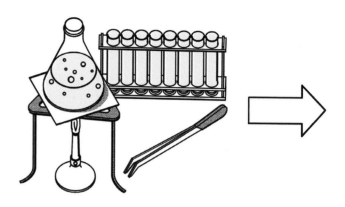

Immersion circulators did not enter the market as a way to cook. Instead, they were first used as equipment in scientific laboratories. Precisely heated water baths are perfect for incubating live cell cultures and testing materials—and basically anything else you'd use a Bunsen burner for.

When sous vide arrived in the food world, the technique wasn't initially used to make food taste better. In the late 1960s, when food-grade plastic films and vacuum packing were mastered by French and American engineers, sous vide was used as a safety measure: The ability to keep packaged foods in a water bath at a certain temperature made pasteurizing and sterilizing easier for labs, hospitals, and large-scale commercial food companies. Originally, vacuum packing and cooking foods sous vide was used to seal and pasteurize industrially prepared foods so that they would have a longer shelf life.

But then in 1974, sous vide made its way into the restaurant scene. (Well, kind of.) French chef Pierre Troisgros wanted to develop a new way to cook foie gras, and he hired Georges Pralus, another chef, to help. The goal? To lose as little fat as possible when cooking. After all, fat is flavor, and foie gras is all about fatty flavor. Through experimentation, Pralus found that the liver lost the least amount of fat when poached at a precise temperature, sealed in plastic.

Around the same time, Bruno Goussault—an economist, inventor, and chef—made similar discoveries for commercial food operations and hospitals. In the 1980s, he teamed up with Chef Joël Robuchon to create a sous vide dining program for the French railroad. This paved the way for Goussault's next career move: He has been the chief scientist at Cuisine Solutions, an American company that specializes in sous vide food preparation and packaging, since 1989.

The technique slowly spread to chefs in the U.S.—largely thanks to the Internet. Chefs began to acquire sous vide circulators for their kitchens in the early 2000s. (Thomas Keller was one of the first.) The only problem: No one really knew how to use them. None of these chefs had come up in the kitchen world using them. No one had spent time experimenting with them. Enter: the website eGullet. The forums on this culinary-minded site were a place for people to geek out on food-related issues, and sous vide was a perfect subject.

On eGullet, explained Boston chef Tony Maws, people like Grant Achatz, Sean Brock, Wyliê Dufresne, and many others "would talk about what they were playing with, and [how they used] different times and temperatures for different proteins. There was a lot of sharing of knowledge, and over time we figured out this technique."

In 2005, sous vide started to really pick up. Joan Roca, a chef in Spain, wrote a book about sous vide that arrived in the U.S. that year (with a slightly rocky translation). Chef Grant Achatz's restaurant, Alinea, also opened—sous vide circulators included. Chef and inventor Dave Arnold began to teach low-temperature cooking classes at the French Culinary Institute.

"Cryovacking, which is more often called sous vide (French for "under vacuum"), is poised to change the way restaurant chefs cook," wrote Amanda Hesser for the *New York Times* in a 2005 story called "Under Pressure." "And like the Wolf stove and the immersion blender, it will probably trickle down to the home kitchen someday."

In 2006, Dufresne battled Mario Batali on *Iron Chef America;* it was the first time sous vide circulators were seen on TV. The demand only grew from there.

The move into home kitchens has also been slow, and largely due to the influx of sous vide circulators with a lower price point, as professional devices cost over $1,000. In 2009, Sous Vide Supreme debuted as the first circulator for less than $500. In 2012, another sous vide circulator company called Nomiku launched, and they started selling machines for $359. In 2016, ChefSteps released their own circulator, called the Joule, for just $199. (In 2017, we named the Joule our top pick for the home cook.)

Introduction

3

What do you need to sous vide?

Pick a Sous Vide Device

Sous vide machines are sleeker, cheaper, and smarter than ever before. We tested seven immersion circulators priced from $129.99 to $274.95. We used each to prepare eggs, salmon, flank steak, pork loin, and beef short ribs. We evaluated accuracy and speed by tracking the water temperature as we programmed each machine to heat and maintain water baths at 149°F/65°C and 190°F/88°C for 3 hours. We also measured weight, height, distance between minimum and maximum water levels, and footprint. All products were purchased online and appear below in order of preference.

	PERFORMANCE	COMMENTS
HIGHLY RECOMMENDED		

Joule
Price **$199**
Height **11 in**
Weight **1 lb, 5 oz**
Footprint **1.8-in diameter**
Time To Heat Bath
To 190°F **22 min**
Average Difference From
Target Temperature **0.2°**
Distance Between Minimum
And Maximum Water
Levels **6.5 in**
Model Number
Stainless Steel

SPEED ★★½
COOKING ★★★
ACCURACY ★★★
EASE OF USE ★★½
VERSATILITY ★★½

This slim, lightweight machine heated water almost as fast as the biggest circulators and was the most accurate in our lineup. Though it doesn't have a display and requires a smartphone to work, its app was intuitive and simple, and its enclosed electronics meant we didn't have to worry about getting any part of the circulator wet. Testers loved its magnetic bottom, which allowed it to stand stably in the center of metal pots. It also had the largest distance between water lines, so we could forgo refilling even during longer cooking projects, and it was small enough to store in a drawer.

RECOMMENDED

Anova Precision Cooker
WI-FI
Price **$199**
Height **15 in**
Weight **2 lb, 6 oz**
Footprint **2.3-in diameter**
Time To Heat Bath
To 190°F **30 min**
Average Difference From
Target Temperature **1.2°**
Distance Between Minimum
And Maximum Water
Levels **3.6 in**
Model Number **A3.2**

SPEED ★★
COOKING ★★★
ACCURACY ★★
EASE OF USE ★★½
VERSATILITY ★★★

A Wi-Fi enabled update of our former winning circulator, this version has many of the same features that we liked in the old model: a sturdy screw-in clamp that can be raised or lowered depending on the vessel height; an adjustable heating port; and easy-to-use, intuitive controls. We liked that its temperature and time could be set either directly on the circulator or in the app. However, it lagged behind our top-ranked model on heating speed and accuracy (it overcooked eggs in multiple tests) and was a little too bulky to be stored in a standard drawer.

KEY	GOOD ★★★	FAIR ★★	POOR ★

RECOMMENDED	PERFORMANCE	COMMENTS

Nomiku Sous Vide
Price **$174.95**
Height **12 in**
Weight **3 lb, 2 oz**
Footprint **3.6 in x 2.4 in**
Time To Heat Bath To
190°F **45 min**
Average Difference From
Target Temperature **0.4°**
Distance Between Minimum
And Maximum Water
Levels **3.5 in**
Model Number **Nom1US**

SPEED ★
COOKING ★★★
ACCURACY ★★½
EASE OF USE ★★½
VERSATILITY ★★★

Testers loved this circulator's big, bright display, which allowed us to check the temperature of the bath from across the room. Though it took 45 minutes just to preheat the bath to 190°F/88°C, its motors were silent and gentle, barely rocking eggs and delicate fillets. We tried the companion smartphone app, but it frequently crashed; it was easier to just set the temperature and timer using the dial on the circulator. Its paper clip–style clamp was easy to attach.

Sansaire Sous Vide Machine
Price **$195.90**
Height **14.5 in**
Weight **3 lb, 12 oz**
Footprint **4-in diameter**
Time To Heat Bath To
190°F **22 min**
Average Difference From
Target Temperature **0.7°**
Distance Between Minimum
And Maximum Water
Levels **3.5 in**
Model Number **N/A**

SPEED ★★½
COOKING ★★★
ACCURACY ★★
EASE OF USE ★★
VERSATILITY ★★½

This large circulator has no app, no timer, no fancy display, but it was quick to heat and easy to set, and it could stand on its own in the middle of any vessel because of its wide, flat base. It didn't require refilling during a 72-hour cooking project, and food emerged juicy and tender. Its clamp attached quickly and securely to pots of all sizes. Some testers lamented the absence of a timer function. It fluctuated a bit more than its competitors during cooking, dipping lower and rising higher than other models. This resulted in a moderate 0.7-degree average fluctuation from the target temperature over the course of 3 hours; delicate ingredients like eggs sometimes emerged over- or undercooked.

RECOMMENDED WITH RESERVATIONS

PolyScience Culinary Creative Series Sous Vide Immersion Circulator
Price **$249.95**
Height **14 in**
Weight **4 lb, 14 oz**
Footprint **3.4 in x 3.3 in**
Time To Heat Bath To
190°F **20 min**
Average Difference From
Target Temperature **1.4°**
Distance Between Minimum
And Maximum Water
Levels **3.5 in**
Model Number **CRC-5AC1B**

SPEED ★★★
COOKING ★★
ACCURACY ★★
EASE OF USE ★★
VERSATILITY ★★

Though this brand makes circulators for labs and restaurant kitchens, this model wasn't as accurate or reliable as we expected. The unit wouldn't heat the water until after we set the timer, and it beeped incessantly once up to temperature. It was also large and bulky, so it felt slightly cramped and unsteady in smaller vessels. Plus, testers were perplexed by a plastic piece on the front of the unit, which was meant to be a cover for the reset button, that repeatedly fell into the bath.

Pick a Container

You can sous vide in a Dutch oven, a large saucepan, a stockpot, or a large plastic container. We call for a 7-quart container in most of our recipes. In some of our recipes, we cook large cuts of meat, like our Peppercorn-Crusted Roast Beef, page 76. For these recipes, we recommend investing in a 12-quart container. (Cambro containers are inexpensive and easy to use, and we recommend buying one for your larger-scale sous vide cooking.)

DUTCH OVEN	PERFORMANCE	COMMENTS
Cuisinart Chef's Classic Enameled Cast Iron Covered Casserole Price **$87.25** Materials **Enameled cast iron** Weight **16.8 lbs** Interior Height **4 ⅜ in** Cooking Surface Diameter **9 ⁷⁄₁₆ in** Interior Color **Light** Model Number **CI670-30CR**	COOKING ★★★ EASE OF USE ★★½ DURABILITY ★★½	With an exceptionally broad cooking surface and low, straight sides, this 7-quart pot was substantial enough to hold and distribute heat evenly, without being unbearably heavy. The looped handles were comfortable to hold, though slightly smaller than ideal. The rim and lid chipped cosmetically when we repeatedly slammed the lid onto the pot.

STOCK POT	PERFORMANCE	COMMENTS
All-Clad Stainless 12-Quart Stock Pot Price **$389.95** Weight **5.5 lb** Material **Stainless steel with aluminum core** Model Number **4512**		This pot was lauded for being "nice and heavy," with "easy-to-grip" handles that "didn't get too hot" (although we still needed potholders). The aluminum core runs up the side of the pot—other pots have aluminum cores only in the bottom, if anywhere—which ensures more even heating than most of us will ever need.

PLASTIC CONTAINER	PERFORMANCE	COMMENTS
Cambro 12-Quart Square Storage Container Price **$22.99** Dishwasher-Safe **Yes** Model Number **12SFSCW135**	CLEANUP ★★★ CAPACITY ★★★	There's a reason that food service professionals use these storage containers. They're sturdy, spacious, and dead simple to use and clean, with no pointless bells or whistles. While they come in a range of sizes, the 12-quart size is necessary to fit most foods we circulate in a water bath.

Buy Some Plastic Bags

Originally, sous vide was done with vacuum-sealed foods—after all the name *sous vide* is French for "under vacuum." But buying a vacuum sealer and special vacuum bags are not a necessity when it comes to sous vide. In fact, we recommend you use zipper-lock freezer bags instead. It's important to use high-quality freezer bags, as low quality bags can contain BPA, which is not safe for cooking (see page 130). Most of our recipes call for 1-gallon bags; some larger cuts of meat call for 2-gallon bags.

RECOMMENDED	PERFORMANCE	COMMENTS
Ziploc Brand Freezer Bags with Easy Open Tabs Price **$5.37 for 28 bags** **($0.19 per bag)** Thickness **2.2 mil** Model Number **UPC #0-25700-00382-3**	LEAKPROOF ★★★ DURABILITY ★★★ EASE OF USE ★★★ FREEZER PROTECTION ★★★	For general use, this bag protected food from freezer burn and ice crystals for more than two months, and it stayed intact when filled with tomato sauce and dropped. For sous vide applications, it rarely leaked and sealed snugly. Ziploc publishes its ingredients; the bags are made of cook-safe polyethylene and are without additives.

Also needed: **binder clips** (to clip your bags of food to the side of the water bath container), **plastic wrap** (for covering your water bath), and **Mason jars** (for making yogurt, pudding, cheesecake, or other custardy recipes).

Optional: Vacuum Sealer

Though they aren't necessary for sous vide cooking, vacuum sealers are useful and are great for storing food. We use them at the test kitchen to help store hundreds of pounds of food weekly. They work by pulling air away and creating a tight seal around the food, blocking it from elements that hasten deterioration. Using a vacuum sealer eliminates the need to carefully remove air from a zipper-lock bag as you prepare your food to cook in a water bath.

HIGHLY RECOMMENDED	PERFORMANCE	COMMENTS
Weston Professional Advantage Vacuum Sealer Price **$189.99** Style **Heat** Vacuum Strength **23 inHg** Model Number **65-0501-W**	EASY TO USE ★★★ PERFORMANCE ★★★	This compact, powerful heat-sealing model kept food fresh for three months. Its intuitive interface has a responsive pulse mode and bright blue lights that indicate its progress. It works with a wide variety of bags, canisters, and rolls.

How do you sous vide?

Sous vide cooking allows you to achieve perfect results with eggs, poultry, meat, and more. But how do you *do* it? You'll find detailed recipes throughout the book. But here let's start with the basics.

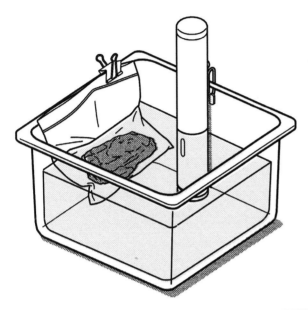

1 Set up your rig

Attach your immersion circulator to a heat-safe container—either a Dutch oven, a stockpot, or a large plastic container like a Cambro. Our recipes require either a 7-quart or 12-quart container. Fill it with water to about 1 inch above the machine's minimum water level line. Since the food will raise the water level once added, avoid filling to the maximum water line.

2 Choose your temp and preheat water

Turn on the machine. Set the machine's temperature to your desired cooking temperature. With sous vide cooking, you typically set the bath to the final internal temperature of the food. The food sits in the bath and slowly comes up to its ideal temperature without any danger of overcooking. Choose a cooking temperature that matches your ideal serving temperature. (There are some exceptions: Eggs and delicate fish fillets are often cooked for a comparatively short amount of time at a temperature that is a higher-than-desired internal temperature to better control the final texture of the cooked food.) Letting the bath preheat helps ensure even cooking. Depending on your machine and target temperature, preheating will take 20 to 30 minutes. Cover the bath with plastic wrap to speed up the preheating process. (Worried about safety? See page 40 for more on pasteurization.)

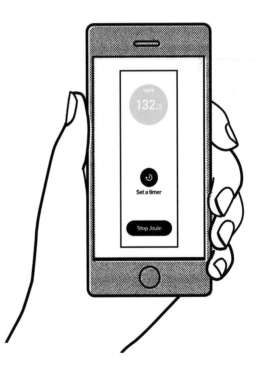

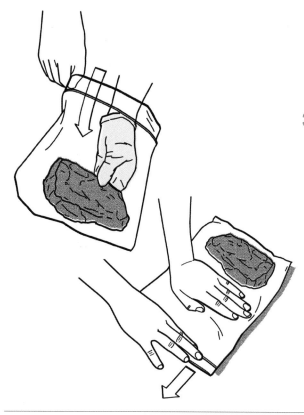

3 Seal food in a bag

Season your food with salt, pepper, and any other aromatics as per the recipe. Place your food in a zipper-lock freezer bag. We recommend adding a small amount of olive or vegetable oil to the bag for meats and fish. To ensure that all food finishes at the same time, make sure the pieces are cut to about the same size and thickness, and lay the food as flat as possible in the bag. Once your food is in the bag, press out as much air as you can, and seal the bag. If cooking above 158°F/70°C, we recommend double bagging your food in order to prevent any water leakage, as high temperatures can weaken the plastic.

4 Submerge the bag

Once the bath is up to temperature, gently lower the bag into the bath. If the ingredients in the bag have a tendency to float, weight the bag down (see page 14 for weight options).

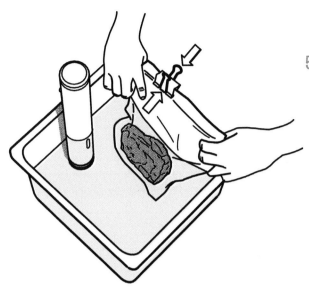

5 Clip bag to container

Clip the corner of the bag to the side of the container with a binder clip, allowing remaining air bubbles to rise to the top of the bag. This step is important because air is a poor conductor of heat and too much of it insulates the food from the hot water bath. Removing air gives the food better contact with the heated water, so it cooks more quickly and evenly.

6 Remove last air bubbles

Open one corner of the zipper and release any remaining air, and then reseal the bag. To prevent cold spots on the food, make sure the bag isn't touching the sous vide machine or cooking vessel. If cooking with multiple bags, make sure they aren't pressing up against each other.

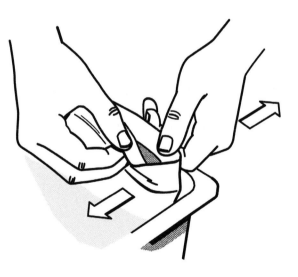

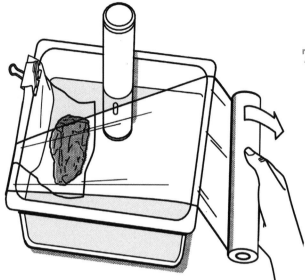

7 Cook your food

It's important to cover the water bath with plastic wrap (or a sous vide–specific lid for your large plastic container) during cooking. For long cook times (from a couple hours to a full day), the cover helps to minimize evaporation (and the need to add more water). For short cook times (less than an hour), the cover helps to keep the temperature as static as possible after adding ingredients to the bath.

8 Relax until time is up

The biggest benefit of sous vide? You don't need to *do* anything once the food is in the water bath (except read a book, play video games, or hang out with family). Note that timing isn't as important for sous vide as it is with traditional cooking methods, but it's still important to keep a passive eye on the time, since the texture of many foods can suffer if they spend too much time in the bath. Most tender cuts of pork, beef, and poultry will be fully cooked in about 1 hour, but they can stay in the bath for about 3 hours without much change to texture. When cooking delicate foods such as eggs or fish, which are often cooked at higher temperatures for less time, you'll want to be extra-vigilant. Too much time for a poached egg can spell disaster.

9 Finishing touches

Remove your food from the bath. Though some foods, such as fish fillets, eggs, vegetables, and pulled pork are ready to enjoy straight out of the bath, most cuts of meat benefit from a quick sear to give the food a crisp crust. How you sear depends on the size and cut of the meat, but whatever method you choose, the goal is to get the searing done as quickly as possible to avoid raising the temperature of the meat further. Make sure you use high heat and dry the food as much as possible before searing.

10 If you're saving for later

If you're not serving the food right away, it's important to rapidly chill the food before storage. Why? Food safety. (See page 40 for more.) Plunge the still-sealed bags into a large ice bath to stop the cooking, let sit until chilled, and then refrigerate it for later.

Questions and Answers

Q *Is sous vide cooking safe?*

A Short answer: Yes. Take a look at our essays on temperature safety (page 40) and plastics (page 130) for more detail.

Q *What should I do if I accidentally get raw chicken juice in my sous vide bath?*

A Don't freak out! Dispose of the water. Thoroughly wash your water bath container. You can gently clean your sous vide device with a no-suds dishwashing detergent (do not submerge the device in soapy water). We also recommend cleaning your device periodically in a vinegar bath. Combine equal parts water and distilled white vinegar in a small pot. Use your sous vide circulator to bring vinegar solution to 140°F/60°C. Once the bath reaches that temperature, the cleaning is complete. This cleaning method also helps remove mineral buildup inside the circulator.

Q *What should I do if my zipper-lock freezer bag springs a leak?*

A Take it out of the bath, and place it in a second bag. Remove as much air as possible, make sure both bags are sealed, and place it gently back in the bath. Follow our air-displacement method on page 11 to remove the rest of the air bubbles.

Q *Is there any way to sous vide if I don't have a sous vide circulator?*

A Not really. Precision and hands-off ease-of-use are two of the most attractive qualities of sous vide for the home cook. Trying to cook sous vide without an immersion circulator forces you to sacrifice both of these attributes. The most effective "hack" for cooking sous vide without a device is to set up a large pot of water on your stovetop, fit it with a thermometer, and fiddle with your burner until you reach your target cooking temperature. But this method is imprecise and requires a lot of babysitting. An immersion circulator accurately controls and maintains the temperature of your water bath so that you don't have to. Long story short: If you want to cook sous vide, get a device.

Q *What if my plastic bag begins to float? What's a good way to weigh it down?*

A We have a "use whatever sinks your boat" policy when it comes to dealing with floating sous vide bags, but here are a few of our favorite methods:

- Clip a large binder clip to the bottom of the sous vide bag, and then fit a heavy spoon into the mouth of the clip.
- For recipes that call for double bagging, pop a couple of heavy spoons into the outer bag.
- Fill a Mason jar or zipper-lock freezer bag with pie weights, and place it on top of the floating bag.
- Place an inverted steamer basket on top of the offending floating bag. Then place additional weights, like heavy spoons or pie weights, on top of the basket.

Q *Do I need to buy a vacuum sealer?*

A No. Vacuum sealers are helpful tools (see page 7), but not necessary for sous vide. A high-quality zipper-lock plastic bag (see page 7) does just fine.

Q *Why do I need to cover my pot when I'm cooking sous vide?*

A Covering your water bath container with plastic wrap or a sous vide–specific lid helps to prevent evaporation (and therefore the need to refill the water bath over the course of long cook times). It also helps bring the water back up to temperature quickly after adding ingredients to the bath, which is especially important when cooking delicate foods like Soft-Poached Eggs (page 20).

Q *Why does my sous vide steak not look super red when I first slice into it? But then it becomes red?*

A Myoglobin, an oxygen-storing protein and the main pigment in meat, is responsible for the color of your steak. Myoglobin changes hues depending on its chemical environment. Without oxygen, myoglobin is dark purple (think of a raw vacuum-sealed steak). When heated, myoglobin loses an electron and turns brown (think of a cooked sous vide steak). And finally, when exposed to oxygen, that myoglobin turns red (sliced steak).

Q *How do I pronounce sous vide?*

A Say it ten times fast: *soo veed.*

Q *How do I know how much is the right amount of water in my bath?*

A You always need enough water to completely immerse the item that you will be cooking sous vide. Keep in mind the principles of displacement—if you are going to be cooking a whole prime rib roast, you don't want to fill your water bath to the brim. Sous vide devices will either have a minimum water fill-line marked on the device itself or will display an error message if the water level gets too low.

Q *Do you have a trick for removing air bubbles that doesn't involve my hands touching hot water?*

A First, it's usually not *that* hot. But if you're looking to avoid the heat, fill a separate container with cold water and carry out the sealing steps (page 11) there, and then transfer your bag to the prepared heated water bath. No poached digits!

Q *How do I get the air out of a bag that's filled with liquid, like for making broth?*

A Our displacement method for removing air bubbles (see page 11) is just as effective with liquid. Just be careful not to spill the contents of the bag before you get it in the water!

Q *What's the deal with the time ranges in these recipes?*

A We love that sous vide allows for a bigger time window for perfectly cooked food compared to most traditional methods. You will notice a lot of the recipes in this book have ranges for the sous vide cooking time. The idea is that any time within a recipe's range will yield a great result. The low end of the range gives the ideal result in the least amount of time, and the upper end of the time range is the limit to which that food can be cooked without any negative impact. If a recipe does not have a range, it's important to hit the exact target time.

What should you sous vide?

10 Recipes to Cook When You Want to Impress

9 Things You Should Never Sous Vide

Popcorn

Fried Rice

Nachos

Pepperoni Pizza

Brioche

Vegetable Lasagna

Twice-Baked Potatoes

Chocolate Souffle

Your Grandmother's Famous Apple Pie

EGGS AND DAIRY

There's no getting around it: Eggs are tricky to cook. The white and the yolk behave differently when subjected to heat. Because they contain different proportions of proteins, fats, and water, they coagulate and set at different temperatures, and they have different final textures. Plus, there's the simple fact that the white of the egg is on the outside—closer to the shell and the heat source—and therefore cooks faster than the yolk.

At America's Test Kitchen, we've devised countless ways to make egg cookery easier, from the quick timing of eggs poached in salted water with vinegar to hard "boiling" eggs in a steamer basket. But bringing sous vide into the equation changes things. Cooking eggs in a low-temperature water bath with a sous vide circulator allows you to cook with a precision absent from traditional methods. And with eggs in particular, this makes a huge difference.

Egg whites begin to thicken at 150 degrees Fahrenheit/65.5 degrees Celsius and fully set at 158°F/70°C, while the yolk begins to thicken at 145°F/62.8°C and fully sets at 180°F/82°C. "An egg soft-cooked at 60°C (140°F) is barely jelled throughout; at 62.8°C (145°F), the yolk is actually firmer than the surrounding white," writes food scientist Harold McGee in the introduction to chef Thomas Keller's *Under Pressure*, the first English-language sous vide cookbook. "Sous vide cooking has opened up new realms of texture and flavor that weren't discernible before and that still aren't fully understood."

Because, really, egg cookery isn't just about temperature. It's also about time (see chart, page 43). Sous vide cooking allows you, the home cook, to play with time in a way that's impossible with traditional cooking methods, giving you the ability to decide exactly what texture you want, no need for winging it or guesswork.

However you like your eggs, one thing is clear: Each temperature degree difference is distinctive in sous vide cooking. "I can look at an egg at any point that's been cooked low temperature," says Dave Arnold, founder of the Museum of Food and Drink and author of *Liquid Intelligence*, "and tell you in this range exactly how hot or cold it was." Arnold calls an egg cooked at 145°F/63°C for about an hour an "in-betweener egg"—not totally set but still creamy (perfect for serving on toast). Meanwhile, Dr. Michael Eades, co-creator of the SousVide Supreme water oven calls an egg cooked at 147°F/64°C for 55 minutes the "perfect custard egg"—a "soft white and a custardy, custardy yolk." When developing our own recipe for Soft-Poached Eggs (page 20), we decided to go for a more traditional texture, one without any liquidy white. Our eggs are more like those you would expect to get for breakfast from the diner down the street. To achieve that, we cook our eggs for a far shorter time (12 minutes) at a higher temperature (167°F/75°C). (Bonus: Cook our sous vide Soft-Poached Eggs at the same time as our sous vide Hollandaise, page 30, and win brunch for a crowd.)

Eggs are perhaps the poster child for innovative sous vide cooking, but there is so much more you can do with this technique—even just in the breakfast realm.

Behold: sous vide Yogurt (page 35). After bringing milk up to 185°F/85°C, cooling it, and mixing it with a starter, we cook our yogurt in Mason jars in a low-temperature water bath for anywhere from 5 to 24 hours (depending on your preference for pucker). Using sous vide removes the need to babysit or monitor the temperature of the yogurt as it incubates—hands off! Sous vide also allows for easy home-made Ricotta (page 37), and even Crème Fraîche (page 38).

Want something a little more out there? Try your hand at our Runny Egg Yolk Sauce (page 32) if you want the experience of a perfect runny yolk on your pasta, your salad, or your burger at literally any time—ready to go, straight from the fridge.

Soft-Poached Eggs

YIELD MAKES 1 TO 16 EGGS
Sous Vide Temperature 167°F/75°C
Sous Vide Time 12 minutes
Active Cooking Time 20 minutes

To Make Ahead Eggs can be rapidly chilled in ice bath for 10 minutes (see page 13) and then refrigerated for up to 5 days. To reheat, lower eggs into water bath set to 140°F/60°C and cook until heated through, at least 15 minutes or up to 60 minutes. Crack into bowls as directed.

Why This Recipe Works Eggs are perhaps the poster child for sous vide cooking: The technique can produce eggs with unique texture; the method is hands-off; and the recipe is easily scalable. Typically, sous vide eggs are cooked at a low temperature (around 145°F/63°C) for at least an hour. This will give you a yolk that is slightly thickened but still runny and a barely set white. We found the white to be too loose when cooked in this temperature range, most of it running off when we cracked into the eggs. Some recipes call for cracking "63-degree eggs" such as these into simmering water to better set the whites. We wanted to ditch that extra step and still produce a perfectly poached egg, so we opted to cook at a higher temperature for a shorter time to set more of the white. This method produced a traditional poached egg—right out of the shell! And with the ability to make these eggs ahead of time—just reheat them in a 140°F/60°C water bath for anywhere from 15 to 60 minutes—this recipe is perfect for the brunch crowd. Be sure to use large eggs that have no cracks and are cold from the refrigerator. Fresher eggs have tighter egg whites and are better suited for this recipe. Serve with crusty bread or toast. Or for a crowd in Eggs Benedict (page 24).

1–16 large eggs, chilled
Salt and pepper

1 Using sous vide circulator, bring water to 167°F/75°C in 7-quart container. Using slotted spoon, gently lower eggs into prepared water bath, cover, and cook for 12 minutes.

2 Meanwhile, fill large bowl halfway with ice and water. Using slotted spoon, transfer eggs to ice bath and let sit until cool enough to touch, about 1 minute. To serve, crack eggs into individual bowls and season with salt and pepper to taste.

Hard-Cooked Eggs

YIELD **MAKES 1 TO 18 EGGS**
Sous Vide Temperature 194°F/90°C
Sous Vide Time 20 minutes
Active Cooking Time 20 minutes, plus chilling time

To Make Ahead Eggs can be rapidly chilled in ice bath for 15 minutes (see page 13) and then refrigerated for up to 5 days. They can be stored in their shells and peeled as needed.

Why This Recipe Works Hard-cooked eggs are a breeze to make with a sous vide circulator. Our goal: Hard-cooked eggs that were easy to peel, with a set but not fudgy yolk. We found that cooking eggs in very hot water (194°F/90°C) rapidly denatured the outermost egg white proteins, causing them to form a solid gel that shrank and pulled away from the membrane. This translated to easy-peeling hard-cooked eggs with set but not overcooked yolks. (When we tested cooking eggs at lower temperatures for longer time periods, the egg whites stuck to the shell membrane, making peeling a frustrating task. And once we got those eggs peeled, their yolks were fudgy instead of firm.) Using sous vide to hard-cook eggs makes scaling the recipe up or down simple; the method and timing is the same for 1 to 18 eggs. So whether you're cooking a snack for yourself or preparing a large batch of deviled eggs for a party, this recipe has got you covered.

1–18 large eggs

1 Using sous vide circulator, bring water to 194°F/90°C in 7-quart container. Using slotted spoon, gently lower eggs into prepared water bath, cover, and cook for 20 minutes.

2 Meanwhile, fill large bowl halfway with ice and water. Using slotted spoon, transfer eggs to ice bath and let sit until chilled, about 15 minutes. Peel before serving.

Eggs Benedict

YIELD SERVES 6
Sous Vide Temperature 167°F/75°C
Sous Vide Time 12 minutes
Active Cooking Time 35 minutes

To Make Ahead Soft-Poached Eggs can be rapidly chilled in ice bath for 10 minutes (see page 13) and then refrigerated for up to 5 days. To reheat, lower eggs into water bath set to 140°F/60°C and cook until heated through, at least 15 minutes or up to 60 minutes.

Why This Recipe Works Eggs Benedict is easy enough for a restaurant to pull off, but even seasoned cooks grow anxious at the idea of tackling this multicomponent dish at home, especially when you want to prepare it for a crowd. Enter sous vide. Making our Soft-Poached Eggs with a sous vide circulator (page 20) ensures perfectly cooked eggs every time. We developed our recipe for sous vide Hollandaise (page 30) at the same temperature as our Soft-Poached Eggs (167°F/75°C) so that they can be made at the same time, in the same water bath. Presto! Add Canadian bacon and some quickly toasted English muffins, and you've got the brunch crowd covered. (Note: While our Soft-Poached Eggs can be made ahead, the Hollandaise cannot.)

12 slices Canadian bacon
 6 English muffins, split and toasted
12 Soft-Poached Eggs (page 20)
 1 recipe Hollandaise (page 30)

 1 Adjust oven rack to middle position and heat oven to 300°F/149°C. Place 1 slice Canadian bacon on each toasted muffin half and arrange on baking sheet; keep warm in oven.

 2 Arrange 1 poached egg on top of each slice of bacon. Spoon 2 tablespoons (30 grams) hollandaise over each egg and serve immediately, passing remaining hollandaise separately.

Classic Deviled Eggs

YIELD MAKES 12 EGGS

Sous Vide Temperature 194°F/90°C

Sous Vide Time 20 minutes

Active Cooking Time 40 minutes, plus chilling time

To Make Ahead Hard-Cooked Eggs can be rapidly chilled in ice bath for 15 minutes (see page 13) and then refrigerated for up to 5 days. They can be stored in their shells and peeled as needed.

Why This Recipe Works The best deviled eggs start with the best hard-cooked eggs. We use our sous vide circulator to make great hard-cooked eggs every time, plus the technique gives us the ability to make from just 1 egg to a whopping 18 (!) eggs without changing the recipe or cooking time. To make sure the eggs were both easy to peel and perfectly cooked, we opted to cook them in a water bath heated to 194°F/90°C. This higher-temperature cooking denatured the outermost egg white proteins, causing them to shrink away from the shell membrane. As a result, the shells easily slipped off of the cooked eggs. Fresh herbs, cider vinegar, Dijon, Worcestershire sauce, and cayenne elevated the flavor of the filling. This recipe can be doubled. If you prefer, use a pastry bag fitted with a large plain or large star tip to fill the egg halves.

6 Hard-Cooked Eggs (page 22)

3 tablespoons (38 grams) mayonnaise

1 tablespoon (4 grams) minced fresh parsley, plus 12 small whole parsley leaves for garnishing

1 teaspoon (5 grams) cider vinegar

1 teaspoon (5 grams) Dijon mustard

¼ teaspoon (1 gram) Worcestershire sauce
   Pinch cayenne pepper

1 Peel eggs and halve lengthwise with paring knife. Transfer yolks to bowl; arrange whites on serving platter. Mash yolks with fork until no large lumps remain. Add mayonnaise and use rubber spatula to smear mixture against side of bowl until thick, smooth paste forms, 1 to 2 minutes. Add minced parsley, vinegar, mustard, Worcestershire, and cayenne and mix until fully incorporated.

2 Transfer yolk mixture to 1-quart zipper-lock freezer bag. Press mixture into 1 corner and twist top of bag. Using scissors, snip ½ inch off filled corner. Squeezing bag, distribute yolk mixture evenly among egg white halves. Garnish with parsley leaves and serve.

Classic Egg Salad

Sous Vide Temperature 194°F/90°C
Sous Vide Time 20 minutes
Active Cooking Time 25 minutes, plus chilling time

To Make Ahead Hard-Cooked Eggs can be rapidly chilled in ice bath for 15 minutes (see page 13) and then refrigerated for up to 5 days. They can be stored in their shells and peeled as needed. Salad can be refrigerated for up to 1 day.

Why This Recipe Works For a creamy, flavorful egg salad with perfectly cooked eggs and just the right amount of crunch, we followed a few simple steps. First, we relied on our Hard-Cooked Eggs (page 22), which are cooked sous vide to yield creamy yolks, tender whites, and no green ring every single time. We chopped the eggs and then combined them with mayonnaise (our tasters dismissed cottage cheese, sour cream, and cream cheese), lemon juice, Dijon mustard, red onion, celery, and parsley. Be sure to use red onion; yellow onion will be too harsh.

6 Hard-Cooked Eggs (page 22)
¼ cup (50 grams) mayonnaise
2 tablespoons (24 grams) minced red onion
1 tablespoon (4 grams) minced fresh parsley
½ celery rib (40 grams), minced
2 teaspoons (10 grams) Dijon mustard
2 teaspoons (10 grams) lemon juice
   Salt and pepper

1 Peel and chop eggs.
2 Mix eggs with remaining ingredients in bowl and season with salt and pepper to taste. Serve.

Hollandaise

YIELD MAKES 1⅓ CUPS (260 GRAMS)
Sous Vide Temperature 167°F/75°C
Sous Vide Time 12 to 30 minutes
Active Cooking Time 25 minutes

To Make Ahead We don't recommend making this recipe in advance.

Why This Recipe Works Hollandaise, one of the five mother sauces of French cuisine, is a brunch classic—and it can be a mother to make. It is an egg-emulsified butter sauce that is similar to mayonnaise in many respects, but must be kept warm to keep the butter fluid. There are a lot of ways to make hollandaise; the most traditional preparations involve a lot of time and temperature-sensitive whisking, double boilers, and stress that could ruin your mellow Sunday brunch vibe. Fret not, we've got you covered with this easy sous vide hollandaise. We started by making a quick reduction with white wine vinegar and shallots, which we then combined with egg yolks, butter, water, lemon juice, and salt in a zipper-lock bag. The short 12-minute sous vide bath at 167°F is conveniently the same time and temperature that we use to cook our Soft-Poached Eggs (page 20). Pulling off show-stopping brunch dishes like Eggs Benedict (page 24) just got a whole lot easier.

3 tablespoons (40 grams) white wine vinegar

1 large shallot (30 grams), sliced thin

10 tablespoons (140 grams) unsalted butter

5 large egg yolks (85 grams), lightly beaten

¼ cup (55 grams) water

2 teaspoons (10 grams) lemon juice

½ teaspoon (3 grams) salt

1 Using sous vide circulator, bring water to 167°F/75°C in 7-quart container. In small saucepan, combine vinegar and shallot and bring to boil over high heat. Cook until vinegar is reduced by half, about 1 minute. Strain mixture through fine-mesh strainer set over small bowl, pressing on shallots to extract as much liquid as possible. Discard shallots.

2 Combine vinegar reduction, butter, egg yolks, water, lemon juice, and salt in 1-quart zipper-lock freezer bag. Seal bag, pressing out as much air as possible. Gently lower bag into prepared water bath until mixture is fully submerged, and then clip top corner of bag to side of water bath container, allowing remaining air bubbles to rise to top of bag. Reopen 1 corner of zipper, release remaining air bubbles, and reseal bag. Cover and cook for at least 12 minutes or up to 30 minutes.

3 Transfer mixture to blender and process until smooth, about 1 minute, scraping down sides of blender jar as needed. Serve immediately.

Variation
Béarnaise
Add 2 sprigs (2 grams) fresh tarragon to saucepan with vinegar and shallots in step 1. Discard with shallots after straining reduction. Stir in 2 tablespoons (8 grams) minced fresh tarragon before serving.

Runny Egg Yolk Sauce

YIELD **MAKES ABOUT 1 CUP (200 GRAMS)**
Sous Vide Temperature 149°F/65°C
Sous Vide Time 32 minutes
Active Cooking Time 20 minutes, plus chilling time

To Make Ahead Sauce can be refrigerated for up to 1 week.

Why This Recipe Works Chefs are obsessed with emulsions because they combine something that is already delicious—rich fat—with a water-based ingredient to create something even more satisfying (think mayonnaise, butter, and cream—all emulsions). And egg yolks are one of nature's top-notch emulsions—a creamy mixture of water, protein, and fat (a full 34 percent!). We love a good runny egg yolk, and this recipe gives us the convenience of pasteurized, perfectly thickened yolks always ready to drizzle on toast, a burger, pasta carbonara, you name it. This recipe safely achieves pasteurization (144°F/62.2°C for at least 6 minutes) and then continues to heat the yolks to create a sauce with the ideal runny texture. Store-bought, in-shell, pasteurized eggs can also be used without any changes to the recipe. The cooking time depends on the number of yolks, so this recipe cannot be scaled up or down without making adjustments. Don't discard the whites— save them to make recipes such as angel food cake or meringue cookies. You can also freeze them for later use.

12 large (200 grams) egg yolks
¼ teaspoon (2 grams) salt

1 Using sous vide circulator, bring water to 149°F/65°C in 7-quart container. Using spatula or ladle, push yolks through fine-mesh strainer into medium bowl; gently whisk yolks and salt until just smooth (do not overwhisk).

2 Pour mixture into 1-quart zipper-lock freezer bag. Seal bag, pressing out as much air as possible. Gently lower bag into prepared water bath until mixture is fully submerged, and then clip top corner of bag to side of water bath container, allowing remaining air bubbles to rise to top of bag. Reopen 1 corner of zipper, release remaining air bubbles, and reseal bag. Cover and cook for 32 minutes.

3 Meanwhile, fill large bowl halfway with ice and water. Transfer bag to ice bath and let sit until chilled, about 10 minutes. Transfer sauce to airtight container or squeeze bottle and refrigerate.

Yogurt

YIELD **MAKES 4 CUPS (965 GRAMS)**
Sous Vide Temperature 110°F /43°C
Sous Vide Time 5 to 24 hours
Active Cooking Time 1 hour, plus chilling time

To Make Ahead Yogurt can be refrigerated for up to 1 week; stir to recombine before serving.

Why This Recipe Works Making yogurt at home is a pretty simple process with delicious results, and it requires just two ingredients: milk and a starter (for this recipe we used a small amount of store-bought yogurt with live cultures). The live cultures—namely *Lactobacillus bulgaricus* and *Streptococcus thermophilus*—are beneficial bacteria that give yogurt the flavor (tangy) and texture (thick) that we love. It doesn't hurt that these cultures are purportedly very good for you, too. First, we heated milk to 185°F/85°C to kill unwanted microorganisms and denature the proteins in the milk. This protein reconfiguration allowed the cultured milk to transform into creamy yogurt rather than separate into curds and whey. We learned that it was important to resist the urge to stir the milk during this heating process. As the proteins denature, they become loose strands eager to tangle with each other; stirring led to small lumps in the end product. We then cooled the milk to 110°F/43.5°C to create a friendly environment for the starter culture and to prevent curdling. We stirred in the yogurt starter, put the mixture into jars, and finally placed the jars in a water bath to incubate. The beauty of using a sous vide circulator for this process was that we could precisely hold our yogurt in the culturing temperature sweet spot without any babysitting. Five hours later, we were rewarded with delicious, tangy homemade yogurt. We found we could leave it for as long as 24 hours; the longer the incubation time, the greater the pucker. The success of this recipe hinges on using yogurt that contains live and active cultures. You will need two 16-ounce Mason jars for this recipe. Be careful not to overtighten the jars before placing them in the prepared water bath; that can cause the glass to crack. This recipe can be doubled.

3¾ cups (845 grams) whole milk
¼ cup (60 grams) plain yogurt with live and active cultures

1 Using sous vide circulator, bring water to 110°F/43.5°C in 7-quart container. Heat milk in large saucepan over medium-low heat, without stirring, until milk registers 185°F/85°C. Strain milk through fine-mesh strainer into 8-cup liquid measuring cup. Let cool until milk registers 110°F/43.5°C, stirring occasionally to prevent skin from forming, about 30 minutes.

2 Combine yogurt and ½ cup (120 grams) cooled milk in small bowl. Gently stir yogurt mixture into remaining cooled milk, and then transfer to two 16-ounce Mason jars and seal; do not overtighten lid. Place jars in prepared water bath, cover, and cook for at least 5 hours or up to 24 hours. Let yogurt cool at room temperature for 15 minutes. Transfer to refrigerator and let sit until fully chilled, about 3 hours. Stir yogurt to recombine before serving.

Variations
Greek Yogurt
Line fine-mesh strainer with double layer of coffee filters and set over large bowl. Transfer completely cooled yogurt to prepared strainer, cover, and refrigerate until 2 cups (450 grams) of liquid have drained into bowl, 7 to 8 hours. Discard drained liquid.

Fruit-on-the-Bottom Yogurt Cups
This recipe will work with any variety of your favorite jam or preserves.

Substitute eight 4-ounce jars for 16-ounce jars. Dollop 1 tablespoon (20 grams) jam or preserves into each jar before transferring yogurt mixture to jars in step 2. Carefully pour off any liquid that has settled on top of yogurt before serving.

Ricotta Cheese

YIELD **MAKES 2 CUPS (400 GRAMS)**
Sous Vide Temperature 190°F/88°C
Sous Vide Time 30 minutes
Active Cooking Time 1 hour, plus chilling time

To Make Ahead Ricotta can be refrigerated for up to 5 days; stir to recombine before using.

Why This Recipe Works For those interested in making their own cheese, homemade ricotta is a great entry-level recipe. *Ricotta* is Italian for "twice cooked," a reference to the traditional ricotta-making process of reheating whey, or the liquid left over from the production of other cheese, and then adding acid to coagulate the milk proteins. This method is called acid-heat coagulation. For our recipe, we started with whole milk and used distilled white vinegar for the acid. Distilled white vinegar, unlike lemon juice (the other common choice), is neutral in flavor and always contains 5 percent acidity. Heating the milk to 190°F/88°C denatured the whey proteins, allowing them to interact and coagulate with their casein counterparts. Using the sous vide technique for this process eliminated the risk of scorched pots and ruined batches of ricotta, a common problem when making it on a stovetop. Once the curds had formed, all that was left to do was strain them through cheesecloth. Cheese making has never been easier. Be sure to use whole milk; milk with other fat percentages will not work as well for this recipe.

8 cups (1.8 kilograms) whole milk
5 tablespoons (75 grams) distilled white vinegar
1 teaspoon (6 grams) salt

1 Using sous vide circulator, bring water to 190°F/88°C in 7-quart container.

2 Whisk together milk, vinegar, and salt in large bowl. Pour mixture into 1-gallon zipper-lock freezer bag. Seal bag, pressing out as much air as possible. Gently lower bag into prepared water bath until mixture is fully submerged, and then clip top corner of bag to side of water bath container, allowing remaining air bubbles to rise to top of bag. Reopen 1 corner of zipper, release remaining air bubbles, and reseal bag. Cover and cook until milk mixture fully separates into solid curds and translucent whey, about 30 minutes. If curds have not separated, cook for additional 10 minutes.

3 Remove bag from water bath and let milk mixture cool for 10 minutes. Meanwhile, set colander over large bowl and line with double layer of cheesecloth. Gently pour cooled milk mixture into prepared colander. Let drain, stirring occasionally, until whey has drained from edges of cheese but center is still very moist, about 30 minutes. Discard drained whey. Gently transfer cheese to now-empty bowl. Stir well to break up large curds and incorporate remaining whey. Cover and refrigerate until fully chilled, about 2 hours.

Crème Fraîche

YIELD MAKES 1 CUP (265 GRAMS)
Sous Vide Temperature 96°F/36°C
Sous Vide Time 12 to 24 hours
Active Cooking Time 20 minutes, plus chilling time

To Make Ahead Crème fraîche can be refrigerated for up to 1 month.

Why This Recipe Works Crème fraîche is a cultured dairy product that is easy to make at home with a sous vide device. Traditionally it is often left to culture—for at least 12 and up to 24 hours—in a warm place. Culturing crème fraîche in a regulated water bath removes the need to manage (or worry about) the temperature of its surroundings during that critical phase. While yogurt is made by culturing milk, crème fraîche starts with heavy cream. For our recipe, we combined a small amount of buttermilk with pasteurized heavy cream, and then we placed this mixture in a warm water bath to culture for 12 hours. We strongly recommend using pasteurized—not ultra-pasteurized—cream for this recipe. Ultra-pasteurized cream is treated at a higher temperature before packaging and thus produces crème fraîche with a more muted flavor. Crème fraîche is a traditional accompaniment for luxurious caviar, or it can be served with fresh berries as an alternative to whipped cream. It's a favorite cultured dairy product to stir into hot braises and stews because, unlike sour cream or yogurt, crème fraîche won't curdle. Curdling occurs when cooking heat causes dairy proteins to denature and form clumps. The high butterfat content of crème fraîche (30 to 40 percent versus 18 to 20 percent of sour cream and roughly 4 percent of yogurt) protects against this clumping by keeping the proteins, which coat the many fat globules, further apart. Different brands of buttermilk contain different live and active cultures, which will produce crème fraîche with subtle flavor differences. Make sure to reserve some of the crème fraîche from your first batch to use as a starter instead of buttermilk for your next batch. You will need one 16-ounce Mason jar for this recipe. Be careful not to overtighten the jar before placing it in the prepared water bath; that can cause the glass to crack.

1 cup (235 grams) pasteurized heavy cream
2 tablespoons (30 grams) cultured buttermilk

1 Using sous vide circulator, bring water to 96°F/36°C in 7-quart container.

2 Combine heavy cream and buttermilk in 16-ounce Mason jar and seal; do not overtighten lid. Transfer jar to water bath, cover, and cook for at least 12 hours or up to 24 hours.

3 Transfer jar to refrigerator and let crème fraîche sit until fully chilled and thickened, about 24 hours. Stir to recombine before serving.

Food Safety and Sous Vide

Key Points

- Sous vide cooking is very safe thanks to its precision and control
- We cook most food at or above 130°F/54.5°C to reduce risk of harmful bacterial growth
- If cooking below 130°F/54.5°C, we sear meat *before* putting it in the water bath to kill surface bacteria
- It's important to rapidly chill foods if you're planning to keep them in the refrigerator
- Don't sous vide raw garlic

So, you've bought a sous vide circulator. You've come home from the grocery store with two nice steaks and some high-quality plastic zipper-lock bags. You heat up the water bath to 130°F/54°C. You're ready to put the steaks in the bags and then into the water bath and walk away for a couple of hours. But then you stop and you think, "Is this really safe?"

Sous vide relies on cooking at low temperatures, often for long periods of time. But when it comes to temperature and time, what is safe?

Food safety is top of our minds, too.

"I believe sous vide is significantly safer than most cooking methods," says Douglas Baldwin, a mathematician at ChefSteps, a Seattle-based food and technology company. He spent months creating pasteurization charts for his own book, *Sous Vide for the Home Cook*. "It's so much more predictable." But there are a few things you need to pay attention to as you cook.

WHAT IS DANGEROUS?

First, let's talk about what's dangerous. A few types of bacteria in particular are responsible for most foodborne illness: *Salmonella, Escherichia coli,* and *Campylobacter jejuni*. (If you're wondering about the safety of cooking in plastic, see page 130.) *Salmonella,* a resilient group of bacteria that is most commonly found in poultry and eggs, is ingested by chickens, and then contaminates their muscle tissue, intestines, and ovaries. *Salmonella* can migrate into the muscle of chickens, meaning that they are contaminated not just on the surface but also inside the meat. *Escherichia coli* is a general group of bacteria that reside in the intestines of many animals, including humans. But if ingested, some strains of *E. coli* can wreak havoc. *Campylobacter jejuni* is a spiral-shaped bacteria that causes one of the most common diarrheal illnesses in humans in America.

Food pathogens won't let you know that they are there. Unlike the microorganisms that let you know when the food in your fridge has spoiled, these pathogens can't be seen, smelled, or tasted. But they can be controlled—with acid, with salt, and even with some spices. But, most important, they can be controlled with temperature.

WHAT IS PASTEURIZATION?

To "pasteurize" is to heat food to a temperature for a certain amount of time in order to reduce enough of the pathogens to deem it safe. We often pasteurize in sous vide cooking.

In the fridge, bacterial action and reproduction slow way down; we can keep food in there for days or weeks without worrying about pathogens growing. And at the temperatures reached when we boil or bake food, the bacteria are killed. It's between those low and high temperatures that bacteria are happiest, so that's where extra care is called for.

When food sits between 40°F/4°C and 140°F/60°C, it is often said to be in the "danger zone" for bacterial growth. It's between these temperatures that potentially harmful bacteria can thrive. But what is not often referenced is that danger—and, thus, safety—isn't just about temperature. It's also about time. "Most people, when they talk about food safety, they oversimplify," explains Baldwin.

For example, the FDA recommends cooking chicken breast meat (which is comprised of 5 percent fat) to 165°F/74°C in order to pasteurize it. When the center of the meat reaches that temperature, virtually 100 percent of *Salmonella* is killed immediately. When brought to 160°F/71°C, it takes 14 seconds to kill the *Salmonella*. At 155°F/68°C, it takes 50 seconds. At 150°F/65.5°C, our favorite temperature for chicken, it takes 3 minutes. We don't recommend cooking chicken at 136°F/58°C—it's a little more like chicken sashimi, really—but you can. It will just take 69 minutes at that temperature to be safe.

With enough time, most food pathogens are killed at 130°F/54.5°C, according to the FDA and Baldwin. For the recipes in this book, this is our magic number.

We cook almost everything either at or above that temperature. (When cooking in a water bath set to 130°F/54.5°C, the food will eventually become that temperature as well.) As an extra precaution, if we plan to cook meat below our magic temperature, the first thing we do is sear it in a hot pan in order to kill off any bacteria on the surface before we circulate (see Butter-Basted Rib-Eye Steak, page 72, and Peppercorn-Crusted Roast Beef, page 76). Of course, nothing is perfect, so if you are immunocompromised or prefer to exercise greater caution for other reasons, please proceed with care. It's important to note that the risk of eating steak prepared to medium-rare in our sous vide recipes is not any different from the risk of eating steak that is grilled to medium-rare. "For the most part, if your steak is seared, then the bacterial load is safe," says Baldwin. "That's why the food code allows you to have seared medium-rare steak."

Safety for ground meat is different than for whole cuts of meat. While the inside of whole cuts of beef are sterile, harmful bacteria can be present throughout ground meat. (Of course *Salmonella* in poultry can be present throughout, whether the meat is ground or whole.)

Also important: Even when food is pasteurized, it isn't safe indefinitely. The food either needs to be eaten immediately, or rapidly chilled and then refrigerated. What does "rapidly chilled" mean? It involves an ice bath (see Introduction, page 13). And once the food is in the refrigerator? Don't leave it there too long. As Dave Arnold, author of *Liquid Intelligence* and an early sous vide adopter, warns, "If you store it improperly, you can get some microaerobic situations, like listeria can grow on cheese and meat slowly at refrigeration."

And one final note: We've chosen not to circulate any raw garlic in this book. This is because garlic is particularly susceptible to *Clostridium botulinum* (or botulism), especially in a warm, anaerobic environment (like sous vide). If we don't cook raw garlic before circulating it, we use granulated garlic powder, or we leave garlic out entirely.

Eggs

As you've seen throughout this chapter, egg cookery is a precise and delicate task. In this chart, we show you the importance of temperature for eggs—just one degree can make a world of change when cooking eggs sous vide, especially when held there for 60 minutes, which is the formula for many classic sous-vide egg recipes.

But, of course, these egg recipes are not dependent on temperature alone. Time is equally important. Our perfect hard-cooked egg is created in a water bath set to 194°F/90°C—no higher, no lower. But an egg cooked at 194°F/90°C for any less than 20 minutes would be too runny and raw. An egg cooked at that temperature for longer than 20 minutes would quickly become chalky and dry. We spent a lot of time testing the perfect temperature and time for our soft-poached egg, and we found that 12 minutes at the (relatively) high temperature of 167°F/75°C set the white just enough to be firm yet tender right out of the shell, while the yolk remained runny.

Follow our recipes for guaranteed perfection, but don't hesitate to do some experimenting of your own, using this chart as a basic guide. It's time to get cracking!

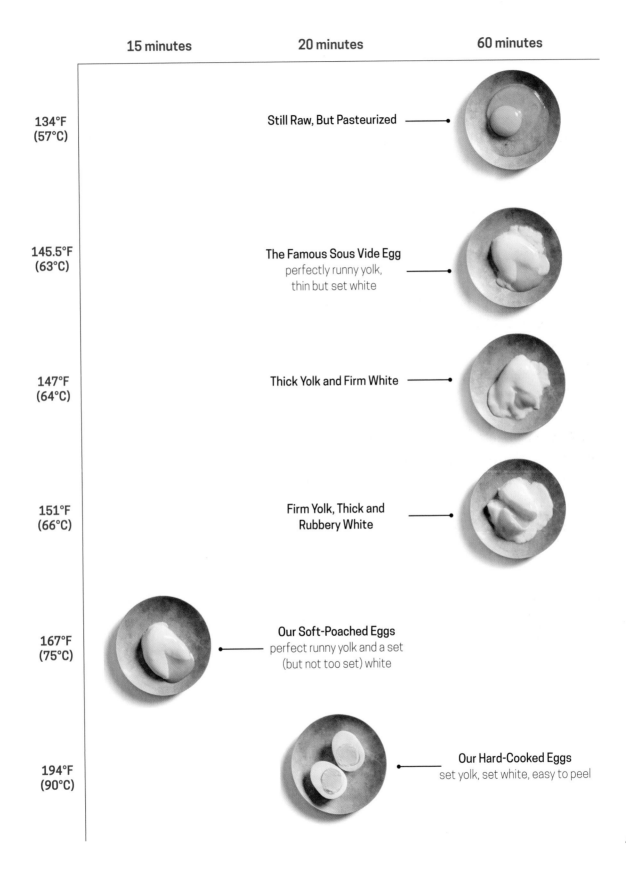

15 minutes	20 minutes	60 minutes

134°F (57°C) — Still Raw, But Pasteurized

145.5°F (63°C) — The Famous Sous Vide Egg
perfectly runny yolk, thin but set white

147°F (64°C) — Thick Yolk and Firm White

151°F (66°C) — Firm Yolk, Thick and Rubbery White

167°F (75°C) — Our Soft-Poached Eggs
perfect runny yolk and a set (but not too set) white

194°F (90°C) — Our Hard-Cooked Eggs
set yolk, set white, easy to peel

POULTRY

"Boneless, skinless chicken breasts are amazing!" said no one, ever. That is, of course, until sous vide came onto the scene.

Chicken breast is an incredibly lean, delicate cut of poultry. It has very little fat, which means it can taste bland. A lack of fat also means that when a chicken breast is eaten, there is nothing to give the perception of moistness. While "the perception of moistness" may not sound particularly enticing, it's actually a key component of flavor. Couple this with the fact that chicken is traditionally cooked to the relatively high temperature of 165 degrees Fahrenheit/74 degrees Celsius (more about this in a bit), and there are a lot of reasons to bet against a delicious outcome.

Sous vide cooking allows us to treat our boneless, skinless chicken breasts right: It lets us cook them at a lower temperature for longer, and it enables us to pair them with flavorful aromatics and easy sauces. How?

First, let's talk about temperature. Traditionally, chicken is cooked to a high temperature in order to keep it safe from the risk of foodborne illnesses. Factory-farmed birds can be contaminated with pathogenic microorganisms such as *Salmonella enterica* and *Campylobacter jejuni*. *Salmonella*, in particular, can migrate into the muscle tissue of chickens, which means that chicken parts and whole chickens can be contaminated not just on the surface, but within. Cooking the meat to 165°F/74°C guarantees ridding the poultry of 100 percent of the *Salmonella* almost immediately.

But cooking chicken to this temperature also causes its muscle fibers to shrink, and enough water is pushed out of the meat that it often emerges from traditional cooking methods decidedly dry.

But wait! It *is* possible to kill all *Salmonella* without bringing chicken to 165°F/74°C. This is because the elimination of *Salmonella* is a function of both time and temperature. (For more on pasteurization, see "Food Safety and Sous Vide," page 40.) For a piece of chicken with 5 percent fat (the higher the fat content, the slower *Salmonella* is killed), it takes less than 10 seconds at 165°F/74°C to kill 100 percent of the *Salmonella*. Drop that temperature to 160°F/71°C and the same kill rate of *Salmonella* (and therefore level of safety) can be achieved by holding the chicken there for around 14 seconds. At 155°F/68°C it takes 50 seconds; at

150°F/65.5°C we get the same effect after 3 minutes. In fact, the USDA commissioned a study that tested cooking chicken at temperatures as low as 136°F/58°C, at which point it takes 69 minutes to render *Salmonella* benign.

The power of sous vide means that chicken breast can be sealed in a bag and cooked at 150°F/65.5°C until the internal temperature matches that of the water bath; holding it there for just 3 minutes ensures complete safety. And because the chicken breasts are cooked at this lower temperature, they emerge from the bag incredibly juicy and tender.

For our Foolproof Poached Chicken (page 46) we do exactly that, cooking boneless, skinless chicken breasts at 150°F/65.5°C for at least 1 hour or up to 3 hours (which guarantees 3 minutes in the safe zone). Flavored with lemon and thyme or soy and ginger—or simply salt and pepper—these juicy, tender breasts are anything but boring. Serve them sliced over a green salad—or turn them into Chicken Salad (page 48). Looking for chicken with crisp skin? We've got you there, too (page 50). After a slightly longer "swim" and then a rest, we crisp the skin by patting the chicken breasts dry with paper towels and then searing them skin side down in a hot pan. Our Peri Peri Chicken (page 53) gives breasts a deep flavor by cooking them with a North African–inspired spice paste.

We adapt our technique for chicken thighs (page 54) by cooking them in a water bath heated to 165°F/74°C—a higher temperature due to the fact that dark meat contains more collagen and fat than lean breasts. After circulating, resting, and patting the thighs dry, we found that pressing them down with a heavy Dutch oven aided in crisping the skin when searing. We get thighs to the perfect ultra-tender texture in a water bath set to 180°F/82°C for our Shredded Chicken Tacos (page 56).

Want to take your sous vide poultry to the next level? Go for Seared Duck Breasts (page 58) for date night. Take our Chicken Liver Mousse (page 60) to your next potluck. Is it Thanksgiving? Look no further than our foolproof Easy Boneless Turkey Breast (page 62). You can thank us later.

Foolproof Poached Chicken

YIELD SERVES 4
Sous Vide Temperature 150°F/65.5°C
Sous Vide Time 1 to 3 hours
Active Cooking Time 25 minutes

To Make Ahead Chicken can be rapidly chilled in ice bath (see page 13) and then refrigerated in zipper-lock bag after step 2 for up to 5 days. To reheat, return sealed bag to water bath set to 150°F/65.5°C for 20 minutes and then proceed with step 3.

Why This Recipe Works Poached chicken gets a bad rap for being tough, dry, and a little squeaky between your teeth. But that's probably because poaching is a relatively imprecise cooking method: If your poaching water's too hot, the meat overcooks; if you leave the meat in the water too long, it overcooks; if you use too little water, the meat—you guessed it—undercooks. There are a lot of variables when poaching chicken. Thankfully, cooking sous vide eliminates most of them. For foolproof poached chicken, we cook chicken breasts at a moderate temperature for about an hour, which results in a juicy, tender texture that's just firm enough that it doesn't fall apart. While this recipe is finished in an hour, you can hold the chicken in the bath for up to 3 hours before the texture starts to change—giving you some flexibility. This perfectly poached chicken is great on its own, sliced over salad, or used in our Chicken Salad recipe (page 48). In addition, this method is a great starting point for experimentation and variation, so feel free to add spices, herbs, or boldly flavored marinades to the bag (just don't add fresh garlic; it is particularly susceptible to botulism).

4 8-ounce (225 grams) boneless, skinless chicken breasts, trimmed
Salt and pepper
¼ cup (56 grams) vegetable oil

1 Using sous vide circulator, bring water to 150°F/65.5°C in 7-quart container.

2 Season chicken with salt and pepper. Place chicken and oil in 1-gallon zipper-lock freezer bag and toss to coat. Seal bag, pressing out as much air as possible. Gently lower bag into prepared water bath until chicken is fully submerged, and then clip top corner of bag to side of water bath container, allowing remaining air bubbles to rise to top of bag. Reopen 1 corner of zipper, release remaining air bubbles, and reseal bag. Cover and cook for at least 1 hour or up to 3 hours.

3 Transfer chicken to paper towel–lined plate and let rest for 5 to 10 minutes. Serve.

Variations

Foolproof Lemon-Thyme Poached Chicken
Combine 1 teaspoon (6 grams) salt, ½ teaspoon (2 grams) pepper, ½ teaspoon (1 gram) garlic powder, ½ teaspoon (1 gram) minced fresh thyme, and 1 teaspoon (2 grams) grated lemon zest in bowl. Sprinkle chicken with salt mixture in step 2.

Foolproof Soy-Ginger Poached Chicken
Omit salt and pepper. Whisk ¼ cup (59 grams) soy sauce, ¼ cup (50 grams) sugar, 1 teaspoon (3 grams) grated fresh ginger, 1 teaspoon (5 grams) toasted sesame oil, and ½ teaspoon (2 grams) white pepper together in bowl. Substitute soy sauce mixture for oil.

Chicken Salad

YIELD **SERVES 4 TO 6**
Sous Vide Temperature 150°F/65.5°C
Sous Vide Time 1 to 3 hours
Active Cooking Time 40 minutes

To Make Ahead Salad can be refrigerated for up to 2 days.

Why This Recipe Works Recipes for chicken salad are only as good as the chicken. If the chicken is dry or flavorless, no amount of dressing or add-ins will camouflage it. How do we ensure silky, juicy, and flavorful chicken? Sous vide, of course. We circulate our chicken breasts at 150°F/65.5°C for anywhere from 1 to 3 hours. Incomparably moist, and perfect every single time, this chicken was a no-brainer for turning into chicken salad. Serve it in a sandwich or spooned over leafy greens.

½ cup (116 grams) mayonnaise
2 tablespoons (30 grams) lemon juice
1 teaspoon (6 grams) Dijon mustard
  Salt and pepper
1 recipe Foolproof Poached Chicken (page 46), chilled and cut into ½-inch pieces
2 celery ribs (120 grams), minced
1 shallot (30 grams), minced
1 tablespoon (2 grams) minced fresh parsley
1 tablespoon (2 grams) minced fresh tarragon

Whisk mayonnaise, lemon juice, mustard, and ¼ teaspoon (1 gram) pepper together in large bowl. Add chicken, celery, shallot, parsley, and tarragon and toss to combine. Season with salt and pepper to taste. Serve.

Crispy-Skinned Bone-In Chicken Breasts

YIELD SERVES 4
Sous Vide Temperature 150°F/65.5°C
Sous Vide Time 1½ to 3 hours
Active Cooking Time 30 minutes

To Make Ahead Chicken can be rapidly chilled in ice bath (see page 13) and then refrigerated in zipper-lock bag after step 2 for up to 5 days. To reheat, return sealed bag to water bath set to 150°F/65.5°C for 20 minutes and then proceed with step 3.

Why This Recipe Works Cooking a perfect skin-on chicken breast is a tall order. You want your chicken to have a juicy, firm interior and a crackling crisp skin. But to get perfectly crisp skin you need to sear the breast after cooking—a hot act that often results in overcooking the lean and delicate meat just beneath. The solution? Cook it sous vide to maintain the ideal temperature and let the chicken rest for 5 to 10 minutes before searing to retain juiciness. To get a really good sear? We aggressively patted the exterior of the chicken dry with paper towels.

4 12-ounce (340 grams) bone-in split chicken breasts, trimmed

Salt and pepper

6 tablespoons (84 grams) vegetable oil

1 Using sous vide circulator, bring water to 150°F/65.5°C in 7-quart container.

2 Season chicken with salt and pepper. Place chicken and ¼ cup (56 grams) oil in 1-gallon zipper-lock freezer bag and toss to coat. Seal bag, pressing out as much air as possible. Gently lower bag into prepared water bath until chicken is fully submerged, and then clip top corner of bag to side of water bath container, allowing remaining air bubbles to rise to top of bag. Reopen 1 corner of zipper, release remaining air bubbles, and reseal bag. Cover and cook for at least 1½ hours or up to 3 hours.

3 Transfer chicken to paper towel–lined plate and let rest for 5 to 10 minutes. Pat chicken thoroughly dry with paper towels. Heat remaining 2 tablespoons (28 grams) oil in 12-inch skillet over medium-high heat until just smoking. Place chicken skin side down in skillet and cook until skin is well-browned and crisp, 4 to 6 minutes. Serve.

Leek and White Wine Pan Sauce

YIELD Makes about ¾ cup

Sauvignon Blanc is our preferred white wine for cooking. Note that this recipe is meant to be started after you have seared the chicken breasts.

Vegetable oil, if needed

1 leek (227 grams), white and light green parts only, halved lengthwise, sliced ¼ inch thick, and washed thoroughly

1 teaspoon (3 grams) all-purpose flour

¾ cup (178 grams) chicken broth

½ cup (118 grams) dry white wine or dry vermouth

1 tablespoon (14 grams) unsalted butter, chilled

2 teaspoons (1 gram) chopped fresh tarragon

1 teaspoon (5 grams) whole-grain mustard

Salt and pepper

1 Pour off all but 2 tablespoons (28 grams) fat from skillet used to sear chicken. (If necessary, add oil to equal 2 tablespoons (28 grams).) Add leek and cook over medium heat until softened and lightly browned, about 5 minutes. Stir in flour and cook for 1 minute. Slowly whisk in broth and wine, scraping up any browned bits and smoothing out any lumps. Bring to simmer and cook until thickened and reduced to ¾ cup, 3 to 5 minutes.

2 Off heat, whisk in butter until melted, and then whisk in tarragon, mustard, and any accumulated meat juices. Season with salt and pepper to taste.

Hoisin-Sesame Pan Sauce

YIELD Makes about ¾ cup

Note that this recipe is meant to be started after you have seared the chicken breasts.

Vegetable oil, if needed

2 teaspoons (10 grams) grated fresh ginger

¼ cup (75 grams) hoisin sauce

½ cup (118 grams) orange juice

½ cup (118 grams) chicken broth

2 scallions (30 grams), sliced thin on bias

1 teaspoon (5 grams) toasted sesame oil

Pepper

1 Pour off all but 1 tablespoon (14 grams) fat from skillet used to sear chicken. (If necessary, add oil to equal 1 tablespoon (14 grams).) Add ginger and cook over medium heat until fragrant, about 15 seconds. Stir in hoisin, orange juice, and broth, scraping up any browned bits. Bring to simmer and cook until liquid is reduced to ¾ cup (175 grams), about 4 minutes.

2 Off heat, stir in scallions, sesame oil, and any accumulated meat juices. Season with pepper to taste.

Peri Peri Chicken

YIELD SERVES 4
Sous Vide Temperature 150°F/65.5°C
Sous Vide Time 1½ to 3 hours
Active Cooking Time 50 minutes, plus marinating time

To Make Ahead Chicken and accumulated juices can be rapidly chilled in ice bath (see page 13) and then refrigerated in zipper-lock bag after step 2 for up to 5 days. To reheat, return sealed bag to water bath set to 150°F/65.5 °C for 20 minutes. Proceed with step 3.

Why This Recipe Works If you've ever found yourself in the United Kingdom, you've probably eaten in, seen, heard of, or smelled a Nando's. This humble fast-casual restaurant empire does one thing and one thing only: chicken. Specifically, they serve *peri peri* chicken. A mouthwatering dish with roots in Africa and the West Indies, it features grilled chicken that has been marinated overnight in a spicy paste. This is our take on it. We start by blending garlic powder, tomato paste, herbs, spices, lemon juice, and dried arbol chiles to make a thick paste. We throw the paste straight into a plastic bag with the chicken to first marinate and then circulate. (Marinating is key to give the salt time to penetrate the meat to both season it and help it retain moisture during cooking.) Because there is little to no evaporation due to the sealed bag, this cooking method produces a considerable amount of juices. We reduce the juices in a pan to intensify the flavors, and then we brush them over the chicken before giving the meat a final broil in the oven to brown the skin. If you can find *peri peri* chiles, use them instead of arbols. For a spicier dish, use the greater amount of chiles.

- 2-5 arbol chiles (1-3 grams), stemmed
- 1 shallot (30 grams), chopped
- 2 tablespoons (28 grams) extra-virgin olive oil
- 1 tablespoon (18 grams) salt
- 1 tablespoon (15 grams) tomato paste
- 2 teaspoons (8 grams) sugar
- 1½ teaspoons (3 grams) paprika
- 1½ teaspoons (6 grams) five-spice powder
- 1 teaspoon (2 grams) garlic powder
- 1 teaspoon (2 grams) grated lemon zest plus 2 tablespoons (30 grams) juice, plus lemon wedges for serving
- ½ teaspoon (1.5 grams) pepper
- ¼ teaspoon (1 gram) cayenne pepper
- 2 bay leaves (1 gram), crumbled
- 4 12-ounce (340 grams) bone-in split chicken breasts, trimmed

1 Process arbols, shallot, oil, salt, tomato paste, sugar, paprika, five-spice powder, garlic powder, lemon zest and juice, pepper, cayenne, and bay leaves in blender until smooth, scraping down sides of blender jar as needed, about 1 minute. Place chicken and chile paste in 1-gallon zipper-lock freezer bag and toss to coat. Seal bag, pressing out as much air as possible. Refrigerate chicken for at least 6 hours or up to 24 hours.

2 Using sous vide circulator, bring water to 150°F/65.5°C in 7-quart container. Gently lower bag into prepared water bath until chicken is fully submerged, and then clip top corner of bag to side of water bath container, allowing remaining air bubbles to rise to top of bag. Reopen 1 corner of zipper, release remaining air bubbles, and reseal bag. Cover and cook chicken for at least 1½ hours or up to 3 hours.

3 Adjust oven rack 6 inches from broiler element and heat broiler. Set wire rack in aluminum foil–lined rimmed baking sheet and spray with vegetable oil spray. Transfer chicken skin side up to prepared rack and let rest while preparing sauce.

4 Pour accumulated juices into 8-inch skillet, bring to simmer over medium heat, and cook until reduced by two-thirds, 3 to 5 minutes. Brush chicken with sauce and broil until skin is crisp and lightly charred, 6 to 8 minutes. Serve with lemon wedges.

Crispy-Skinned Chicken Thighs

YIELD SERVES 4
Sous Vide Temperature 165°F/74°C
Sous Vide Time 1½ to 4 hours
Active Cooking Time 35 minutes

To Make Ahead Chicken and accumulated juices can be rapidly chilled in ice bath (see page 13) and then refrigerated in zipper-lock bag after step 2 for up to 5 days. To reheat, return sealed bag to water bath set to 150°F/65.5°C for 20 minutes. Proceed with step 3.

Why This Recipe Works Of all the common parts of a chicken, the thigh ought to be MVP. With more pockets of fat and collagen than breasts, thighs contain great potential for flavor. We found cooking thighs at a higher temperature (180°F/82°C) resulted in a fall-apart texture, while lower temperatures (160°F/71°C) left the thighs a bit too chewy. An intermediate temperature (165°F/74°C) gave the best balance of a cohesive but tender texture, and a juicy interior. We use a Dutch oven to press the thighs while searing. This method maximizes contact with the surface of the pan, giving us an even layer of crispy, crackly skin. To reduce cleanup, wrap the bottom of the pot with aluminum foil in step 3. Be sure to double bag the chicken thighs to protect against seam failure.

4 7-ounce (200 grams) bone-in chicken thighs, trimmed
  Salt and pepper
6 tablespoons (84 grams) vegetable oil

1 Using sous vide circulator, bring water to 165°F/74°C in 7-quart container.

2 Season chicken with salt and pepper. Place chicken and ¼ cup (56 grams) oil in 1-gallon zipper-lock freezer bag and toss to coat. Seal bag, pressing out as much air as possible. Place bag into second 1-gallon zipper-lock freezer bag and seal. Gently lower bag into prepared water bath until chicken is fully submerged, and then clip top corner of bag to side of water bath container, allowing remaining air bubbles to rise to top of bag. Reopen 1 corner of zipper, release remaining air bubbles, and reseal bag. Cover and cook for at least 1½ hours or up to 4 hours.

3 Transfer chicken to paper towel–lined plate and let rest for 5 to 10 minutes. Pat chicken dry with paper towels. Heat remaining 2 tablespoons (28 grams) oil in 12-inch skillet over medium-high heat until just smoking. Place chicken skin side down in skillet. Place heavy pot on top of chicken to press it flat and cook until skin is well-browned and very crisp, 4 to 6 minutes. Serve.

Mango-Peach Chutney
YIELD Makes about 2 cups
Avoid adding the cilantro to the chutney before it is fully cooled, or the cilantro will wilt.

1 tablespoon (14 grams) vegetable oil
2 ripe but firm mangos, peeled and chopped (3 cups/567 grams)
1 shallot (30 grams), minced
1 tablespoon (5 grams) grated fresh ginger
⅓ cup (79 grams) white wine vinegar
½ cup (160 grams) peach preserves
¼ cup (5 grams) minced fresh cilantro

Heat oil in 12-inch nonstick skillet over medium-high heat until shimmering. Cook mangos until lightly browned, about 5 minutes. Stir in shallot and ginger and cook until fragrant, about 1 minute. Stir in vinegar and peach preserves, bring to simmer, and cook until thickened and measures about 2 cups, about 5 minutes. Transfer to bowl and let cool to room temperature, about 2 hours. Stir in cilantro. (Chutney can be refrigerated for up to 1 week; bring to room temperature before serving.)

Tangy Corn Relish

YIELD Makes about 2½ cups

You can substitute 1½ cups (170 grams) frozen corn kernels for 2 ears corn.

- ¼ cup (50 grams) sugar
- 2 tablespoons (18 grams) all-purpose flour
- 1½ teaspoons (9 grams) salt
- 1 teaspoon (3 grams) pepper
- 1 cup (236 grams) distilled white vinegar
- 2 tablespoons (30 grams) water
- 2 ears corn, kernels cut from cobs (1½ cups/170 grams)
- 1 red bell pepper (226 grams), stemmed, seeded, and chopped fine
- ½ onion (70 grams), chopped fine
- ½ teaspoon (1 gram) yellow mustard seeds
- ¼ teaspoon (0.5 grams) celery seeds

Whisk sugar, flour, salt, and pepper together in large saucepan. Slowly whisk in vinegar and water until incorporated. Stir in corn, bell pepper, onion, mustard seeds, and celery seeds and bring to simmer. Cook, stirring occasionally, until vegetables are tender and mixture has thickened slightly and measures about 2½ cups, about 40 minutes. Transfer to bowl and let cool to room temperature, about 2 hours, before serving. (Relish can be refrigerated for up to 1 week; bring to room temperature before serving.)

Shredded Chicken Tacos (*Tinga de Pollo*)

YIELD SERVES 6
Sous Vide Temperature 180°F/82°C
Sous Vide Time 3 to 5 hours
Active Cooking Time 50 minutes

To Make Ahead Chicken and sauce can be rapidly chilled in ice bath (see page 13) and then refrigerated in zipper-lock bag after step 4 for up to 5 days. To reheat, return sealed bag to water bath set to 150°F/65.5°C for 20 minutes. Proceed with step 5.

Why This Recipe Works *Tinga de pollo* is typically made by poaching and then shredding breast meat, preparing a tomato-chipotle sauce separately, and then combining the two at the end. That's a real missed opportunity for building flavor, but luckily, cooking sous vide offers a way to maximize flavor and produce perfect shredded chicken goodness. First, we skipped the chicken breasts and opted for thighs: They're juicier, more flavorful, and those pockets of fat and collagen are better suited for a long, extended cooking time. Searing the thighs at the start gave extra flavor to the sauce, which we blended before bagging it all up. Circulating the meat and sauce together allowed the flavors to marry and develop over a long period of time without having to stand over a simmering pot or carefully watch an oven. But the best part of this recipe? All the work is done up front, so at the end of the sous vide cooking time, all you have to do is empty the bag into a big bowl, shred the meat, and serve it to all of your family and friends. Be sure to double bag the chicken thighs to protect against seam failure.

Chicken

- 2 pounds (900 grams) boneless, skinless chicken thighs, trimmed
  Salt and pepper
- 2 tablespoons (28 grams) vegetable oil
- 1 onion (140 grams), halved and sliced thin
- 2 tablespoons (32 grams) minced canned chipotle chile in adobo sauce
- 1 teaspoon (2 grams) garlic powder
- 1 teaspoon (2.5 grams) ground cumin
- ¼ teaspoon (1 gram) ground cinnamon
- 1 14.5-ounce (410 grams) can fire-roasted diced tomatoes, drained
- ½ teaspoon (2 grams) brown sugar
- 1 teaspoon (3 grams) grated lime zest plus 2 tablespoons (30 grams) juice

Tacos

- 12–18 (6-inch) corn tortillas, warmed
- 1 avocado, halved, pitted, and cut into ½-inch pieces
- 2 ounces (57 grams) Cotija cheese, crumbled (½ cup)
- 6 scallions (90 grams), minced
  Minced fresh cilantro
  Lime wedges

1 For the chicken Using sous vide circulator, bring water to 180°F/82°C in 7-quart container.

2 Pat chicken dry with paper towels and season with salt and pepper. Heat 1 tablespoon (14 grams) oil in 12-inch skillet over medium-high heat until just smoking. Brown half of chicken, 3 to 4 minutes per side; transfer to plate. Repeat with remaining chicken.

3 Heat remaining 1 tablespoon (14 grams) oil in now-empty skillet until shimmering. Add onion and cook until softened and lightly browned, 4 to 6 minutes. Stir in chipotle, garlic powder, cumin, and cinnamon and cook until fragrant, about 1 minute. Stir in tomatoes and sugar, scraping up any browned bits. Transfer mixture to blender and process until smooth, 30 to 45 seconds, scraping down sides of blender jar as needed.

4 Place chicken and any accumulated juices and sauce in 1-gallon zipper-lock freezer bag and toss to coat. Seal bag, pressing out as much air as possible. Place bag into second 1-gallon zipper-lock freezer bag and seal. Gently lower bag into prepared water bath until chicken is fully submerged, and then clip top corner of bag to side of water bath container, allowing remaining air bubbles to rise to top of bag. Reopen 1 corner of zipper, release remaining air bubbles, and reseal bag. Cover and cook for at least 3 hours or up to 5 hours.

5 Transfer chicken and sauce to large bowl, let cool slightly, and then shred chicken into bite-size pieces using 2 forks. Stir in lime zest and juice and season with salt and pepper to taste.

6 For the tacos Spoon chicken into center of each tortilla and serve, passing avocado, Cotija, scallions, cilantro, and lime wedges separately.

Seared Duck Breasts

YIELD **SERVES 4**
Sous Vide Temperature 135°F/57°C
Sous Vide Time 1½ to 2 hours
Active Cooking Time 50 minutes

To Make Ahead Cherry sauce can be refrigerated for up to 1 week; bring to room temperature before serving. We don't recommend making the duck in advance.

Why This Recipe Works With crispy skin and a juicy, pink interior, a properly cooked duck breast is a special treat that often proves just as satisfying as a good butter-basted steak (page 72). Traditionally, duck breasts are pan-seared from start to finish. But this method requires experience, precise timing, and a watchful eye. The meat can go from perfectly pink to tough and gray in a flash. To guarantee perfectly cooked meat, rendered fat, and crispy skin every time, sous vide is a great option. We found that a gentle cooking temperature of 135°F/57°C for 90 minutes produced duck with a uniform, tender, and juicy texture throughout. To render out as much fat as possible—a key step—we scored the skin and then preseared it for a few minutes before giving the duck breasts their low-temperature bath. Searing the breasts a final time helped to render even more fat and made the skin super-crisp. We serve our duck breasts with a buttery grapefruit and balsamic sauce. This recipe cooks the duck breasts to a precise medium (our preferred serving temperature).

- 4 10-ounce (284 grams) boneless duck breasts, skin and fat cap trimmed to ¼ inch
- 8 sprigs (4 grams) fresh thyme
- 6 garlic cloves, peeled and smashed
  Salt and pepper
- 2 tablespoons (28 grams) vegetable oil

1 Using sous vide circulator, bring water to 135°F/57°C in 7-quart container.

2 Using sharp knife, cut slits ½ inch apart in crosshatch pattern in duck skin and fat cap, being careful not to cut into meat. Pat duck dry with paper towels. Place duck skin side down in cold 12-inch nonstick skillet. Heat skillet over medium-high heat and cook until fat begins to render and skin is lightly browned, 6 to 8 minutes. Flip duck, add thyme sprigs and garlic to skillet, and cook until second side of breasts are opaque, about 30 seconds. Transfer duck and thyme sprigs to large plate. Discard garlic and fat left in skillet and wipe clean with paper towels.

3 Season duck with salt and pepper. Place duck and thyme sprigs in 1-gallon zipper-lock freezer bag. Seal bag, pressing out as much air as possible. Gently lower bag into prepared water bath until duck is fully submerged, and then clip top corner of bag to side of water bath container, allowing remaining air bubbles to rise to top of bag. Reopen 1 corner of zipper, release remaining air bubbles, and reseal bag. Cover and cook for at least 1½ hours or up to 2 hours.

4 Transfer duck to paper towel–lined plate and let rest for 5 to 10 minutes. Pat duck dry with paper towels. Heat oil in now-empty skillet over medium-high heat until just smoking. Place duck skin side down in skillet and cook until well-browned and crisp, 2 to 4 minutes. Transfer to cutting board and slice into ½-inch-thick slices. Serve.

Grapefruit-Balsamic Sauce
YIELD Makes about ¾ cup
The success of this sauce depends on using fresh grapefruit juice.

- 2 tablespoons (30 grams) balsamic vinegar
- 2 tablespoons (28 grams) sugar
- 2 cups (472 grams) chicken broth
- 1 cup (236 grams) fresh grapefruit juice
  Salt and pepper
- 4 tablespoons (56 grams) unsalted butter, cut into 4 pieces and chilled

Bring vinegar and sugar to simmer in 12-inch skillet over medium-high heat and cook until thickened and syrupy, about 2 minutes. Stir in chicken broth, grapefruit juice, and 1 teaspoon (2 grams) pepper, bring to simmer, and cook until mixture is reduced to about ½ cup (140 grams), 10 to 14 minutes. Off heat, whisk in butter, one piece at a time, until sauce is smooth and glossy. Season with salt to taste.

Cherry-Port Sauce

YIELD Makes about 1½ cups

You can substitute an equal amount of frozen sweet cherries for the fresh cherries; do not defrost them. This sauce is best served at room temperature.

10 ounces (284 grams) fresh sweet cherries, pitted and halved

2 cups (472 grams) dry red wine

¾ cup (150 grams) sugar

¼ cup (60 grams) chicken broth

¼ cup (60 grams) plus 1 tablespoon (15 grams) red wine vinegar

¼ cup (60 grams) ruby port

Bring cherries, wine, sugar, broth, ¼ cup (60 grams) vinegar, and port to simmer in medium saucepan. Cook, stirring occasionally, until mixture measures about 1½ cups (450 grams), about 30 minutes. Transfer to bowl and let cool to room temperature, about 2 hours. Stir in remaining 1 tablespoon (15 grams) vinegar.

Chicken Liver Mousse

YIELD MAKES ABOUT 3 CUPS (600 GRAMS)
Sous Vide Temperature 154°F/68°C
Sous Vide Time 30 minutes to 2 hours
Active Cooking Time 50 minutes, plus chilling and
resting time

To Make Ahead Mousse can be refrigerated for up
to 3 days.

Why This Recipe Works Leave it to the French to take the lowliest of poultry parts and transform it into something rich, decadent, and just as worthy of being on a charcuterie plate as a fancy Iberico ham. Traditionally, to make chicken liver mousse the chicken livers are gently cooked in an aromatic base until they are just pink, and then the mixture gets blended together until it's smooth. Unfortunately, this method is fairly imprecise: The livers tend to cook unevenly and often overcook, resulting in a grainy texture and metallic aftertaste. But sous vide makes chicken liver mousse easy. It guarantees even cooking and, as a result, the perfect texture, every time. To give the mousse its traditional vibrant color, we used pink curing salt. Curing salt goes by many names, including DQ Curing Salt and Insta Cure #1, but it's most commonly labeled pink salt. You can find it in specialty food stores or online. (Do not substitute Morton's Tender Quick or Insta Cure #2.) If omitting the pink salt, increase the table salt to 1 teaspoon in step 3.

1 tablespoon (14 grams) vegetable oil
1 tablespoon (14 grams) unsalted butter,
   plus 11 tablespoons (154 grams) cut into
   ½-inch pieces and chilled
2 shallots (60 grams), sliced thin
3 garlic cloves (15 grams), sliced thin
½ teaspoon (1 gram) minced fresh thyme,
   plus extra for serving
   Salt and pepper
¾ cup (180 grams) brandy
1 pound (450 grams) chicken livers, rinsed,
   patted dry, and trimmed
½ teaspoon (4 grams) pink curing salt (optional)
   Flake sea salt

1 Using sous vide circulator, bring water to 154°F/68°C in 7-quart container.

2 Heat oil and 1 tablespoon (14 grams) butter in 10-inch skillet over medium heat until butter is melted. Add shallots, garlic, thyme, and ¼ teaspoon (1.5 grams) salt and cook until shallots are softened and lightly browned, 3 to 5 minutes. Off heat, add brandy and let warm through, about 5 seconds. Return skillet to medium heat and cook until brandy has reduced by about two-thirds, 3 to 5 minutes.

3 Season livers with pink curing salt, if using, ½ teaspoon (1.5 grams) salt, and ¼ teaspoon (1.5 grams) pepper. Place livers and shallot mixture in 1-gallon zipper-lock freezer bag. Seal bag, pressing out as much air as possible. Gently lower bag into prepared water bath until livers are fully submerged, and then clip top corner of bag to side of water bath container, allowing remaining air bubbles to rise to top of bag. Reopen 1 corner of zipper, release remaining air bubbles, and reseal bag. Cover and cook livers for at least 30 minutes or up to 2 hours.

4 Transfer liver-shallot mixture to food processor and process until smooth, about 30 seconds, scraping down sides of bowl as needed. With processor running, add remaining 11 tablespoons (154 grams) chilled butter, 1 piece at a time, and process until emulsified, about 2 minutes.

5 Strain mousse through fine-mesh strainer into bowl, pressing on solids to extract as much mousse as possible; discard solids. Season with salt and pepper to taste. Stir mousse to combine, transfer to serving dish or individual ramekins, cover tightly with plastic wrap, and refrigerate until fully set, at least 6 hours or up to 3 days. Before serving, let mousse sit at room temperature for about 30 minutes, then sprinkle with flake sea salt and thyme.

Easy Boneless Turkey Breast

YIELD SERVES 6 TO 8
Sous Vide Temperature 145°F/63°C
Sous Vide Time 3½ to 5 hours
Active Cooking Time 45 minutes

To Make Ahead Turkey can be rapidly chilled in ice bath (see page 13) and then refrigerated in zipper-lock bag after step 2 for up to 5 days. To reheat, return sealed bag to water bath set to 145°F/63°C for 30 minutes. Proceed with step 3.

Why This Recipe Works The words "turkey breast" do not bring to mind the image of moist, succulent meat and crispy skin—but they should. We took the breasts off of the breastbone for easy handling and better crisping of the skin. A long bath delivered tender, juicy meat with a uniform texture. Resting the turkey before searing to crisp the skin helped retain juiciness. You can make any number of turkey breasts ahead of time and sear them off as needed. If using a self-basting or a kosher turkey breast, do not salt the breast halves in step 2.

- 1 7-pound (3.18 kilogram) bone-in turkey breast
- ½ cup plus 2 tablespoons (140 grams) vegetable oil
-    Salt and pepper

1 Using sous vide circulator, bring water to 145°F/63°C in 7-quart container.

2 Using sharp knife, cut along rib cage of breast to remove breast halves; discard bones. Trim excess skin from turkey and season with salt and pepper. Place one breast half and ¼ cup (56 grams) oil in 1-gallon zipper-lock freezer bag. Repeat with second breast half. Seal bags, pressing out as much air as possible. Gently lower bags into prepared water bath until turkey is fully submerged, and then clip top corner of each bag to side of water bath container, allowing remaining air bubbles to rise to top of bags. Reopen 1 corner of each zipper, release remaining air bubbles, and reseal bags. Cover and cook for at least 3½ hours or up to 5 hours.

3 Transfer turkey to paper towel–lined plate and let rest for 5 to 10 minutes. Pat turkey dry with paper towels. Heat remaining 2 tablespoons (28 grams) oil in 12-inch skillet over medium-high heat until just smoking. Place turkey skin side down in skillet and cook, adjusting position with tongs as needed, until well-browned and crisp, 4 to 6 minutes. Transfer turkey to carving board and slice into ½-inch-thick slices. Serve.

All-Purpose Gravy
YIELD Makes about 2 cups

- 3 tablespoons (42 grams) vegetable oil
- 1 small onion (140 grams), chopped
- 1 small carrot (60 grams), peeled and chopped
- 1 small celery rib (60 grams), chopped
-    Salt and pepper
- ¼ cup (50 grams) all-purpose flour
- 4 cups (945 grams) chicken broth
- ¼ cup (60 grams) dry white wine
- 2 sprigs (1 gram) fresh thyme
- 1 bay leaf (0.5 grams)

1 Heat oil in large saucepan over medium heat until shimmering. Add onion, carrot, celery, and ½ teaspoon (3 grams) pepper and cook over medium heat until vegetables are softened and well browned, about 8 minutes. Stir in flour and cook for 1 minute. Slowly whisk in broth and wine, scraping up any browned bits and smoothing out any lumps. Stir in thyme sprigs and bay leaf, bring to simmer, and cook until gravy is thickened and reduced to 3 cups, about 15 minutes.

2 Strain gravy through fine-mesh strainer into bowl, pressing on solids to extract as much liquid as possible; discard solids. Season with salt and pepper to taste.

Red Bell Pepper Chutney

YIELD Makes about 2 cups

Avoid adding the parsley to the chutney before it is fully cooled or the parsley will wilt. This recipe is best served at room temperature.

- 1 tablespoon (14 grams) extra-virgin olive oil
- 1 red onion (140 grams), chopped fine
- 4 red bell peppers (32 grams), stemmed, seeded, and cut into ½-inch pieces
- 1 cup (236 grams) white wine vinegar
- ½ cup plus 2 tablespoons (125 grams) sugar
- 2 garlic cloves (10 grams), peeled and smashed
- 1 1-inch piece ginger (7 grams), peeled, sliced into thin coins, and smashed
- 1 teaspoon (3 grams) yellow mustard seeds
- 1 teaspoon (6 grams) salt
- ½ teaspoon (2 grams) red pepper flakes
- ¼ cup (5 grams) minced fresh parsley

Heat oil in large saucepan over medium heat until shimmering. Add onion and cook until softened, about 5 minutes. Stir in bell peppers, vinegar, sugar, garlic, ginger, mustard seeds, salt, and pepper flakes. Bring to simmer and cook until thickened and measures about 2 cups (500 grams), about 40 minutes. Transfer to bowl and let cool to room temperature, about 2 hours. Discard garlic and ginger, and stir in parsley. (Chutney can be refrigerated for up to 1 week; bring to room temperature before serving.)

Meat Cookery and Sous Vide

Key Points

- Meat consists of muscle fibers, connective tissue, water, and fat
- Sous vide provides precision and prevents moisture loss
- Enzymatic action around 130°F/54°C can give meat an incredibly tender texture

Humans learned to cook meat for three main reasons: It gets rid of microbes that could make us sick; it turns bland pink lumps into delicious meals; and it changes meat's physical structure in crucial ways to make it more eatable and digestible. This is possible because of the microscopic structure of meat and what happens when it is heated—whether with traditional cooking methods or sous vide.

MICROSCOPIC MEAT AND POULTRY BASICS

Whether it comes from a cow, pig, or chicken, meat and poultry consists primarily of muscle fibers, water, connective tissue, and fat. Muscle tissue resembles many bundles of wire, each surrounded by a covering of connective tissue. Each bundle is made up of numerous muscle fibers. These fibers are made up of many smaller structures called myofibrils. Cooking changes the structure of those muscle fibers, and whether a piece of meat comes out tough or tender depends on cooking time and cooking temperature. When red meat and poultry are heated, the long protein molecules begin to contract, first (between 104°F/40°C and 145°F/63°C) in diameter, and then (above 145°F/63°C) in length. A single muscle fiber can shrink to half its original length during the cooking process.

When proteins contract, they squeeze out some of the liquid trapped within their structure. The rate of moisture loss becomes significant around 140°F/60°C, the temperature at which the connective tissue surrounding the muscle fibers begins to tighten as well, squeezing the fibers even more firmly. Raw muscle fibers contain a lot of water (around 75 percent!), and this water loss can cause a cooked piece of meat to end up quite tough. We rest meat after cooking via traditional high-heat methods, allowing the contracted proteins to relax and draw some moisture back in.

The connective tissue surrounding the fiber bundles is a membranous, translucent covering that consists of cells and protein filaments. It provides both structure and support to muscles. Collagen, the predominant protein in connective tissue, is composed of three protein chains tightly wound together in a triple-stranded helix and is therefore almost unchewable when raw.

But collagen begins to relax when it hits heat, unwinding into individual strands. This happens very slowly at temperatures as low as 122°F/50°C and far more rapidly between 160°F/71°C and 180°F/82°C. Eventually, the triple helix of collagen turns into gelatin, a single-stranded protein able to tenderize meat, retain up to 10 times its weight in moisture, and add a thick richness to the sauces of a braised dish. Tough, collagen-heavy meats are often held in the higher temperature range for a few hours to encourage the triple helix of collagen to unwind and form gelatin more quickly.

THE BENEFITS OF SOUS VIDE

Precision We know a lot about the science of cooking meat, but that doesn't make all of our cooking foolproof. A roast comes out dry and mealy instead of succulent, and the middle of a steak is still too rare though the outside is perfectly crusted. Sous vide gives us precision, allowing us to cook meat (and poultry) to an exact temperature all the way through, guaranteeing that you will never again overcook your fancy rib-eye.

Preventing Moisture Loss Most tender cuts of red meat are best cooked to medium-rare—or around 130°F/54°C—so that cooking is finished before the muscle fibers really begin to squeeze out all of the moisture within. But when cooked to medium-rare in a skillet, the outer layers of a piece of meat soar well above 140°F/60°C—the temperature at which the moisture loss really picks up. Sous vide gives us the ability to cook these cuts to a precise medium-rare from end to end, and with no hot spots. This is why we don't need to rest meat cooked sous vide in order to retain moisture: We are cooking most meat below 140°F/60°C. That said, we do rest meat before searing in order to let the temperature fall a bit and reduce risk of overcooking when the meat is in the hot skillet.

Turning Tough Cuts Tender Collagen proteins unwind into moisture-holding gelatin at temperatures as low as 122°F/50°C. Sous vide cooking allows us to hold tough, collagen-heavy cuts of meat at lower temperatures for longer periods of time and get the same tenderizing effect as braising.

But that's not all. Enzymes are also at work during low-temperature sous vide cooking. In living animals, one of the functions of these proteins is the turnover and reprocessing of other proteins around them. In meat, many of the enzymes are still active, and if handled correctly, they can work wonders on the cook's behalf. Dry-aging beef is a classic example: Beef is held at a steady temperature between 33°F/0.5°C and 40°F/4°C for 30 days or more. In this temperature range, enzymes in the meat work slowly to break down protein, resulting in much more tender steaks.

In meat, there are two important enzymes that work to break down protein: calpain and cathepsin. Calpains break down the proteins that hold the muscle fibers in place. Cathepsins break apart a range of meat proteins, and can even weaken the collagen in the muscles' connective tissue. Breaking down protein imparts a meatier umami taste (due to the formation of amino acids) and, given enough time, tenderizes the meat—that is, if the environment is right.

The activity of these enzymes is largely based on temperature—and the amount of time held there. The rate at which they break down the protein in a cut of meat increases as the temperature of the meat rises. This is why sous vide cooking allows us to make enzyme-tenderized meat in hours, not days. Calpains cause proteins to fall apart around 105°F/40°C, so they're not very helpful in sous vide, but cathepsins are. Although they begin to break down proteins around 122°F/50°C degrees, the breakdown is a long process, and cathepsin activity is still going on during a lengthy cook at 130°F/54°C. Our Peppercorn-Crusted Roast Beef, page 76, is a prime example of enzymes in action. (This is also why you would not want to cook fish for a long period of time sous vide. These enzymes are also active in fish, and too much time in the presence of tenderizing enzymes can make fish protein—which is quite tender to start with—mushy.)

So, as you cook your Perfect Seared Steaks (page 70), Shredded Chicken Tacos (page 56), and Perfect Prime Rib (page 78), think about what's going on under the surface: the deliberate movement of proteins, enzymes, and water, working together to create the ultimate finished dish.

Chicken Breasts

While egg cookery can be tricky, a complicated dance that depends on each and every degree and minute, chicken breasts are a bit more forgiving. To cook tender and juicy chicken breasts using sous vide, discovering the perfect temperature was paramount. Time is important, too, but less so. Our chicken breast recipes can circulate for anywhere between 1 and 3 hours.

To find the perfect temperature, associate editor Tim Chin cooked a lot of chicken breasts. And we mean a lot. He cooked samples starting at 140°F/60°C and, degree by degree, up to 160°F/71°C. Our team of tasters tried each sample and rated the results. In this chart, you'll see what we found. The difference between chicken cooked at 140°F/60°C and 160°F/71°C is immense, and our preference is for smack in the middle.

Important to note: Traditionally, chicken breasts are cooked to at least 165°F/74°C. At that temperature, according to the FDA, the possibility of *Salmonella* is virtually zero. But you don't have to cook chicken breasts to that temperature to guarantee safety. Lower temperatures can also render them safe—they just need to cook for longer. (See page 40 for more.)

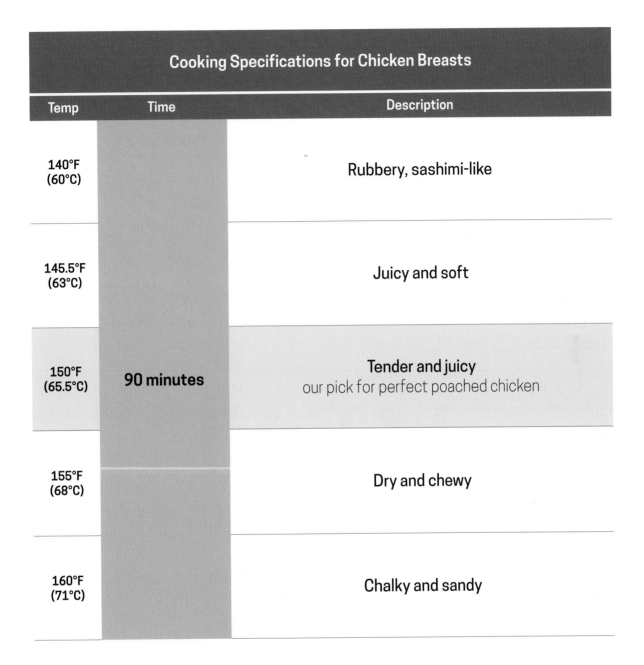

Cooking Specifications for Chicken Breasts

Temp	Time	Description
140°F (60°C)		Rubbery, sashimi-like
145.5°F (63°C)		Juicy and soft
150°F (65.5°C)	90 minutes	**Tender and juicy** our pick for perfect poached chicken
155°F (68°C)		Dry and chewy
160°F (71°C)		Chalky and sandy

MEAT

For most home cooks, the first test of their brand-new sous vide circulator is a steak. A simple steak. About 1½ inches thick. Set the water bath to 130 degrees Fahrenheit/54.5 degrees Celsius for the perfect medium-rare. Put nothing but salt and pepper and a drizzle of oil in the bag along with the steak. Seal it. Circulate it. Sear it—fast—on the stove. Done.

This steak is perfect. It's juicy and tender, rosy and pink from end to end. One bite and you realize: Steak can be this perfect from here on out.

And that's why many home cooks—not to mention professional chefs—choose sous vide. "A circulator means you can produce professional results without the learning curve," says Dave Arnold, a sous vide expert and author of *Liquid Intelligence*. To put it bluntly: "People don't want the first 100 steaks they bought to suck."

"It shifts the responsibility toward the recipe writer," adds Arnold. Well, you've come to the right place.

To create the recipes in this meat chapter, we had our 16 Joules circulating hundreds of pounds of meat in a parade of Dutch ovens and large plastic containers over the course of 10 straight weeks. We ate steaks; we tasted roasts; we played around with lamb cooked to 130°F/54.5°C, 133°F/56°C, and 136°F/58°C degrees (check out page 100 to find out where we landed). By the end of testing, we'll admit that the vegetable chapter was starting to sound pretty good.

Still, we learned about what cooking sous vide can do for meat. (Spoiler: A lot.)

First, the technique allows you to cook precisely (and perfectly!) every time because the water bath temperature is so carefully controlled. As a result, sous vide helps prevent moisture loss: The muscle fibers in meat really begin to contract and squeeze out internal juices above 140°F/60°C. With traditional high-heat cooking methods, the outside of a seared steak regularly surpasses this temperature before the interior reaches its target, resulting in a gray band of overcooked meat. Sous vide allows us to keep all parts of the cut below 140°F/60°C. Sous vide also enables us to make tough cuts very tender by dissolving collagen and fat, even at very low temperatures over time. (Check out "Meat Cookery and Sous Vide" on page 64 for more.)

And then there are the enzymes. Take the Peppercorn-Crusted Roast Beef (page 76). This holiday-ready roast is no prime rib. Instead, we opt for chuck roast, a relatively tough cut that is often cooked at a temperature high enough to achieve a fall-apart braised texture after a few hours. Sous vide, however, allows us to cook this roast at a far lower temperature usually reserved for prime steaks (133°F/56°C) for 24 hours straight. Enzymes, the wily little proteins present in meat that slowly break down tough collagen, are activated at that temperature—a few degrees higher and they cease to do anything. The end result? A chuck roast that eats like prime rib, minus the expense. (If prime rib is what you're going for, though, we're here to help. Check out page 78.)

We've created a world of meat dishes to tackle using sous vide, ranging from the classic (see Osso Buco, page 81) to the creative (see Sichuan Twice-Cooked Pork Belly, page 92). We've got you covered for date night (Seared Thick-Cut Pork Chops with Port-Cherry Pan Sauce, page 82) and game night (Beer Braised Brats, page 97). Our tender yet still-sliceable Porchetta (page 88) and the salty-sweet pork dish Char Siu (page 91) are perfect for surprisingly low-stress dinner parties. We've even got Easter taken care of: Spiral-Sliced Ham (page 99).

Perfect Seared Steaks

YIELD SERVES 4
Sous Vide Temperature 130°F/54.5°C
Sous Vide Time 1½ to 3 hours
Active Cooking Time 30 minutes

To Make Ahead We don't recommend making this recipe in advance.

Why This Recipe Works Cooking steaks sous vide is a game changer. The water bath technique takes all of the risk, guesswork, and stress out of the dinner-preparation equation. With sous vide, steaks are cooked to the same temperature, and thus same doneness (of your choosing!), all the way through. This eliminates the gray band of over-cooked meat around the exterior of steaks, which often occurs with traditional pan-roasted methods. Once your sous vide steaks are taken out of the water bath, all that's left to do is to give them a quick sear in a screaming hot pan to create the Maillard browning and flavorful crust. This recipe was developed for tender steaks such as strip, rib eye, shell sirloin, top sirloin, and tenderloin; avoid tougher cuts such as top round, bottom round, blade, and flank, as they would require a longer cook time. Serve with Red Wine–Peppercorn Pan Sauce or Mustard-Fennel Pan Sauce (recipes follow), if desired.

2 pounds (900 grams) boneless beef steaks,
   1 to 1½ inches thick, trimmed
Salt and pepper
7 tablespoons (98 grams) vegetable oil

1 Using sous vide circulator, bring water to 130°F/54.5°C in 7-quart container.

2 Season steaks with salt and pepper. Place steaks and ¼ cup (56 grams) oil in 1-gallon zipper-lock freezer bag and toss to coat. Arrange steaks in single layer and seal bag, pressing out as much air as possible. Gently lower bag into prepared water bath until steaks are fully submerged, and then clip top corner of bag to side of water bath container, allowing remaining air bubbles to rise to top of bag. Reopen 1 corner of zipper, release remaining air bubbles, and reseal bag. Cover and cook for at least 1½ hours or up to 3 hours.

3 Transfer steaks to paper towel–lined plate and let rest for 5 to 10 minutes. Pat steaks dry with paper towels. Heat remaining 3 tablespoons (42 grams) oil in 12-inch skillet over medium-high heat until just smoking. Sear steaks, about 1 minute per side, until well browned. Transfer to cutting board and slice into ½-inch-thick slices. Serve.

Red Wine–Peppercorn Pan Sauce
YIELD Makes about ½ cup
Note that this recipe is meant to be started after you have seared the steaks. Use a good quality medium-bodied wine, such as a Côtes du Rhône or Pinot Noir, for this sauce.

Vegetable oil, if needed
1 large shallot (30 grams), minced
½ cup (113 grams) dry red wine
¾ cup (168 grams) chicken broth
2 teaspoons (8 grams) packed brown sugar
3 tablespoons (42 grams) unsalted butter,
   cut into 3 pieces and chilled
1 teaspoon (3 grams) coarsely ground pepper
¼ teaspoon (0.5 grams) balsamic vinegar
Salt

1 Pour off all but 1 tablespoon (14 grams) fat from skillet used to sear steak. (If necessary, add oil to equal 1 tablespoon (14 grams).) Add shallot and cook over medium heat until softened, 1 to 2 minutes. Stir in wine, scraping up any browned bits. Bring to simmer and cook until wine is reduced to glaze, about 3 minutes.

2 Stir in broth and sugar and simmer until reduced to ⅓ cup, 4 to 6 minutes. Off heat, whisk in butter, 1 piece at a time, until melted and sauce is thickened and glossy.

Whisk in pepper, vinegar, and any accumulated meat juices. Season with salt to taste. Serve immediately.

Mustard-Fennel Pan Sauce

YIELD Makes about ½ cup

Note that this recipe is meant to be started after you have seared the steaks. Sauvignon Blanc is our preferred white cooking wine.

Vegetable oil, if needed

1 shallot (30 grams), minced

½ teaspoon (1.5 grams) fennel seeds, cracked

½ cup (113 grams) chicken broth

¼ cup (56 grams) dry white wine

1½ tablespoons (27 grams) Dijon mustard

2 tablespoons (28 grams) unsalted butter, cut into 2 pieces and chilled

1 teaspoon (1 gram) chopped fresh tarragon

Salt and pepper

1 Pour off all but 1 tablespoon (14 grams) fat from skillet used to sear steak. (If necessary, add oil to equal 1 tablespoon (14 grams).) Add shallot and fennel seeds and cook over medium heat until shallot is softened, 1 to 2 minutes. Stir in broth, wine, and mustard, scraping up any browned bits. Bring to simmer and cook until liquid is reduced to ½ cup, about 6 minutes.

2 Off heat, whisk in butter, 1 piece at a time, until melted and sauce is thickened and glossy. Whisk in tarragon and any accumulated meat juices and season with salt and pepper to taste. Serve immediately.

Butter-Basted Rib-Eye Steaks

YIELD SERVES 4
Sous Vide Temperature 125°F/52°C
Sous Vide Time 2 to 3 hours
Active Cooking Time 40 minutes

To Make Ahead We don't recommend making this recipe in advance.

Why This Recipe Works A nicely cooked rib-eye steak is a culinary showstopper but is also a challenge to pull off. The risk of over- or undercooking—and therefore ruining an expensive cut of meat—can make cooking a thick-cut rib eye at home an intimidating endeavor. But with the help of sous vide, preparing steak at home is suddenly a sure bet. Cooking sous vide allows you to control the precise temperature (and therefore doneness) of a steak, cooking it to the exact same temperature throughout. This means your steak is perfectly cooked every time. Sous vide steaks are often seared in a hot pan after cooking in the water bath to give them the exterior Maillard browning that we love. For these rib eyes, we up the ante with butter basting. This technique involves continuously spooning hot fat over the steaks to quickly create a nice deep-brown crust. Bonus: It also gives them the nutty flavor of browned butter. That butter is reserved and used as a rich sauce to be drizzled over the top for a decadent steak dinner. Because these steaks cook at a slightly lower temperature to allow enough time to properly butter baste without overcooking, we also quickly sear them before they go into the water bath to reduce the risk of bacterial growth. This recipe moves quickly once you start searing in step 3, so have everything prepared and within arm's reach before you start.

2 2-pound (900 grams) bone-in rib-eye steaks, about 2 inches thick, trimmed
Salt and pepper
½ cup (112 grams) vegetable oil
3 tablespoons (42 grams) unsalted butter
1 large shallot (30 grams), peeled and quartered lengthwise through root end
2 garlic cloves (10 grams), peeled and smashed
5 sprigs (3 grams) fresh thyme

1 Using sous vide circulator, bring water to 125°F/52°C in 7-quart container.

2 Pat steaks dry with paper towels and season with salt and pepper. Heat 1 tablespoon (14 grams) oil in 12-inch skillet over medium-high heat until just smoking. Cook steaks, 1 minute per side. Place steaks in 2 separate 1-gallon zipper-lock freezer bags. Add 2 tablespoons (14 grams) oil to each bag. Seal bags, pressing out as much air as possible. Gently lower bags into prepared water bath until steaks are fully submerged, and then clip top corner of each bag to side of water bath container, allowing remaining air bubbles to rise to top of bag. Reopen 1 corner of each zipper, release remaining air bubbles, and reseal bags. Cover and cook for at least 2 hours or up to 3 hours.

3 Transfer steaks to paper towel–lined plate and let rest for 5 to 10 minutes. Pat steaks dry with paper towels. Heat remaining 3 tablespoons (42 grams) oil in clean 12-inch skillet over medium-high heat until just smoking. Place steaks in skillet and cook, without moving, for 30 seconds. Flip steaks and continue to cook for 30 seconds.

4 Slide steaks to back of skillet, opposite handle, and add butter to front of skillet near handle. When butter has melted, add shallot, garlic, and thyme sprigs. Holding skillet handle, tilt skillet so butter pools near base of handle. Using metal spoon, baste steaks with butter and aromatics, concentrating on areas where crust is less browned. Continuously baste steaks, flipping every 30 seconds, until well browned on both sides, about 3 minutes.

5 Reduce heat to medium and transfer steaks to cutting board. Using tongs, stand each steak on its side in skillet and cook, rotating as needed, until well browned on edges, about 1 minute; return to cutting board. Strain seasoned butter into small bowl; discard solids. Carve steaks off bones, then slice into ¼-inch-thick slices. Serve with seasoned butter.

Variations

Rib-Eye Steaks with Coffee-Chile Butter

Substitute 2 tablespoons (10 grams) whole coffee beans, cracked, for garlic cloves and ½ teaspoon (0.5 grams) red pepper flakes for thyme.

Rib-Eye Steaks with Rosemary-Orange Butter

Substitute 8 (2-inch) strips orange zest for garlic and 1 sprig (0.5 grams) fresh rosemary for thyme.

Rib-Eye Steaks with Green Peppercorn–Star Anise Butter

Substitute 2 teaspoons (6 grams) whole green peppercorns, cracked, for garlic and 5 star anise pods (3 grams), cracked, for thyme.

Short Rib "Pot Roast"

To Make Ahead Short ribs can be rapidly chilled in ice bath (see page 13) and then refrigerated in zipper-lock bags after step 4 for up to 3 days. To reheat, return sealed bags to water bath set to 160°F/71°C, and let sit for 30 minutes. Proceed with step 5.

Why This Recipe Works Beef short ribs are a prime example of how the precise control of time and temperature afforded by sous vide cooking can affect a piece of meat. Short ribs are a tougher cut, with a good amount of collagen and intramuscular fat so they are traditionally braised to a fall-apart texture. But with sous vide, you can achieve short ribs that have a texture similar to a medium-rare steak or you can deliver a more traditional flaky, braised texture—or land almost anywhere in between. For this recipe, we were looking for a fall-apart tender, pot roast-style texture, so we decided on a higher-temperature water bath (160°F/71°C) while keeping the cooking time under 24 hours. This cooking time and temperature combination allowed us to break down this tough cut's intramuscular collagen, tenderizing the meat while keeping it moist and preserving a rosy interior from edge to edge. To make things even easier, we frontloaded the work. We quickly seared the short ribs, and then we built a sauce with traditional pot roast ingredients: *mirepoix*, tomato paste, red wine, beef broth, and herbs. We bagged up the beef and sauce together for their sous vide bath. Afterward, we strained the sauce and briefly reduced it on the stovetop, we poured it over the tender short ribs and finished the dish with a sprinkling of fresh parsley. Easy pot roast, no pot or roasting required. Make sure that the ribs are at least 4 inches long and 1 inch thick. Be sure to double-bag the ribs to protect against seam failure.

3½ pounds (1.5 kilograms) boneless beef short ribs, trimmed
    Salt and pepper
2 tablespoons (28 grams) vegetable oil
1 large onion (350 grams), chopped
2 celery ribs (80 grams), chopped
1 carrot (80 grams), peeled and chopped
1 tablespoon (15 grams) tomato paste
1 garlic clove (5 grams), minced
1 cup (225 grams) dry red wine
1 cup (225 grams) beef broth
8 sprigs (4 grams) fresh thyme
2 bay leaves (1 gram)
2 tablespoons (8 grams) minced fresh parsley

1 Using sous vide circulator, bring water to 160°F/71°C in 7-quart container.

2 Pat ribs dry with paper towels and season with salt and pepper. Heat 1 tablespoon (14 grams) oil in Dutch oven over medium-high heat until just smoking. Brown half of ribs on all sides, 8 to 12 minutes; transfer to plate. Repeat with remaining 1 tablespoon (14 grams) oil and ribs.

3 Add onion, celery, carrot, ¼ teaspoon (1 gram) salt, and ¼ teaspoon (1 gram) pepper to fat left in pot and cook over medium heat until softened and lightly browned, 8 to 10 minutes. Stir in tomato paste and garlic and cook until fragrant, about 1 minute. Stir in wine, scraping up any browned bits, and cook until reduced by half, 2 to 4 minutes. Stir in broth and simmer for 2 minutes. Transfer mixture to blender and process until smooth, about 1 minute.

4 Divide ribs, sauce, thyme sprigs, and bay leaves between two 1-gallon zipper-lock freezer bags and toss to coat. Arrange ribs in single layer and seal bags, pressing out as much air as possible. Place each bag in second 1-gallon zipper-lock freezer bag and seal bags. Gently lower bags into prepared water bath until ribs are fully submerged, and then clip top corner of each bag to side of water bath container, allowing remaining air bubbles to rise to top of bag. Reopen 1 corner of each zipper, release remaining air bubbles, and reseal bags. Cover and cook for at least 20 hours or up to 24 hours.

5 Using tongs, transfer ribs to serving dish. Tent with aluminum foil and let rest while finishing sauce. Strain cooking liquid through fine-mesh strainer into medium saucepan, pressing on solids to extract as much liquid as possible; discard solids. Bring to simmer over medium heat and cook until reduced to 2 cups, 4 to 6 minutes. Season with salt and pepper to taste. Spoon sauce over ribs, sprinkle with parsley, and serve.

Peppercorn-Crusted Roast Beef

YIELD SERVES 10 TO 12

Sous Vide Temperature 133°F/56°C

Sous Vide Time 18 to 24 hours

Active Cooking Time 1 hour, plus at least 18 hours salting time

To Make Ahead We don't recommend making this recipe in advance.

Why This Recipe Works When it comes to holiday beef roasts, chuck isn't really known for being the go-to for medium-rare resplendence (we're looking at you, prime rib). But that's a real shame since chuck is among the most flavorful cuts of beef available—and the cheapest per pound, to boot. This cut has plenty of fat and connective tissue, making it tough and chewy when it's cooked to medium-rare in a conventional oven. With most traditional methods of cooking, you have two options: low and slow until it's tender, or braised and broken down. Neither method gives you pink, tender, juicy meat. But with sous vide we can have it all: A fork-tender, juicy, medium-rare chuck roast. Circulating the roast at a low temperature for 24 hours allows enough time to break down intramuscular collagen, tenderizing the meat while preserving a rosy, medium-rare interior from edge to edge. We were inspired by the folks at ChefSteps to pair this roast with a generous herb crust, making it easily customizable and ready to pair with all sorts of sauces. And best of all, it won't break the bank over the holidays. We prefer a combination of all three different peppercorns here, but you can use a single type. Serve with Yogurt-Herb Sauce (recipe follows), if desired.

- 1 5-pound (2.3 kilograms) boneless beef chuck-eye roast, pulled into 2 pieces at natural seam and trimmed of large pieces of fat

  Kosher salt and pepper

- 2 tablespoons (28 grams) vegetable oil

- 1 egg white (30 grams)

- ¼ cup (30 grams) coarsely ground black, green, and pink peppercorns

- 2 tablespoons (20 grams) flake sea salt

1 Sprinkle beef with 4 teaspoons (16 grams) kosher salt. Arrange pieces side by side along natural seam, and then tie together at 1 inch intervals to create 1 evenly shaped roast. Transfer roast to large plate and refrigerate, uncovered, at least 24 hours or up to 96 hours.

2 Using sous vide circulator, heat water to 133°F/56°C in 12-quart container.

3 Heat oil in 12-inch skillet over medium-high heat until just smoking. Brown roast on all sides, 6 to 8 minutes. Season roast with pepper and place into 2-gallon zipper-lock freezer bag. Seal bag, pressing out as much air as possible. Gently lower bag into prepared water bath until roast is fully submerged, and then clip top corner of bag to side of water bath container, allowing remaining air bubbles to rise to top of bag. Reopen 1 corner of zipper, release remaining air bubbles, and reseal bag. Cover and cook for at least 18 hours or up to 24 hours.

4 Adjust oven rack to middle position and heat oven to 475°F/246°C. Set wire rack in aluminum foil–lined rimmed baking sheet and spray with vegetable spray. Transfer roast to prepared rack and let rest for 10 to 15 minutes. Pat roast dry with paper towels.

5 Whisk egg white in bowl until frothy, about 30 seconds. Combine peppercorns and flake sea salt in shallow dish. Brush roast on all sides with egg white, then coat with peppercorn mixture, pressing to adhere. Return roast to prepared rack and roast until surface is evenly browned and fragrant, 15 to 20 minutes, rotating sheet halfway through roasting.

6 Transfer roast to carving board and slice into ½-inch-thick slices and serve.

Variations

Za'atar-Crusted Roast Beef
Substitute ½ cup (60 grams) za'atar for peppercorns.

Rosemary–Mustard Seed Crusted Roast Beef
Process ¼ cup (42 grams) mustard seeds and 3 table-spoons (25 grams) peppercorns in spice grinder under coarsely ground. Transfer to shallow dish and stir in ⅓ cup (25 grams) chopped rosemary. Substitute rosemary mixture for peppercorns.

Yogurt-Herb Sauce
YIELD Makes about 2 cups
Do not substitute low-fat or nonfat yogurt here.

- 2 cups (490 grams) plain whole-milk yogurt
- ¼ cup (16 grams) minced fresh parsley
- ¼ cup (16 grams) minced fresh chives
- 2 teaspoons (4 grams) grated lemon zest plus ¼ cup (60 grams) juice
- 2 garlic cloves (10 grams), minced
  Salt and pepper

Whisk all ingredients together in bowl and season with salt and pepper to taste. Cover and refrigerate for at least 30 minutes to allow flavors to meld. (Sauce can be refrigerated for up to 4 days.)

Perfect Prime Rib

YIELD SERVES 6 TO 8
Sous Vide Temperature 133°F/56°C
Sous Vide Time 16 to 24 hours
Active Cooking Time 1 hour 15 minutes,
plus at least 24 hours salting time

To Make Ahead We don't recommend making this recipe in advance.

Why This Recipe Works In the land of celebratory roasts, the prime rib stands as king. But cooking this cut of beef properly is a challenge. And when you're dropping upward of 100 bucks on a quality rib roast, you're going to want to cook it well. Luckily, sous vide allows you to do just that. We start by removing the ribs to expose all sides of the roast before salting it and letting it sit overnight. The salt slowly moves toward the center of the meat, enhancing the beefy flavor while dissolving some of the proteins. Presearing the roast built flavor before it went into its low-temperature bath. After 16 to 24 hours at 133°F/56°C, the roast's connective tissue had broken down, producing a buttery texture. A flash under the broiler crisped up the fat cap to create a nice crust. Look for a roast with an untrimmed fat cap ideally ½ inch thick. We prefer the flavor and texture of prime-grade prime rib, but a choice-grade roast will work. Serve with Horseradish–Sour Cream Sauce or Mint Persillade (recipes follow), if desired. Note that this recipe requires salting and refrigerating the roast at least 24 hours before cooking.

1 7-pound (3.2 kilograms) first-cut beef standing rib roast (3 bones)
   Kosher salt and pepper
1 tablespoon (14 grams) vegetable oil

1 To remove bones from roast, use sharp knife and run it down length of bones, following contours as closely as possible; set bones aside. Cut slits in surface layer of fat on roast, spaced 1 inch apart, in crosshatch pattern, being careful to cut down to, but not into, meat. Rub 2 tablespoons (24 grams) salt over entire roast and into slits. Place meat back on bones (to save space in refrigerator), transfer to plate, and refrigerate, uncovered, at least 24 hours or up to 96 hours.

2 Using sous vide circulator, bring water to 133°F/56°C in 12-quart container.

3 Separate meat and bones; set aside bones. Heat oil in 12-inch skillet over medium-high heat until just smoking. Sear sides and top of roast until browned, 6 to 8 minutes (do not sear side where roast was cut from bone). Place meat back on ribs so bones fit where they were cut, and let cool for 10 minutes. Tie meat to bones between ribs with 2 lengths of kitchen twine.

4 Season roast with pepper and place in 2-gallon zipper-lock freezer bag. Seal bag, pressing out as much air as possible. Gently lower bag into prepared water bath until roast is fully submerged, and then clip top corner of bag to side of water bath container, allowing remaining air bubbles to rise to top of bag. Reopen 1 corner of zipper, release remaining air bubbles, and reseal bag. Cover and cook for at least 16 hours or up to 24 hours.

5 Adjust oven rack to middle position and heat broiler. Set wire rack in aluminum foil–lined rimmed baking sheet and spray with vegetable spray. Transfer roast, fat side up, to prepared rack and let rest for 10 to 15 minutes. Pat roast dry with paper towels. Broil until surface of roast is browned and crisp, 4 to 8 minutes.

6 Transfer roast to carving board and discard ribs. Slice meat into ¾-inch-thick slices. Serve.

Horseradish–Sour Cream Sauce
YIELD Makes about 2 cups
Buy refrigerated prepared horseradish, not the shelf-stable kind, which contains preservatives and additives.

1 cup (230 grams) sour cream
1 cup (240 grams) prepared horseradish, drained
   Salt and pepper

Whisk sour cream, horseradish, 1½ teaspoons (9 grams) salt, and ¼ teaspoon (1 gram) pepper together in bowl. Cover and refrigerate for at least 30 minutes to allow flavors to meld. Season with salt and pepper to taste. (Sauce can be refrigerated for up to 2 days.)

Mint Persillade

YIELD Makes about 1½ cups

This sauce makes a great accompaniment to prime rib.

2½ cups (35 grams) fresh mint leaves

2½ cups (35 grams) fresh parsley leaves

  6 garlic cloves (30 grams), peeled

  6 anchovy fillets (24 grams), rinsed and patted dry

2 teaspoons (4 grams) grated lemon zest plus 2½ tablespoons (38 grams) juice

  Salt and pepper

¾ cup (168 grams) extra-virgin olive oil

1 Pulse mint, parsley, garlic, anchovies, lemon zest, ½ teaspoon (3 grams) salt, and ⅛ teaspoon (1 gram) pepper in food processor until finely chopped, 15 to 20 pulses. Add lemon juice and pulse briefly to combine.

2 Transfer mixture to medium bowl and slowly whisk in oil until incorporated. Cover and let sit at room temperature for at least 1 hour to allow flavors to meld. Season with salt and pepper to taste. (Sauce can be refrigerated for up to 2 days. Bring to room temperature and whisk to recombine before serving.)

Osso Buco

YIELD SERVES 4
Sous Vide Temperature 176°F/80°C
Sous Vide Time 24 to 26 hours
Active Cooking Time 1 hour 15 minutes

To Make Ahead Shanks can be rapidly chilled in ice bath (see page 13) and then refrigerated in zipper-lock bag after step 6 for up to 3 days. To reheat, return sealed bag to water bath set to 176°F/80°C for 1 hour and then proceed with step 7.

Why This Recipe Works Osso buco is a classic Milanese dish of braised veal shanks in a hearty sauce of vegetables, wine, and tomato. While the ingredients are simple, the resulting flavors are rich and satisfying. That's because veal shanks contain a significant amount of fatty marrow. The marrow renders as the shanks braise, contributing earthy flavor to the sauce and effectively basting the meat in its own fat. Traditional preparations require hours of babysitting the stove or oven. By cooking our osso buco sous vide, we make this dish relatively hands-off. First, we presear the shanks to develop some good browning in our pan and on our meat. We reduce a sauce of onion, carrot, celery, garlic, wine, and tomato to create a paste, which we throw right into the bag with our shanks. As the shanks cook, juices accumulate and rehydrate the paste, resulting in a velvety sauce with tons of meaty flavor. After 24 hours, nearly all the fat and collagen have been rendered, and we're left with fork-tender, fall-apart meat. Be sure to double-bag the shanks to protect against seam failure.

- 1 large onion (280 grams), chopped
- 2 carrots (160 grams), peeled and chopped
- 2 celery ribs (120 grams), chopped
- 8 garlic cloves (40 grams), minced
- 1 14.5-ounce can (411 grams) diced tomatoes, drained
- 4 12-ounce (340 grams) veal shanks, 2 inches thick, trimmed and tied around equator
-    Salt and pepper
- ¼ cup (56 grams) vegetable oil
- 2 tablespoons (32 grams) tomato paste
- 1¼ cups (290 grams) dry white wine
- 4 bay leaves (1 gram)
- ¼ cup (5 grams) chopped fresh parsley

1 Using sous vide circulator, bring water to 176°F/80° C in 7-quart container.

2 Pulse onion, carrots, celery, and garlic in food processor until finely chopped, 12 to 14 pulses; transfer to bowl. Pulse tomatoes in now-empty processor until finely chopped, 8 to 10 pulses.

3 Pat shanks dry with paper towels and season with salt and pepper. Heat 2 tablespoons (28 grams) oil in 12-inch skillet over medium-high heat until just smoking. Brown shanks, 3 to 4 minutes per side; transfer to plate.

4 Heat remaining 2 tablespoons (28 grams) oil in now-empty skillet over medium heat until shimmering. Add vegetable mixture, ¾ teaspoon (5 grams) salt, and ¾ teaspoon (2 grams) pepper and cook until softened and lightly browned, 16 to 20 minutes.

5 Stir in tomato paste and cook until fragrant, about 1 minute. Stir in wine, scraping up any browned bits, and cook until almost completely evaporated, 4 to 6 minutes. Stir in tomatoes and cook until mixture is thick and lightly browned, 16 to 20 minutes.

6 Transfer mixture to 2-gallon zipper-lock freezer bag. Add shanks and bay leaves and toss to coat. Arrange shanks in single layer and seal bag, pressing out as much air as possible. Place bag into second 2-gallon zipper-lock freezer bag and seal bag. Gently lower bag into prepared water bath until shanks are fully submerged, and then clip top corner of bag to side of water bath container, allowing remaining air bubbles to rise to top of bag. Reopen 1 corner of zipper, release remaining air bubbles, and reseal bag. Cover and cook for at least 24 hours or up to 26 hours.

7 Transfer shanks to serving dish, leaving sauce in bag. Discard bay leaves. Stir parsley into sauce and season with salt and pepper to taste. Pour sauce over shanks and serve.

Seared Thick-Cut Pork Chops

YIELD SERVES 4
Sous Vide Temperature 140°F/60°C
Sous Vide Time 2 to 3 hours
Active Cooking Time 40 minutes

To Make Ahead Chops can be rapidly chilled in ice bath (see page 13) and then refrigerated in zipper-lock bag after step 2 for up to 3 days. To reheat, return sealed bag to water bath set to 140°F/60°C for 30 minutes and then proceed with step 3.

Why This Recipe Works Without a lot of fat to insulate and moisten pork chops, traditional versions of this recipe can go from perfect to overcooked in a flash. But with sous vide, there's no worry of that. Our thick-cut chops cooked at 140°F/60°C for 2 to 3 hours before a quick sear in a hot pan. Serve with Porcini-Marsala Pan Sauce or Port-Cherry Pan Sauce (recipes follow), if desired.

- 4 12-ounce (340 grams) bone-in pork rib or center-cut chops, about 1½ inches thick, trimmed
   Salt and pepper
- 6 tablespoons (84 grams) vegetable oil

1 Using sous vide circulator, bring water to 140°F/60°C in 7-quart container.

2 Season chops with salt and pepper. Divide chops and ¼ cup (56 grams) oil between two 1-gallon zipper-lock freezer bags and toss to coat. Arrange chops in single layer and seal bag, pressing out as much air as possible. Gently lower bags into prepared water bath until chops are fully submerged, and then clip top corner of each bag to side of water bath container, allowing remaining air bubbles to rise to top of bag. Reopen 1 corner of zipper, release remaining air bubbles, and reseal bag. Cover and cook for at least 2 hours or up to 3 hours.

3 Transfer chops to paper towel–lined plate and let rest for 5 to 10 minutes. Pat chops dry with paper towels. Heat 1 tablespoon (14 grams) oil in 12-inch skillet over medium-high heat until just smoking. Place 2 chops in skillet and cook until well browned on first side, 1 to 2 minutes, lifting once halfway through cooking to redistribute fat underneath each chop. Flip chops and continue to cook until well browned on second side, 1 to 2 minutes. Transfer chops to plate and tent with aluminum foil. Repeat with remaining 1 tablespoon (14 grams) oil and chops. Serve.

Porcini-Marsala Pan Sauce

YIELD Makes about ½ cup

Note that step 1 can be completed while pork chops are circulating. Step 2 is meant to be started after you have seared the chops. It is worth spending a little extra for a moderately priced dry Marsala ($10 to $12 per bottle).

- ¾ cup (168 grams) chicken broth
- ¼ ounce (7 grams) dried porcini mushrooms, rinsed
   Vegetable oil, if needed
- 1 shallot (30 grams), minced
- ½ cup (113 grams) dry Marsala
- 2 tablespoons (28 grams) unsalted butter, cut into 2 pieces and chilled
- 1 tablespoon (4 grams) minced fresh parsley
   Salt and pepper

1 Microwave ½ cup (113 grams) broth and mushrooms in covered bowl until steaming, about 1 minute. Let sit until softened, about 5 minutes. Drain mushrooms through fine-mesh strainer lined with coffee filter, reserving drained liquid, and chop mushrooms.

2 Pour off all but 1 tablespoon (14 grams) fat from skillet used to sear pork chops. (If necessary, add oil to equal 1 tablespoon (14 grams).) Add shallot and cook over medium heat until softened, 1 to 2 minutes. Off heat, stir in Marsala, scraping up any browned bits. Return skillet to medium heat and simmer until Marsala is reduced to glaze, about 3 minutes.

3 Stir in remaining ¼ cup (56 grams) broth, reserved soaking liquid, and mushrooms. Bring to simmer and cook until liquid is reduced to ⅓ cup, 4 to 6 minutes. Off heat, whisk in butter, 1 piece at a time, until melted and sauce

is thickened and glossy. Whisk in parsley and any accumulated meat juices. Season with salt and pepper to taste. Serve immediately.

Port-Cherry Pan Sauce

YIELD Makes about ½ cup

Note that this recipe is meant to be started after you have seared the chops. We prefer to use less expensive ruby port for this sauce.

    Vegetable oil, if needed
1 shallot (30 grams), minced
¾ cup (168 grams) port
¼ cup (60 grams) balsamic vinegar
¼ cup (40 grams) dried tart cherries
2 sprigs (1 gram) fresh thyme
2 tablespoons (28 grams) unsalted butter, cut into 2 pieces and chilled
    Salt and pepper

1 Pour off all but 1 tablespoon (14 grams) fat from skillet used to sear pork chops. (If necessary, add oil to equal 1 tablespoon (14 grams).) Add shallot and cook over medium heat until softened, 1 to 2 minutes. Stir in port, vinegar, cherries, and thyme sprigs, scraping up any browned bits. Bring to simmer and cook until liquid is reduced to ¼ cup, about 8 minutes.

2 Off heat, discard thyme sprigs. Whisk in butter, 1 piece at a time, until melted and sauce is thickened and glossy. Whisk in any accumulated meat juices. Season with salt and pepper to taste. Serve immediately.

Seared Pork Tenderloin Steaks

YIELD SERVES 4
Sous Vide Temperature 140°F/60°C
Sous Vide Time 1 to 2 hours
Active Cooking Time 40 minutes

To Make Ahead Steaks can be rapidly chilled in ice bath (page 13) and then refrigerated in zipper-lock bag after step 2 for up to 3 days. To reheat, return sealed bag to water bath set to 140°F / 60°C for 30 minutes and then proceed with step 3.

Why This Recipe Works We began by lightly pounding our pork tenderloin to create two flat sides that would be easy to sear. Halving the tenderloin crosswise created moderately sized steaks that would be easy to maneuver. Submerged in a 140°F/60°C water bath, the pork was guaranteed to remain moist and tender and cook evenly from edge to edge. For great browning, we made sure to pat the pork dry before searing it in a hot skillet. Serve with Scallion-Ginger Relish (recipe follows), if desired.

2 1-pound (450 grams) pork tenderloins, trimmed
    Salt and pepper
¼ cup (56 grams) vegetable oil

   1 Using sous vide circulator, bring water to 140°F/60°C in 7-quart container.

   2 Pound tenderloins to 1-inch thickness. Halve each tenderloin crosswise into 2 steaks. Sprinkle each steak with ½ teaspoon (3 grams) salt and ⅛ teaspoon (0.5 grams) pepper. Place steaks and 2 tablespoons (28 grams) oil in 1-gallon zipper-lock freezer bag and toss to coat. Arrange steaks in single layer and seal bag, pressing out as much air as possible. Gently lower bag into prepared water bath until steaks are fully submerged, and then clip top corner of bag to side of water bath container, allowing remaining air bubbles to rise to top of bag. Reopen 1 corner of zipper, release remaining air bubbles, and reseal bag. Cover and cook for at least 1 hour or up to 2 hours.

   3 Transfer steaks to paper towel–lined plate and let rest for 5 to 10 minutes. Pat steaks dry with paper towels. Heat remaining 2 tablespoons (28 grams) oil in 12-inch skillet over medium-high heat until just smoking. Brown steaks, 1 to 2 minutes per side. Transfer to cutting board and slice into ¾-inch-thick slices. Serve.

Scallion-Ginger Relish
YIELD Makes about ⅔ cup
We like the complexity of white pepper in this recipe; don't substitute black pepper.

6 scallions (100 grams), white and green parts separated and sliced thin
2 teaspoons (12 grams) grated fresh ginger
½ teaspoon (1 gram) ground white pepper
½ teaspoon (1 gram) grated lime zest plus 2 teaspoons (10 grams) juice
¼ cup (56 grams) vegetable oil
2 teaspoons (10 grams) soy sauce

Combine scallion whites, ginger, pepper, and lime zest in heatproof bowl. Heat oil in small saucepan until shimmering. Pour oil over scallion mixture. (Mixture will bubble.) Stir until well combined and let cool completely, about 15 minutes. Stir in scallion greens, lime juice, and soy sauce. Let mixture sit for 15 minutes to allow flavors to meld. Serve.

Indoor Pulled Pork

YIELD **SERVES 6 TO 8**
Sous Vide Temperature 165°F/74°C
Sous Vide Time 20 to 24 hours
Active Cooking Time 50 minutes

To Make Ahead Pork can be rapidly chilled in ice bath (see page 13) and then refrigerated in zipper-lock bags after step 3 for up to 3 days. To reheat, return sealed bags to water bath set to 165°F/74°C for 1 hour and then proceed with step 4.

Why This Recipe Works Pulled pork can often be a huge project—especially if you want to do it on the grill or in a smoker. But it is possible to streamline the process and make it a little more convenient. Unfortunately, recipes for this kind of indoor pulled pork often produce mushy, water-logged meat that's swimming in sauce in order to mask all that blandness. But by cooking the pork sous vide, we can achieve proper texture at a lower, more stable temperature than in traditional methods—which means less moisture loss, and more succulent meat. And a long, 24-hour cooking time breaks down almost all fat and collagen, making the pork shreddable but not mushy. We coat the pork in an aggressively seasoned spice paste to ensure flavorful meat. To give this dish a boost, we make a tangy sauce from the cooking juices. Slap this stuff on pillowy potato rolls and you've got yourself some flavor-packed barbecue sand-wiches—right at home, any time of year. Pork butt roast is often labeled Boston butt in the supermarket. Serve the pork on hamburger rolls with pickle chips and thinly sliced onion. Feel free to substitute the South Carolina Mustard Barbecue Sauce (recipe follows). Alternatively, use 2 cups of your favorite barbecue sauce thinned with ¾ cup of the defatted pork cooking liquid in step 5. Be sure to double-bag the pork to protect against seam failure.

Pork

- ¼ cup (56 grams) vegetable oil
- 2 teaspoons (12 grams) salt
- 2 tablespoons (25 grams) sugar
- 2 tablespoons (18 grams) pepper
- 2 tablespoons (14 grams) smoked paprika
- 1 tablespoon (9 grams) garlic powder
- 1 teaspoon (2 grams) cayenne pepper
- ¼ cup (60 grams) yellow mustard
- 1 tablespoon (15 grams) liquid smoke
- 1 5-pound (2.3 kilograms) boneless pork butt roast, trimmed and halved

Lexington Vinegar Barbecue Sauce

- 1 cup (236 grams) cider vinegar
- ½ cup (140 grams) ketchup
- ½ cup (118 grams) water
- 1 tablespoon (12.5 grams) sugar
- ¾ teaspoon (1 gram) red pepper flakes
  Salt and pepper

1 **For the pork** Using sous vide circulator, bring water to 165°F/74°C in 12-quart container.

2 Whisk oil, salt, sugar, pepper, paprika, garlic powder, and cayenne together in medium bowl. Microwave until bubbling and fragrant, about 3 minutes, stirring halfway through microwaving. Stir in mustard and liquid smoke.

3 Divide pork and spice mixture between two 2-gallon zipper-lock freezer bags and toss to coat. Seal bags, pressing out as much air as possible. Place bags in second 2-gallon zipper-lock freezer bag and seal bag. Gently lower bags into prepared water bath until pork is

fully submerged, and then clip top corner of each bag to side of water bath container, allowing remaining air bubbles to rise to top of bag. Reopen 1 corner of zipper, release remaining air bubbles, and reseal bag. Cover and cook for at least 20 hours or up to 24 hours.

4 Transfer pork to cutting board and reserve cooking liquid. Let pork cool slightly, and then shred into bite-size pieces using 2 forks; discard excess fat.

5 For the barbecue sauce Pour cooking liquid into fat separator, let settle for 5 minutes, and then transfer ¾ cup (185 grams) defatted liquid to medium bowl; discard remaining liquid. Whisk in vinegar, ketchup, water, sugar, pepper flakes, ¾ teaspoon (5 grams) salt, and ½ teaspoon (1.5 grams) pepper. Toss pork with 1 cup (250 grams) sauce and season with salt and pepper to taste. Serve, passing remaining sauce separately.

Variation

South Carolina Mustard Sauce

Substitute the following ingredients for the Lexington Vinegar Barbecue Sauce: 1 cup (240 grams) yellow mustard, ½ cup (118 grams) distilled white vinegar, ¼ cup packed (50 grams) light brown sugar, ¼ cup (75 grams) Worcestershire sauce, 2 tablespoons (36 grams) hot sauce, 1 teaspoon (7 grams) salt, and 1 teaspoon (3 grams) pepper.

Porchetta

YIELD SERVES 8 TO 10
Sous Vide Temperature 145°F/63°C
Sous Vide Time 20 to 24 hours
Active Cooking Time 1 hour 10 minutes

To Make Ahead Pork can be rapidly chilled in ice bath (see page 13) and then refrigerated in zipper-lock bags after step 6 for up to 3 days. To reheat, return sealed bags to water bath set to 145°F/63°C for 30 minutes and then proceed with step 7.

Why This Recipe Works Traditionally, Italian porchetta is a whole pig that is spit-roasted to produce fall-apart tender, rich pieces of slow-cooked pork, aromatic with garlic, fennel seeds, rosemary, and thyme. It's served with pieces of crisp skin on a crusty roll. Seeing as most people don't have a rotisserie in their kitchen, or access to whole pigs, porchetta is a tricky recipe to adapt for cooking at home. After testing a few different cuts, we settled on pork butt, which is cut from the upper portion of the shoulder and has a good amount of fat to keep the meat moist and flavorful without making it over the top decadent (as can be the case with pork belly, another common choice). We cut the pork butt in half to allow for even seasoning and easy slicing when serving. We seasoned both pieces with salt and then rubbed them down with a simple garlic-herb paste before sending them to the water bath. A low-and-slow sous vide bath allowed the collagen in the meat to transform into moisture-retaining gelatin. This kept the roast juicy and tender but still sliceable. Once the pork had finished cooking in the water bath, we quickly blasted it in a hot oven to crisp up and brown the fat cap to mimic traditional porchetta's crispy pork skin. In sum? Roast pork just got a whole lot better. Pork butt roast is often labeled Boston butt in the supermarket. If fennel seeds are unavailable, substitute ¼ cup of ground fennel.

3 tablespoons (27 grams) fennel seeds
½ cup (25 grams) fresh rosemary leaves
¼ cup (12 grams) fresh thyme leaves
12 garlic cloves (60 grams), peeled
Kosher salt and pepper
½ cup (112 grams) extra-virgin olive oil
1 5-pound (2.3 kilograms) boneless pork butt roast, trimmed

1 Using sous vide circulator, bring water to 145°F/63°C in 12-quart container.

2 Grind fennel seeds in spice grinder or mortar and pestle until finely ground. Transfer ground fennel to food processor and add rosemary, thyme, garlic, 1 tablespoon (9 grams) pepper, and 2 teaspoons (6 grams) salt. Pulse mixture until finely chopped, 10 to 15 pulses. Add oil and process until smooth paste forms, 20 to 30 seconds.

3 Using sharp knife, cut slits in surface layer of fat on roast, spaced 1 inch apart, in crosshatch pattern, being careful not to cut into meat. Cut roast in half with grain into 2 equal pieces.

4 Turn each roast on its side so fat cap is facing away from you, bottom of roast is facing toward you, and newly cut side is facing up. Starting 1 inch from short end of each roast, use boning or paring knife to make slit that starts 1 inch from top of roast and ends 1 inch from bottom, pushing knife completely through roast. Repeat making slits, spaced 1 to 1½ inches apart, along length of each roast, stopping 1 inch from opposite end (you should have 6 to 8 slits).

5 Turn roast so fat cap is facing down. Rub sides and bottom of each roast with 2 teaspoons (6 grams) salt, taking care to work salt into slits from both sides. Rub herb paste onto sides and bottom of each roast, taking care to work paste into slits from both sides. Flip roast so that fat cap is facing up. Using 3 pieces of kitchen twine per roast, tie each roast into compact cylinder.

6 Combine 1 tablespoon (9 grams) salt and 1 teaspoon (3 grams) pepper in small bowl. Rub fat cap of each roast with salt mixture, taking care to work mixture into cross-hatches. Place each roast in 1-gallon zipper-lock freezer bag. Seal bags, pressing out as much air as possible. Gently lower bags into prepared water bath until roasts are fully submerged, and then clip top corner of each bag to side

of water bath container, allowing remaining air bubbles to rise to top of bag. Reopen 1 corner of zipper, release remaining air bubbles, and reseal bag. Cover and cook for at least 20 hours or up to 24 hours.

7 Adjust oven rack to middle position and heat oven to 500°F/260°C. Set wire rack in aluminum foil–lined rimmed baking sheet and spray with vegetable spray. Transfer roasts, fat side up, to prepared rack, leaving at least 2 inches between roasts. Discard twine and pat roasts dry with paper towels. Roast until exteriors of roasts are well browned, about 20 minutes.

8 Transfer roasts to carving board and let rest for 5 to 10 minutes. Slice roasts ½ inch thick and serve.

Char Siu

YIELD SERVES 8 TO 10
Sous Vide Temperature 149°F/65°C
Sous Vide Time 12 to 16 hours
Active Cooking Time 1 hour, plus at least 10 hours marinating time

To Make Ahead Pork can be rapidly chilled in ice bath (see page 13) and then refrigerated in zipper-lock bags after step 3 for up to 3 days. To reheat, return sealed bags to water bath set to 149°F/65°C for 30 minutes and then proceed with step 4.

Why This Recipe Works The smell of fatty, sweet, slow-roasted *char siu* is familiar for anyone who frequents Chinatown. *Char siu* literally means "fork roast," since it is usually skewered with long forks and roasted over a fire. We wanted pork that strikes a balance between chewy, juicy, and just tender. Enter, sous vide: A longer, extended cooking time renders just enough collagen to tenderize the meat without having it fall apart. A quick glaze and broil makes the pork fragrant and delicious. Pork butt roast is often labeled Boston butt in the supermarket. To help give the pork its traditional vibrant color, we use red food dye and pink curing salt, though neither are required. Curing salt goes by many names, including DQ Curing Salt and Insta Cure #1, but it's most commonly labeled pink salt. You can find it in specialty food stores or through online retailers such as butcher-packer.com. (Do not substitute Morton's Tender Quick or Insta Cure #2.) Serve in steamed buns or over rice.

1 4-pound (2 kilograms) boneless pork butt roast, trimmed and sliced crosswise into ¾-inch-thick steaks

1 cup (260 grams) soy sauce

1 cup (7 ounces/200 grams) sugar

¾ cup (220 grams) hoisin sauce

½ cup (114 grams) Shaoxing Chinese rice wine or dry sherry

¼ cup (60 grams) grated fresh ginger

2 tablespoons (25 grams) toasted sesame oil

4 garlic cloves (20 grams), minced

1 tablespoon (15 grams) red food coloring (optional)

2 teaspoons (5 grams) five-spice powder

½ teaspoon (2 grams) ground white pepper

⅛ teaspoon (1 gram) pink curing salt (optional)

¾ cup (263 grams) honey

1 Whisk soy sauce, sugar, hoisin, rice wine, ginger, sesame oil, garlic, food coloring, if using, five-spice powder, and pepper together in large bowl. Measure out and reserve 1 cup (200 grams) marinade in refrigerator. Whisk pink curing salt, if using, into remaining marinade. Add steaks and toss to coat. Cover and refrigerate for at least 10 hours or up to 16 hours.

2 Using sous vide circulator, bring water to 149°F/65°C in 7-quart container.

3 Remove steaks from marinade, letting excess drip off. Divide pork between two 1-gallon zipper-lock freezer bags. Seal bags, pressing out as much air as possible. Gently lower bags into prepared water bath until steaks are fully submerged, and then clip top corner of each bag to side of water bath container, allowing remaining air bubbles to rise to top of bag. Reopen 1 corner of zipper, release remaining air bubbles, and reseal bag. Cover and cook for at least 12 hours or up to 16 hours.

4 Whisk honey and reserved marinade together in medium saucepan. Cook over medium heat, stirring frequently, until reduced to about 1 cup (350 grams), 4 to 8 minutes.

5 Adjust oven rack 6 inches from broiler element and heat broiler. Set wire rack in aluminum foil–lined rimmed baking sheet and spray with vegetable spray. Transfer steaks to prepared rack and pat dry with paper towels. Brush top of steaks with half of glaze and broil until mahogany, 2 to 6 minutes per side. Brush both sides of steaks with remaining glaze and broil until top is dark mahogany and lightly charred, 2 to 6 minutes. Transfer steaks, charred side up, to cutting board and let rest for 10 minutes. Slice steaks crosswise into ½-inch-thick strips and serve.

Sichuan Twice-Cooked Pork Belly

YIELD SERVES 4
Sous Vide Temperature 170°F/77°C
Sous Vide Time 8 to 9 hours
Active Cooking Time 1 hour 15 minutes

To Make Ahead Pork belly can be rapidly chilled in ice bath (see page 13) and then refrigerated in zipper-lock bag after step 2 for up to 3 days. To reheat, return sealed bag to water bath set to 170°F/77°C for 30 minutes and then proceed with step 3.

Why This Recipe Works Twice-cooked pork belly is the perfect indulgence—it's fatty, succulent, and full of flavor. A Chinese dish from the Sichuan province, twice-cooked pork belly traditionally starts by first simmering a pork belly in water until it is just cooked through. Then it is chilled to firm it up, sliced into thin pieces, and finally crisped in a hot wok with vegetables and a fiery sauce. For our recipe, we substitute a sous vide method for the initial simmer. By cooking the belly sous vide, we don't leave flavor behind in a pot of water. In fact, we boosted flavor by cooking the belly with a little Asian broad bean chili paste, and then used the accumulated porky cooking juices in the sauce. The final dish is deeply satisfying—savory and spicy with pork belly that is tender, chewy, and crisp all at once. If you love bacon, then you need sous vide pork belly in your life. Be sure to ask for a flat, rectangular center-cut section of skinless pork belly that's 1½ inches thick with roughly equal amounts of meat and fat. If you can only find skin-on pork belly, prepare it as directed, then cut off skin before slicing in step 3. Asian broad bean chili paste (or sauce) is also known as *doubanjiang* or toban djan; our favorite, Pixian, is available online. Lee Kum Kee Chili Bean Sauce is a good supermarket option. Bird chiles are dried red Thai chiles. You can substitute green bell peppers for cubanelle peppers, if desired. The pork belly has a tendency to splatter during searing in step 4; use a splatter guard to minimize oil splattering. Be sure to double bag the pork to protect against seam failure.

1 1½-pound (680 grams) skinless center-cut fresh pork belly, about 1½ inches thick

¼ cup (64 grams) Asian broad bean chili paste

1 teaspoon (5 grams) vegetable oil

2 cubanelle peppers (230 grams), stemmed, seeded, and cut into 1-inch pieces

2 garlic cloves (10 grams), minced

1 tablespoon (10 grams) grated fresh ginger

10 bird chiles (7 grams), finely ground (1 tablespoon)

¼ cup (60 grams) Shaoxing Chinese rice wine or dry sherry

¼ cup (60 grams) water

2 tablespoons (36 grams) hoisin sauce

2 teaspoons (6 grams) fermented black beans, chopped coarse

8 scallions (60 grams), white parts sliced thin, green parts cut into 1-inch pieces

1 Using sous vide circulator, bring water to 170°F/77°C in 7-quart container.

2 Rub pork with 1 tablespoon (16 grams) chili paste and place in 1-gallon zipper-lock freezer bag. Seal bag, pressing out as much air as possible. Place bag in second 1-gallon zipper-lock freezer bag and seal bag. Gently lower bag into prepared water bath until pork is fully submerged, and then clip top corner of bag to side of water bath container, allowing remaining air bubbles to rise to top of bag. Reopen 1 corner of zipper, release remaining air bubbles, and reseal bag. Cover and cook for at least 8 hours or up to 9 hours.

3 Fill large bowl halfway with ice and water. Submerge zipper-lock bag in ice bath and let sit until pork is chilled, about 15 minutes. Transfer pork to cutting board and pat dry with paper towels. Transfer congealed cooking liquid to small bowl. Slice pork lengthwise into 2-inch-wide strips, and then slice strips crosswise into ¼-inch-thick pieces.

4 Heat oil in 12-inch nonstick skillet over medium-high heat until shimmering. Add half of pork in even layer and cook until browned, 2 to 3 minutes per side; transfer to bowl. Repeat with remaining pork. Pour off all but 2 tablespoons fat from skillet.

5 Add peppers to fat left in skillet and cook over medium-high, without stirring, until lightly charred, about 3 minutes. Stir in garlic, ginger, and bird chile and cook until fragrant, about 30 seconds. Stir in rice wine and water, scraping up any browned bits, and cook until liquid is reduced by half, about 15 seconds.

6 Stir in remaining 3 tablespoons (60 grams) chili paste, reserved cooking liquid, hoisin, and fermented black beans. Add pork and scallion greens and toss to coat. Transfer to serving dish and sprinkle with scallion whites.

Cochinita Pibil

YIELD SERVES 8 TO 10
Sous Vide Temperature 155°F/68.5°C
Sous Vide Time 22 to 26 hours
Active Cooking Time 1 hour 15 minutes

To Make Ahead Pork can be rapidly chilled in ice bath (see page 13) and then refrigerated in zipper-lock bag after step 2 for up to 3 days. To reheat, return sealed bag to water bath set to 155°F/68.5°C for 30 to 45 minutes and then proceed with step 3.

Why This Recipe Works *Cochinita pibil* is the pride of the Yucatan peninsula—a dish of smoky, slow-roasted pork marinated in a special blend of ingredients, including cinnamon, allspice, and achiote (annatto) seed. *Cochinita* means "baby pig," and the real-deal recipes use a whole suckling pig. Traditionally the whole thing is wrapped in banana leaves and then buried in a *pib*—a pit with a fire at the bottom. Here we use pork butt roast, and we employed a two-stage "grill-and-swim" cooking process to make things a little more convenient and a lot juicier. Pregrilling the meat added great flavor, while low-and-slow sous vide cooking produced especially succulent meat—no pib required. We did all the prep up front, so once the pork was finished cooking, we just chopped the meat up and served it to our lucky friends and family. Now that you don't have to fire up your grill on taco night, you can focus on curating that sweet summertime playlist you've been meaning to put together. Pork butt roast is often labeled Boston butt in the supermarket. We prefer the flavor of canela cinnamon and Mexican oregano here; however, conventional varieties will work. Serve with white rice or in warmed corn tortillas with any combination of the following: spicy salsa, pickled red onions, thinly sliced radishes, thinly sliced scallions, crumbled *queso fresco* or cotija cheese, and lime wedges.

25 garlic cloves (150 grams), unpeeled
 2 tablespoons (28 grams) vegetable oil
¼ cup (40 grams) annatto seeds
 1 tablespoon (10 grams) peppercorns
 1 (4-inch) stick (8 grams) canela cinnamon
 1 tablespoon (7 grams) allspice berries
 2 tablespoons (3 grams) Mexican oregano
¼ cup (65 grams) orange juice

¼ cup (60 grams) cider vinegar
    Salt and pepper
 1 teaspoon (4 grams) liquid smoke
 1 4-pound (2 kilograms) boneless pork butt roast, trimmed and halved
 1 onion (200 grams), sliced into ¾-inch-thick rounds
 8 ounces (226 grams) banana leaf, cut into long strips and bruised
 8 bay leaves (2 grams)

1 Cook garlic in 12-inch skillet over high heat, shaking occasionally, until blackened on most sides, 8 to 10 minutes. Transfer garlic to bowl, let cool slightly, then peel away skins; wipe skillet clean with paper towels.

2 Heat oil in now-empty skillet over medium heat until shimmering. Add annatto seeds, peppercorns, cinnamon stick, allspice berries, and oregano, cover, and cook, shaking skillet frequently, for 30 seconds. Transfer spice mixture to blender along with garlic, orange juice, vinegar, 1 tablespoon (18 grams) salt, and liquid smoke. Process until smooth paste forms, about 3 minutes, scraping down sides of blender jar as needed. Transfer ¼ cup (60 grams) spice paste to large bowl, add pork, and toss to coat; reserve remaining spice paste.

3A For Charcoal Grill Open bottom vent completely. Light large chimney starter filled with charcoal briquettes (6 quarts/2 kilograms). When top coals are partially covered with ash, pour evenly over half of grill. Set cooking grate in place, cover, and open lid vent completely. Heat grill until hot, about 5 minutes.

3B For Gas Grill Turn all burners to high, cover, and heat grill until hot, about 15 minutes. Leave all burners on high.

4 Clean and oil cooking grate. Place pork and onions on grill over flames and cook until well charred on first side, 3 to 4 minutes. Flip pork and onions and continue to cook until well charred on second side, 2 to 3 minutes. Return pork to now-empty bowl. Continue to cook onions, flipping as needed, until softened, about 4 minutes; transfer to small bowl.

5 Meanwhile, using sous vide circulator, bring water to 155°F/68.5°C in 12-quart container.

6 Add onions to blender with reserved spice paste and process until smooth, 1 to 2 minutes. Divide pork, spice paste, banana leaves, and bay leaves between two 1-gallon zipper-lock bags and toss to coat. Seal bags, pressing out as much air as possible. Gently lower bags into prepared water bath until pork is fully submerged, and then clip top corner of bags to side of water bath container, allowing remaining air bubbles to rise to top of bag. Reopen 1 corner of zipper, release remaining air bubbles, and reseal bag. Cover and cook for at least 22 hours or up to 26 hours.

7 Transfer pork to cutting board, let cool slightly, and then chop into rough ½-inch pieces. Strain cooking liquid through fine-mesh strainer set over large bowl; discard solids. Add pork to cooking liquid and toss to combine. Season with salt and pepper to taste and serve.

Beer-Braised Brats

YIELD SERVES 4
Sous Vide Temperature 170°F/76.5°C
Sous Vide Time 45 minutes to 3 hours
Active Cooking Time 45 minutes

To Make Ahead Bratwurst can be rapidly chilled in ice bath (see page 13) and then refrigerated in zipper-lock bag after step 2 for up to 3 days. To reheat, return sealed bag to water bath set to 170°F/76.5°C for 15 minutes and then proceed with step 3.

Why This Recipe Works Bratwursts and beer are a classic combination that need little introduction, but that's not to say that the beer-braised brat (a tailgating staple!) couldn't use a little help. Many recipes yield soggy sausages and bland onions floating in hot beer, but with the help of sous vide cooking, we are able to solve these problems. To deliver juicy sausages infused with the right amount of beer flavor, we cook the brats sous vide with a mild lager and a little salt added to the bag. While the brats are swimming in the water bath, we brown some onions on the stovetop and then cook them down with a little whole-grain mustard plus more beer. Once the brats are cooked through, we give them a quick post–sous vide sear in a pan to crisp up and brown the exteriors. Loaded in sub rolls and topped with the beer-happy onions, these are better beer brats. Be sure to double bag the brats to protect against seam failure.

1½ pounds (675 grams) bratwurst (6 sausages)

1½ cups (375 grams) mild lager, such as Budweiser

 Salt and pepper

 3 tablespoons (42 grams) vegetable oil

 2 onions (350 grams), halved and sliced thin

 2 garlic cloves (10 grams), minced

 ½ teaspoon (1 gram) caraway seeds

 2 tablespoons (40 grams) whole-grain mustard

 1 teaspoon (7 grams) honey

 1 teaspoon (5 grams) cider vinegar

 6 (6-inch) sub rolls

1 Using sous vide circulator, bring water to 170°F/77°C in 7-quart container.

2 Place bratwursts, ½ cup (125 grams) beer, and ½ teaspoon (3 grams) salt in 1-gallon zipper-lock freezer bag. Arrange sausages in single layer and seal bag, pressing out as much air as possible. Place bag in second 1-gallon zipper-lock freezer bag and seal bag. Gently lower bag into prepared water bath until sausages are fully submerged, then clip top corner of bag to side of water bath container, allowing remaining air bubbles to rise to top of bag. Reopen 1 corner of zipper, release remaining air bubbles, and reseal bag. Cover and cook for at least 45 minutes or up to 3 hours.

3 Heat 2 tablespoons (28 grams) oil in 12-inch nonstick skillet over medium heat until shimmering. Add onion, ¼ teaspoon (1 gram) salt, and ¼ teaspoon (1 gram) pepper and cook until softened and lightly browned, 5 to 7 minutes. Stir in garlic and caraway seeds and cook until fragrant, about 30 seconds. Stir in remaining 1 cup (250 grams) beer, mustard, honey, and vinegar. Increase heat to medium-high and cook, stirring occasionally, until onion mixture is thickened, about 8 minutes. Transfer to small bowl and set aside. Wipe skillet clean with paper towels.

4 Transfer bratwursts to paper towel–lined plate and pat dry with paper towels. Heat remaining 1 tablespoon (14 grams) oil in now-empty skillet over medium-high heat until just smoking. Brown bratwursts on all sides, about 1 to 2 minutes. Serve in rolls topped with onion mixture.

Spiral-Sliced Ham

YIELD **SERVES 12 TO 14**
Sous Vide Temperature 140°F/60°C
Sous Vide Time 3 to 8 hours
Active Cooking Time 45 minutes

To Make Ahead We don't recommend making this recipe ahead of time.

Why This Recipe Works A glazed holiday ham is one of those old-school traditions that will never go out of style. Since it's already cooked, there are not too many places to go awry: All you have to do is reheat the ham, glaze it with a sweet or tangy sauce, and you're good to go. But in the interest of bringing ham into the 21st century (and freeing up some oven space for you next holiday meal), we're here to make it even better and more foolproof. Reheating the ham sous vide guarantees that the meat is evenly heated from edge to edge, eliminating cold spots and the need to obsessively maul your beautiful ham with an instant-read thermometer. Since cooking sous vide all but eliminates evaporation, the meat stays moist and flavorful. But the best part? If your ham comes from the store in convenient vacuum-sealed packaging, you can just drop the whole thing in your water bath and forget about it—no extra-extra-large bag needed. To finish this holiday centerpiece, we lacquer our ham with a couple of coats of cherry-port glaze in a hot oven, which gives the exterior a rich mahogany sheen. For easy carving, we prefer a shank-end spiral-sliced ham, but a butt-end ham will also work. Make sure that vacuum-sealed ham has no visible tears or breaks in the packaging to ensure that the ham reheats properly. Note that this recipe requires a 12-quart container.

1 7-pound (3.2 kilograms) spiral-sliced bone-in ham
½ cup (118 grams) ruby port
½ cup (160 grams) cherry preserves
1 cup packed (200 grams) dark brown sugar
  Pepper

1 Using sous vide circulator, heat water to 140°F/60°C in 12-quart container.

2 Place ham into 2-gallon zipper-lock freezer bag and seal bag, pressing out as much air as possible. Gently lower bag into prepared water bath until ham is fully submerged, and then clip top corner of bag to side of water bath container, allowing remaining air bubbles to rise to top of bag. Reopen 1 corner of zipper, release remaining air bubbles, and reseal bag. Cover and cook for at least 3 hours or up to 8 hours.

3 Cook port in small saucepan over medium heat until reduced to 2 tablespoons (35 grams), about 5 minutes. Stir in cherry preserves, sugar, and 1 teaspoon (4 grams) pepper and cook, stirring occasionally, until sugar dissolves and mixture is thick, syrupy, and reduced to 1 cup, 5 to 10 minutes; set aside.

4 Adjust oven rack to lower-middle position and heat oven to 475°F/246°C. Set wire rack in aluminum foil-lined rimmed baking sheet and spray with vegetable oil spray. Transfer ham, cut side down, to prepared rack and brush with half of glaze. Cook ham until glaze becomes sticky, 5 to 10 minutes. Brush ham with remaining glaze and cook until glaze becomes sticky and light mahogany, 5 to 10 minutes. Carve and serve.

Spice-Rubbed Leg of Lamb with Chermoula

YIELD SERVES 6 TO 8
Sous Vide Temperature 131°F/55°C
Sous Vide Time 20 to 24 hours
Active Cooking Time 1 hour 15 minutes, plus at least 4 hours salting time

To Make Ahead Lamb can be rapidly chilled in ice bath (see page 13) and then refrigerated in zipper-lock bag after step 4 for up to 3 days. To reheat, return sealed bag to water bath set to 131°F/55°C for 1 hour and then proceed with step 5.

Why This Recipe Works Cooking a leg of lamb can be a little intimidating. But swapping in a butterflied leg of lamb for the usual bone-in or boned, rolled, and tied leg provided us with a number of benefits: thorough seasoning, a great ratio of crust to meat, and even cooking. To balance out the potential gamy flavor in lamb, we rub ours with an intense harissa-style paste (a popular North African hot-pepper paste) and let it marinate to intensify the flavors. Circulating the lamb for 24 hours at a low temperature yields a rosy, medium-rare interior from edge to edge that's about as tender as filet mignon. We coat the lamb with even more harissa paste as soon as it comes out of the bath before blasting it under the broiler to char and crisp up the exterior. With a bright, tangy chermoula sauce on top, this is one lamb roast that's sure to impress at any holiday. We prefer the subtler flavor of lamb labeled "domestic" or "American" for this recipe.

Lamb

- 5 tablespoons (70 grams) extra-virgin olive oil
- 4 teaspoons (9 grams) paprika
- 1 tablespoon (6 grams) ground cumin
  Salt and pepper
- 1 teaspoon (2.5 grams) garlic powder
- ¾ teaspoon (2 grams) ground turmeric
- ¼ teaspoon (0.5 grams) cayenne pepper
- ¼ teaspoon (0.5 grams) ground cinnamon
- ¼ teaspoon (0.5 grams) ground ginger
- ¼ cup (42 grams) oil-packed sun-dried tomatoes, patted dry
- ¼ cup (30 grams) pitted brine-cured green olives
- 1 3-pound (1.4 kilograms) boneless half leg of lamb

Chermoula

- 1½ cups (20 grams) fresh cilantro leaves
- ½ cup (112 grams) extra-virgin olive oil
- ¼ cup (60 grams) lemon juice (2 lemons)
- 8 garlic cloves (40 grams), minced
- 1 teaspoon (2 grams) ground cumin
- 1 teaspoon (2 grams) paprika
- ¾ teaspoon (5 grams) salt
- ¼ teaspoon (1 gram) cayenne pepper

1 For the lamb Whisk oil, paprika, cumin, 1 teaspoon (6 grams) salt, garlic powder, ¾ teaspoon (2 grams) pepper, turmeric, cayenne, cinnamon, and ginger in small bowl. Microwave until bubbling and fragrant, about 3 minutes, stirring halfway through microwaving. Transfer spice mixture to food processor. Add tomatoes and olives and process until smooth paste forms, about 1 minute, scraping down sides of bowl as needed. Measure out and reserve half of paste in refrigerator.

2 Place lamb on cutting board with fat cap facing down. Using sharp knife, trim any pockets of fat and connective tissue from underside of lamb. Flip lamb over, trim fat cap so it's between ⅛ and ¼ inch thick, and pound roast to even 1-inch thickness. Cut slits in surface layer of fat, spaced 1 inch apart, in crosshatch pattern, being careful not to cut into meat. Season both sides of lamb with salt and rub with remaining harissa. Place lamb in 2-gallon zipper-lock freezer bag and arrange in even layer. Seal bag, pressing out as much air as possible. Refrigerate lamb for at least 4 hours or up to 24 hours.

3 Using sous vide circulator, bring water to 131°F/55° C in 7-quart container.

4 Gently lower bag into prepared water bath until lamb is fully submerged, and then clip top corner of bag to side of water bath container, allowing remaining air bubbles to rise to top of bag. Reopen 1 corner of zipper, release remaining air bubbles, and reseal bag. Cover and cook for at least 20 hours or up to 24 hours.

5 For the chermoula Process all ingredients in food processor until smooth, about 1 minute, scraping down sides of bowl as needed. Transfer to bowl and set aside for serving.

6 Adjust oven rack 6 inches from broiler element and heat broiler. Set wire rack in aluminum foil–lined rimmed baking sheet and spray with vegetable oil spray. Transfer lamb, fat side up, to prepared rack and let rest for 10 to 15 minutes.

7 Pat lamb dry with paper towels, and then spread reserved paste over top. Broil until lightly charred, 6 to 8 minutes. Transfer lamb to carving board and slice thin against grain. Serve with chermoula.

Heat Transfer and Sous Vide

Key Points

- High heat cooking methods (like the broiler) make heat move quickly
- Gentle cooking methods (like sous vide) mean heat moves more slowly
- Sous vide cooking ensures even heating—and cooking—all the way through your food
- Thick ingredients take longer to cook than thin ingredients
- Shape matters; a chicken cutlet will cook faster than a meatball
- The density of the ingredient being cooked also affects how quickly heat will penetrate to the center

When you broil a steak to perfection and then slice it open, you'll notice that the dark brown crust covers a paler brown layer right under the surface. This gives way to a grayish-brown layer, then a grayish-pink layer, and then, depending on your taste, a rosy pink in the center. It's not just dinner: It's a delicious way to visualize the way heat moves. This color gradient illustrates how the meat cooks. The heat of the broiler strikes most intensely on the surface of the steak, and travels steadily from there to the center.

The trick, of course, is to time that traveling heat right. You want to broil (or sear or roast) your steak for just enough time—so that at the moment the center of the meat is cooked just to your liking, the surface is not yet dried out or charred. This isn't simple work. A broiler can run over 500°F/260°C, and if you, like us, are into medium-rare steaks, the goal is to stop cooking the meat as soon as the center reaches 130°F/54°C. Talk about chaotic precision.

THE GENTLE HEAT OF SOUS VIDE

Cut open a sous-vide steak, however, and it's the same color all the way through. That's by design: if the water bath is set to 130°F/54°C, then the whole steak, inside and out, will become exactly 130°F/54°C—and not a degree more.

The great advantage of cooking sous vide, as demonstrated time and again in this book, is that there is no fear of cooking unevenly; you can dial in the exact grade of doneness you prefer; and you can walk away from the kitchen for hours without overcooking your meal.

The disadvantage is that sous vide cookery can take significantly longer than the broiler method. The nature of heat is that it always moves through a material from a hotter region to a colder region—in the case of your steak, from the outside, where you apply heat, to the inside. And the bigger the difference in temperatures between the hot region and the cold region, the faster it moves. So heat will penetrate to the center of a steak that's under a hot flame quite a bit faster than if the same steak is in a bath of warm water.

That means that in order to ensure our sous-vide meat is done—to ensure that the gentle heat has made its way all the way into the center and cooked it—we leave it in the bath for at least 1½ hours.

Since sous vide–cooked meat is the same temperature all the way through, it requires an additional step to brown the exterior. By searing it with high heat, we make sure that stage happens as quickly as possible, before the heat has a chance to travel into the interior and start to cook more than just the surface.

THICKNESS, SHAPE, AND MATERIAL MATTER

Because of the way heat travels, the thickness of the food being cooked in a sous vide water bath makes a big difference. A steak that's 1-inch thick might take 1½ hours to cook all the way through (see Perfect Seared Steaks, page 70); a steak that's twice as thick will take significantly more than twice as long.

The shape of the food is an important consideration too: Since the heat has to move from the surface to the center, a 2-ounce cut of thin steak, which doesn't have a lot of distance between its surface and its center, heats through a lot faster than a 2-ounce meatball.

Finally, the type of food matters too, because heat travels at different rates through different kinds of materials. A piece of lean meat carries heat efficiently (see Foolproof Poached Chicken, page 46); fattier cuts take a little longer, because fat acts as an insulator, slowing down the passage of heat (see Peppercorn-Crusted Roast Beef, page 76). Fruits and vegetables (see page 134) contain a lot of air, both inside their flesh—an apple can be made of 25 percent air, believe it or not—as well as among and around their irregular geometry, such as the spaces between florets of broccoli. This is why we generally add liquid to the cooking bag. The liquid fills up those spaces, allowing for a more even cook, as well as adding flavor.

Cooking food in a water bath is gentle and, often, slow. But once you understand the different factors that go into how much time is needed, the precision is worth it.

Steak

Most people know how they want their steak. Medium-rare. Rare. Well done. To get your steak exactly there, temperature means (almost) everything. Temperature is the difference between medium-rare and medium-well—and, depending on the type of person you are, getting the wrong side of that medium coin will make you very unhappy.

We tested cooking steaks in a sous vide water bath heated to temperatures starting at 120°F/49°C and going up incrementally through 155°F/68°C. After their swim, we quickly seared them before serving. For our preferred medium-rare steak, we cook at 130°F/54°C. Go by this chart for your perfect level of doneness, or check out our recipe on page 70.

Don't forget: Time is important for cooking steaks, too. It takes longer to bring a thick steak to a precise temperature than a thin steak. To keep the tender texture of steaks like strip or rib eye, it's important not to cook them for too long. We found the ideal time for a tender, 1 to 2-inch-thick steak to be between 1½ and 3 hours in the water bath.

Cooking Specifications for Tender Steaks (Rib Eye, Strip, or Sirloin, 1 to 2 inches thick)		
Temp	Time	Description
120–125°F (49–52°C)		Rare
126–134°F (52–57°C)	90 minutes to 3 hours	Medium-Rare
135–144°F (57–62°C)		Medium
145–154°F (63–68°C)		Medium-Well
155–160°F (68–71°C)		Well Done

SEAFOOD

We've spent a lot of space in this book talking about how easy it is to overcook different foods (eggs, poultry, beef), how overcooking those foods can really mess up the great meal you had planned, and how using sous vide can prevent a cooking disaster. That all remains true. But this time, when we talk about the ease of overcooking an ingredient, we *really* mean business: Seafood is especially easy to overcook.

When it comes to fish (or scallops or octopus or lobster), just a couple degrees north (or south) of your temperature destination can wreak havoc on the final texture. But cooking fish and other seafood sealed in plastic in a precisely heated water bath guarantees perfection, every time.

Sous vide originally became popular with chefs in America because of its seafood potential, explains Dave Arnold, sous vide expert and author of *Liquid Intelligence*. Chefs were very interested in what cooking fish at low temperatures could do. "Whole fish would show up to the table looking like a piece of jewelry," he notes. "But [this fish] has a dense and kind of fudgy texture that was very polarizing."

We aren't here to give you fudgy fish. But we are grateful for what sous vide did to seafood cookery. We use sous vide to cook fish and other seafood—ingredients that are often in grave danger of overcooking via traditional high-heat methods—to perfection.

We start with salmon. Poached salmon may not sound especially exciting, but these fillets emerge from a 125 degrees Fahrenheit/52 degrees Celsius water bath so silky that you will want to put them on salads or serve them with one of our vibrant relishes multiple times a week. For something a bit fancier, our Miso-Marinated Salmon (page 111) finishes in the oven to gain an umami-heavy, caramelized crust. (Because of that final blast of heat, this salmon cooks at a lower sous vide temperature: 110°F/43.5°C.) We give halibut the sous vide treatment, too—alone (well, with browned butter) on page 113 and as part of a Spicy Fish Taco on page 114.

Due to their small size and delicate nature, shrimp can overcook with lightning speed. We keep them juicy and moist by cooking them in a 140°F/60°C water bath, which turned out to be our preferred temperature for lobster as well. Go with classic Shrimp Cocktail (page 119) or

Spanish-Style Spicy Shrimp with Olive Oil and Garlic (page 117), best served with crusty bread or over pasta. Frozen lobster tails emerge succulent: Whether simply poached in butter (page 125) and served as is, or prepared in New England Lobster Rolls (page 127), is up to you.

Sous vide makes producing the work of art that is our Tuna Salade Niçoise (page 120) easy: We cook all of the components, an otherwise daunting list, for this show-stopping summer salad in one water bath. First comes the tuna, poached with olive oil to a perfect rosy finish. After a slight rise in water temperature, the potatoes, green beans, and eggs all go into the bath to cook at the same temperature. All you need to add is crunchy lettuce, fresh tomatoes, and a lemon-herb vinaigrette.

Octopus has the potential to be meaty and tender. Unfortunately, it is often cooked to an unforgivably chewy texture. This is because octopus, even in the world of seafood, is particularly difficult to cook correctly. To tenderize this delicious cephalopod, it needs to be cooked either very quickly at a high temperature or for a very long time at a low one. Sous vide allows us to cook octopus at a precise and relatively low temperature for up to 5 hours, melting the tough and chewy connective tissue into succulent gelatin before a quick char on the grill. We serve it with celery, bell pepper, orange, and olives, all dressed in a Spanish-inspired vinaigrette (see page 122).

Finally: scallops. Our unique recipe pairs delicate scallops with a creamy, spicy sauce. After cooking the mollusks at 120°F/49°C, we top them with a Sriracha-spiked mayonnaise and then use a brûlée torch to brown the whole lot. The result? A guaranteed conversation starter.

Whichever recipe you do decide to start with, know that throughout this chapter we tried hard not to make too many jokes about fish "swimming" in a water bath.

Perfect Poached Salmon

YIELD SERVES 4
Sous Vide Temperature 125°F/52°C (farmed)
Sous Vide Time 30 to 45 minutes
Active Cooking Time 15 minutes, plus at least 30 minutes salting time

To Make Ahead We don't recommend making this recipe in advance.

Why This Recipe Works Salmon is well suited to sous vide cooking. Even though it is a relatively fatty fish, it can go from juicy and silky (our ideal) to chalky and dry (aka overcooked) in a flash—especially with high-heat cooking methods. The precision of low-temperature sous vide cooking eliminates this problem. We cooked salmon to just the right temperature—125°F/52°C for farmed, 120°F/49°C for wild—giving us a tender and silky fish, every time. Before cooking the fillets, we sprinkled them with a dry brine, a mixture of salt and sugar that thoroughly seasoned the salmon and also dissolved some of the proteins in the fish, forming a gel that could hold on to more moisture. It's important to set the water bath to 120°F/49°C if using wild salmon. With naturally firmer flesh and less fat to provide lubrication, wild salmon can taste dry if cooked at the same temperature as fattier farmed salmon. When the wild varieties are cooked at a slightly lower temperature, their muscle fibers contract less and therefore retain more moisture. If using skin-on fillets, the skin can be easily peeled off after cooking. Serve with Grapefruit-Basil Relish, Tangerine-Ginger Relish, or Orange-Avocado Relish (recipes follow), if desired.

- 2 teaspoons (12 grams) salt
- 2 teaspoons (8 grams) sugar
- 1 2-pound (900 grams) skinless salmon fillet, quartered
- 1 tablespoon vegetable oil

1 Combine salt and sugar in small bowl. Sprinkle salmon evenly on all sides with salt mixture and place on wire rack set in rimmed baking sheet. Refrigerate for at least 30 minutes or up to 45 minutes.

2 Using sous vide circulator, bring water to 125°F/52°C in 7-quart container.

3 Pat salmon dry with paper towels and brush with oil on all sides. Individually wrap each fillet with plastic wrap, and then place in single layer in 1-gallon zipper-lock freezer bag. Seal bag, pressing out as much air as possible. Gently lower bag into prepared water bath until fillets are fully submerged, and then clip top corner of bag to side of water bath container, allowing remaining air bubbles to rise to top of bag. Reopen 1 corner of zipper, release remaining air bubbles, and reseal bag. Cover and cook for at least 30 minutes or up to 45 minutes.

4 Gently transfer salmon to cutting board and discard plastic. Pat fillets dry with paper towels. Serve.

Grapefruit-Basil Relish
YIELD Makes about 1 cup

- 2 red grapefruits (about 340 grams each)
- 1 small shallot (15 grams), minced
- 2 tablespoons (8 grams) chopped fresh basil
- 2 teaspoons (10 grams) lemon juice
- 2 teaspoons (10 grams) extra-virgin olive oil
  Salt and pepper
  Sugar

Cut away peel and pith from grapefruits. Cut grapefruits into 8 wedges, then slice crosswise into ½-inch-thick pieces. Place grapefruit pieces in strainer set over bowl and let drain for 15 minutes; measure out and reserve 1 tablespoon (15 grams) drained juice. Combine reserved juice, shallot, basil, lemon juice, and oil in bowl. Stir in grapefruits and let sit for 15 minutes. Season with salt, pepper, and sugar to taste. (Relish can be refrigerated for up to 2 days.)

Variations

Tangerine-Ginger Relish

Substitute 4 tangerines (about 100 grams each) for grapefruits; quarter tangerines before slicing crosswise. Substitute 1½ teaspoons (9 grams) grated fresh ginger for shallot and 1 thinly sliced scallion (15 grams) for basil.

Orange-Avocado Relish

Substitute 1 large orange (185 grams) for grapefruits; quarter orange before slicing crosswise. Substitute 2 tablespoons (8 grams) minced fresh cilantro for basil and 4 teaspoons (20 grams) lime juice for lemon juice. Add 1 diced avocado (170 grams) and 1 small minced jalapeño chile (35 grams) to juice mixture with orange.

Miso-Marinated Salmon

YIELD SERVES 4
Sous Vide Temperature 110°F/43.5°C (farmed)
Sous Vide Time 30 to 45 minutes
Active Cooking Time 20 minutes, plus at least 5 hours marinating time

To Make Ahead We don't recommend making this recipe in advance.

Why This Recipe Works Miso-glazed salmon has the potential to deliver succulent, umami-rich fish with a beautifully laquered exterior. But all too often the salmon ends up with an overcooked, chewy interior due to the extended broiling process typically necessary for the glaze. We wanted fish that was silky and moist but still had that contrasting caramelized crust. We were able to achieve this by cooking the salmon sous vide at an especially low temperature—110°F/43.5°C—before putting it under the broiler. This allowed us to keep the fish supertender even after that final blast of heat in the oven. If using wild salmon, set the water bath to 105°F/40.5°C. If using skin-on fillets, the skin can be easily peeled off after cooking.

½ cup (160 grams) white miso

¼ cup (50 grams) sugar

3 tablespoons (45 grams) sake

3 tablespoons (45 grams) mirin

1 2-pound (900 grams) skinless salmon fillet, quartered

Lemon wedges

1 Whisk miso, sugar, sake, and mirin in medium bowl until sugar and miso are dissolved (mixture will be thick). Dip each fillet into miso mixture to evenly coat all sides. Place salmon in single layer in 1-gallon zipper-lock freezer bag and pour any remaining miso mixture over fillets. Seal bag, pressing out as much air as possible, and refrigerate for at least 5 hours or up to 20 hours.

2 Using sous vide circulator, bring water to 110°F/43.5°C in 7-quart container.

3 Gently lower bag into prepared water bath until fillets are fully submerged, and then clip top corner of bag to side of water bath container, allowing remaining air bubbles to rise to top of bag. Reopen 1 corner of zipper, release remaining air bubbles, and reseal bag. Cover and cook for at least 30 minutes and up to 45 minutes.

4 Adjust oven rack 4 to 5 inches from broiler element and heat broiler. Place wire rack in rimmed baking sheet and cover with aluminum foil. Gently transfer salmon fillets, skinned side down, to prepared sheet, leaving 1 inch between fillets. Broil salmon until deeply browned, 4 to 5 minutes. Transfer to serving platter and serve with lemon wedges.

Thick-Cut Halibut Fillets with Lemon Browned Butter

YIELD SERVES 4

Sous Vide Temperature 120°F/49°C

Sous Vide Time 30 to 45 minutes

Active Cooking Time 30 minutes, plus at least 30 minutes salting time

To Make Ahead We don't recommend making this recipe in advance.

Why This Recipe Works As with most fish, halibut is easily overcooked. Cooking fish sous vide allowed us to guarantee a perfectly cooked piece of fish, one that was moist and tender without the need for stovetop babysitting. For our thick-cut halibut fillets, we started by sprinkling the fish with a dry brine, a mixture of salt and sugar. This helped to evenly season the fish throughout, not just on the surface. We then cooked the fillets at 120°F/49°C for a silky, delicate texture (if you prefer your fish to be fully opaque, set your sous vide bath to 135°F/57°C). We paired the halibut with a rich browned-butter sauce brightened with lemon. Capers lent pops of briny acidity. We prefer to prepare this recipe with halibut, but firm-fleshed white fish such as cod or hake that is between 1 and 1½ inches thick can be substituted.

Fish

- 2 teaspoons (12 grams) salt
- 2 teaspoons (8 grams) sugar
- 4 6- to 8-ounce (170–225 grams) skinless halibut fillets, 1 to 1½ inches thick
- 1 tablespoon (14 grams) vegetable oil

Browned Butter

- 1 lemon (190 grams)
- 4 tablespoons (56 grams) unsalted butter, cut into 4 pieces
- 1 small shallot (14 grams), minced
- 2 tablespoons (30 grams) capers, rinsed
- 2 tablespoons (8 grams) chopped fresh parsley
  Salt and pepper

1 Combine salt and sugar in small bowl. Sprinkle halibut evenly on all sides with salt mixture and place on wire rack set in rimmed baking sheet. Refrigerate for at least 30 minutes and up to 45 minutes.

2 For the fish Using sous vide circulator, bring water to 120°F/49°C in 7-quart container.

3 Pat halibut dry with paper towels and brush with oil on all sides. Individually wrap each fillet with plastic wrap, and then arrange in single layer in 1-gallon zipper-lock freezer bag. Seal bag, pressing out as much air as possible. Gently lower bag into prepared water bath until fillets are fully submerged, then clip top corner of bag to side of water bath container, allowing remaining air bubbles to rise to top of bag. Reopen 1 corner of zipper, release remaining air bubbles, and seal bag fully. Cover and cook for at least 30 minutes or up to 45 minutes.

4 For the browned butter Cut away peel and pith from lemon. Holding fruit over small bowl, use paring knife to slice between membranes to release segments. Cut segments crosswise into ½-inch pieces. Squeeze membranes over bowl to release juice; discard membranes and seeds.

5 Cook butter in small saucepan over medium heat, swirling constantly, until butter melts and turns dark golden brown and has nutty aroma, 4 to 5 minutes. Stir in shallot and cook until fragrant, about 30 seconds. Off heat, stir in capers, parsley, and lemon segments and juice. Season with salt and pepper to taste; cover to keep warm.

6 Gently transfer halibut to cutting board and discard plastic. Pat fillets dry with paper towels and transfer to dinner plates. Spoon sauce over fillets and serve.

Seafood

113

Spicy Fish Tacos

YIELD SERVES 4
Sous Vide Temperature 110°F/43.5°C
Sous Vide Time 30 to 45 minutes
Active Cooking Time 30 minutes, plus at least 1 hour marinating time

To Make Ahead We don't recommend making this recipe in advance.

Why This Recipe Works Fish tacos can look beautiful, overflowing with fresh ingredients and contrasting textures and colors. But that first bite? Disappointing, overcooked fish. We wanted a fish taco with bold flavors—and, most important, perfectly cooked fish. We started by making a chipotle-based paste that would act as a marinade for our thick halibut fillets and also as the base for a zesty sauce to spread on the tortillas. Once the fish had finished marinating, we cooked the halibut sous vide at a very low temperature to keep it moist, and then blasted it quickly under the broiler to firm up the flesh and lightly char the marinade. Topped with a refreshing cabbage slaw, these fish tacos will put you in an endless-summer state of mind. We prefer halibut here but cod or hake are good substitutes.

- 4 teaspoons (19 grams) vegetable oil
- 1 teaspoon (3 grams) chili powder
- 1 teaspoon (1 gram) ground coriander
- 1 teaspoon (0.5 grams) dried oregano
   Salt
- ½ teaspoon (0.5 grams) ground cumin
- ¼ cup (60 grams) minced canned chipotle chile in adobo sauce
- 1 tablespoon (15 grams) tomato paste
- 1 tablespoon (15 grams) honey
- ¼ cup (48 grams) lime juice (2 limes)
- 2 1-pound (450 grams) skinless halibut fillets, 1 to 1½ inches thick
- ½ small head green cabbage, cored and sliced thin (4 cups/225 grams)
- 6 tablespoons (24 grams) chopped fresh cilantro
- 4 scallions (24 grams), sliced thin
- ¼ cup (50 grams) mayonnaise
- ¼ cup (50 grams) sour cream
- 2 garlic cloves (10 grams), minced
- 12 (6-inch) corn tortillas, warmed
   Lime wedges

1 Heat 1 tablespoon (14 grams) oil, chili powder, coriander, oregano, 1 teaspoon (6 grams) salt, and cumin in small saucepan over medium heat, stirring constantly, until fragrant and some bubbles form, 2 to 3 minutes. Stir in chipotle, tomato paste, and honey until well combined. Off heat, stir in 2 tablespoons (24 grams) lime juice and let cool for 5 minutes. Measure out and reserve 2 tablespoons (40 grams) chipotle mixture in small bowl.

2 Sprinkle halibut evenly on all sides with 2 teaspoons (12 grams) salt, then spread remaining chipotle mixture over fish. Place each fillet in separate 1-gallon zipper-lock freezer bag. Seal bags, pressing out as much air as possible, and refrigerate for at least 1 hour or up to 24 hours.

3 Using sous vide circulator, bring water to 110°F/43.5°C in 7-quart container.

4 Gently lower bags into prepared water bath until fillets are fully submerged, and then clip top corner of each bag to side of water bath container, allowing remaining air bubbles to rise to top of bag. Reopen 1 corner of zipper, release remaining air bubbles, and reseal bag. Cover and cook for at least 30 minutes or up to 45 minutes.

5 Combine cabbage, ¼ cup (16 grams) cilantro, scallions, ¼ teaspoon (1 gram) salt, remaining 2 tablespoons (24 grams) lime juice, and remaining 1 teaspoon (5 grams) oil in bowl and set aside. Stir mayonnaise, sour cream, garlic, and remaining 2 tablespoons (8 grams) cilantro into reserved chipotle mixture until combined. Season sauce with salt and pepper to taste.

6 Adjust oven rack 4 to 5 inches from broiler element and heat broiler. Place wire rack in rimmed baking sheet and cover with aluminum foil. Gently transfer halibut fillets to prepared sheet and broil until fish is firm and chipotle mixture begins to char, 4 to 5 minutes. Using knife or spatula, portion halibut into 12 equal pieces. Spread sauce evenly onto warm tortillas and top with fish and cabbage. Serve with lime wedges.

Spanish-Style Spicy Shrimp with Olive Oil and Garlic

YIELD SERVES 4 TO 6
Sous Vide Temperature 140°F/60°C
Sous Vide Time 30 minutes
Active Cooking Time 40 minutes

To Make Ahead We don't recommend making this recipe in advance.

Why This Recipe Works The Spanish tapa *gambas al ajillo* is a simple dish of shrimp quickly cooked in an abundant amount of olive oil with garlic and chiles. Served with crusty bread and a glass of wine, it's a great way to start a meal. For our sous vide version, we started by boosting the flavor of our olive oil by infusing it with shrimp shells, garlic, and pepper flakes. After straining the mixture, we bagged up the oil with our shrimp. We set the water bath to 140°F/60°C—our preferred temperature for both shrimp and lobster since it keeps them both tender and moist. Finishing the dish off with a touch of sherry vinegar added brightness while chopped parsley gave it some fresh color. For this recipe, we prefer to use extra-large shrimp (21 to 25 per pound/450 grams) but jumbo (16 to 20 per pound/450 grams) and large (26 to 30 per pound/450 grams) will work as well. Serve with crusty bread or make it a meal over pasta. Shrimp have a tendency to float when placed in a sous vide water bath, which can lead to uneven cooking. Use weights to make sure the shrimp are fully immersed during cooking (see page 14).

1½ pounds (675 grams) extra-large shrimp (21 to 25 per pound/450 grams), peeled and deveined, shells reserved
   Salt
¾ cup (168 grams) extra-virgin olive oil
8 garlic cloves (40 grams), sliced thin
1 teaspoon (2 grams) red pepper flakes
1 teaspoon (5 grams) sherry vinegar
2 tablespoons (8 grams) chopped fresh parsley

1 Using sous vide circulator, bring water to 140°F/60°C in 7-quart container.

2 Sprinkle shrimp with ½ teaspoon (3 grams) salt and set aside. Heat oil in Dutch oven over medium heat until shimmering. Add shrimp shells and ½ teaspoon (3 grams) salt and cook, stirring occasionally, until shells turn deep orange, 6 to 8 minutes. Add garlic and pepper flakes and cook, stirring frequently, until garlic is golden brown and oil is rust-colored and aromatic, 2 to 4 minutes. Strain oil through fine-mesh strainer into medium bowl, pressing on shrimp shells with rubber spatula to extract as much oil as possible; discard solids. Allow oil to cool for at least 5 minutes.

3 Transfer shrimp and oil to 1-gallon zipper-lock freezer bag and toss to coat. Arrange shrimp in single layer and seal bag, pressing out as much air as possible. Gently lower bag into prepared water bath, weight bag (see page 14) until shrimp are fully submerged, and then clip top corner of each bag to side of water bath container, allowing remaining air bubbles to rise to top of bag. Reopen 1 corner of zipper, release remaining air bubbles, and reseal bag. Cover and cook for 30 minutes.

4 Transfer shrimp and oil to serving bowl. Stir in vinegar and sprinkle with parsley. Serve immediately.

Shrimp Cocktail

YIELD **SERVES 6 TO 8**
Sous Vide Temperature 140°F/60°C
Sous Vide Time 45 minutes
Active Cooking Time 1 hour

Make Ahead Strategy Cooked and chilled shrimp and cocktail sauce can be refrigerated for up to 24 hours.

Why This Recipe Works Shrimp cocktail is a dish well suited to (and well named for) a cocktail party. But, often-times, it's one worth skipping over. After all, who wants rubbery, flavorless shrimp? (Bueller? Bueller?) But with sous vide, we were able to make shrimp cocktail right—and it's dead simple to do. (No need for flavored poaching liquids or time-sensitive, off-heat cooking tricks here.) We simply deveined jumbo shrimp, keeping them in their shells to impart extra shrimp flavor—shells contain lots of umami-boosting glutamates and nucleotides, which are absorbed by the shrimp meat during cooking. We lightly seasoned our deveined, shell-on shrimp with salt, bagged them up, and cooked them at our preferred temperature for shrimp, 140°F/60°C. After cooking, we quickly chilled and peeled the shrimp—and with that, we were ready to go. Paired with our punchy cocktail sauce, this is an easy improvement on a party-food mainstay. For this recipe, we prefer to use jumbo shrimp (16 to 20 per pound/450 grams), but extra-large shrimp (21 to 25 per pound/450 grams) will work as well. Buy refrigerated prepared horseradish, not the shelf-stable kind, which contains preservatives and additives. Shell-on shrimp have a tendency to float when placed in a sous vide water bath, which can lead to uneven cooking. Use weights to make sure the shrimp are fully immersed during cooking (see page 14).

Shrimp

- 2 pounds (900 grams) shell-on jumbo shrimp (16 to 20 per pound/450 grams)
- ½ teaspoon (3 grams) salt

Cocktail Sauce

- 1 cup (280 grams) ketchup
- ¼ cup (60 grams) prepared horseradish
- 1 teaspoon (6 grams) Worcestershire sauce
- 1 teaspoon (5 grams) lemon juice
- ½ teaspoon (1 gram) Old Bay seasoning
- ⅛ teaspoon (0.5 grams) cayenne pepper

1 For the shrimp Using sous vide circulator, bring water to 140°F/60°C in 7-quart container.

2 Using kitchen shears or sharp paring knife, cut through shell and meat of shrimp and devein but do not remove shell. Sprinkle shrimp with salt, and divide between two 1-gallon zipper-lock freezer bags. Arrange shrimp in single layer and seal bags, pressing out as much air as possible. Gently lower bags into prepared water bath, weight bags (see page 14) until shrimp are fully submerged, then clip top corner of each bag to side of water bath container, allowing remaining air bubbles to rise to top of bag. Reopen 1 corner of zipper, release remaining air bubbles, and reseal bag. Cover and cook for at least 45 minutes or up to 1 hour.

3 Meanwhile, fill large bowl halfway with ice and water. Transfer zipper-lock bags to prepared ice bath and let sit until chilled, about 15 minutes. Transfer shrimp to colander and peel, leaving tails intact; discard shrimp shells.

4 For the cocktail sauce Whisk all ingredients in bowl until combined. Serve shrimp with sauce.

Seafood

Tuna Salade Niçoise

YIELD SERVES 4
Sous Vide Temperature 120°F/49°C and 194°F/90°C
Sous Vide Time 1½ hours
Active Cooking Time 1¼ hours, plus at least
30 minutes resting time

To Make Ahead Tuna, potatoes, green beans, and eggs can be rapidly chilled in ice bath (see page 13) and then refrigerated for up to 24 hours.

Why This Recipe Works Salade Niçoise is a show-stopping dish with a daunting ingredient list. Sous vide streamlines the process: We gently cooked tuna steaks with olive oil and then raised the temperature of the water bath to cook the vegetables and eggs. Use small red potatoes measuring 1 to 2 inches in diameter. If niçoise olives are not available, substitute another small, black, brined olive. Vegetables have a tendency to float when placed in a sous vide water bath, which can lead to uneven cooking. Use weights to make sure the potatoes and green beans are fully immersed during cooking (see page 14).

Tuna

- 2 teaspoons (12 grams) salt
- 2 teaspoons (8 grams) sugar
- 2 8-ounce (225 grams) tuna steaks, about 1 inch thick
- ¾ cup (155 grams) extra-virgin olive oil

Vinaigrette

- ¼ cup (60 grams) lemon juice (2 lemons)
- 1 shallot (30 grams), minced
- 2 tablespoons (8 grams) chopped fresh basil
- 1 tablespoon (4 grams) minced fresh thyme
- 2 teaspoons (12 grams) Dijon mustard

Salad

- 1¼ pounds (560 grams) small red potatoes, unpeeled, quartered
- 2 teaspoons (10 grams) extra-virgin olive oil
- 8 ounces (225 grams) green beans, trimmed and halved crosswise
- 4 large eggs

- 1 head Bibb lettuce (8 ounces/225 grams), leaves separated and torn into bite-size pieces
- 8 ounces (225 grams) cherry tomatoes, halved
- 1 small red onion (about 4 ounces/112 grams), halved and sliced thin
- ½ cup (80 grams) pitted niçoise olives
- 2 tablespoons (18 grams) capers, rinsed (optional)

1 For the tuna Combine salt and sugar in small bowl. Sprinkle tuna evenly on all sides with salt mixture and place on wire rack set in rimmed baking sheet. Refrigerate for at least 30 minutes or up to 45 minutes.

2 Using sous vide circulator, bring water to 120°F/49°C in 7-quart container.

3 Pat tuna steaks dry with paper towels and season with pepper. Place steaks and oil in 1-gallon zipper-lock freezer bag. Seal bag, pressing out as much air as possible. Gently lower bag into prepared water bath until steaks are fully submerged, and then clip top corner of bag to side of water bath container, allowing remaining air bubbles to rise to top of bag. Reopen 1 corner of zipper, release remaining air bubbles, and reseal bag. Cover and cook for 30 minutes.

4 Transfer steaks to plate and reserve oil. Allow tuna to cool for 5 to 10 minutes, then cover and refrigerate until ready to serve. Raise temperature of water bath to 194°F/90°C.

5 For the vinaigrette Whisk lemon juice, shallot, basil, thyme, mustard, and oil reserved from tuna in medium bowl and season with salt and pepper to taste; set aside.

6 For the salad Combine potatoes, 1 teaspoon (5 grams) oil, and ½ teaspoon (3 grams) salt in clean 1-gallon zipper-lock freezer bag. Seal bag, pressing out as much air as possible. Combine green beans, remaining

1 teaspoon (5 grams) oil, and ¼ teaspoon (1.5 grams) salt in second 1-gallon zipper-lock freezer bag. Seal bag, pressing out as much air as possible. Place each bag in second 1-gallon zipper-lock freezer bag and seal bags. Gently lower bag with potatoes into prepared water bath, weight bag (see page 14) until potatoes are fully submerged, then clip top corner of bag to side of water bath container, allowing remaining air bubbles to rise to top of bag. Reopen 1 corner of zipper, release remaining air bubbles, and reseal bag. Cover and cook for 40 minutes. Gently add eggs to water bath and continue to cook for 5 minutes. Add bag with green beans to water bath, repeating process of weighting bag and removing air bubbles, and continue to cook vegetables and eggs for 15 minutes.

7 Meanwhile, fill large bowl halfway with ice and water. Using slotted spoon or tongs, carefully transfer eggs and zipper-lock bag with green beans to ice bath and let sit until chilled, 5 to 10 minutes. Transfer green beans to large bowl. Peel and quarter eggs; set aside.

8 Transfer potatoes to medium bowl. Whisk vinaigrette to recombine, then add ¼ cup (65 grams) vinaigrette to bowl with potatoes and toss to coat. Season with pepper to taste.

9 Add lettuce, tomatoes, red onion, and half of remaining vinaigrette to bowl with green beans and toss to combine. Season with salt and pepper to taste. Arrange greens mixture on large serving platter. Arrange potatoes over salad, followed by olives, capers (if using), and eggs. Slice tuna ½ inch thick and arrange over center of salad. Serve immediately, passing remaining vinaigrette separately.

Spanish Grilled Octopus Salad with Orange and Bell Pepper

YIELD **SERVES 4 TO 6**
Sous Vide Temperature 175°F/79.5°C
Sous Vide Time 5 hours
Active Cooking Time 1 hour

To Make Ahead Octopus can be rapidly chilled in ice bath (see page 13) and then refrigerated for up to 3 days.

Why This Recipe Works Octopus can be tricky to cook well. It has tough connective tissue that needs to be broken down into succulent gelatin, and it often skirts the thin lines between tender, chewy, and straight-up mushy. As a result, many (often dubious) tenderizing techniques have circulated (pun intended) within the octopus recipe world. But as it turns out, a great—and reliable—way to turn this cephalopod's connective tissue into gelatin is extended low-heat cooking. Enter sous vide. Cooking low-and-slow for 5 hours gave us perfectly tender octopus. After its bath, we gave it a quick char on a superhot grill, sliced it, and paired it with a Spanish-inspired vinaigrette. We added refreshing celery, bell pepper, orange segments, briny olives, and parsley to the mix for a bright and bold salad. Octopus can be found cleaned and frozen in the seafood section of specialty grocery stores and Asian markets. We recommend using octopus from either Spain or Portugal. Be sure to rinse the defrosted octopus well, as sand can collect in the suckers. The octopus's membrane-like skin is easiest to peel while still warm, so be sure to do so as soon as it's cool enough to handle. You can thaw frozen octopus in a large container under cold running water; it will thaw in about 2 hours. Be sure to double-bag the octopus to protect against seam failure. Note that this recipe requires a 12-quart container.

1 4-pound (1.8 kilograms) octopus, rinsed
½ cup plus 3 tablespoons (154 grams) extra-virgin olive oil
1 tablespoon (6 grams) smoked paprika
4 bay leaves (1 gram)
1 teaspoon (1 gram) lemon zest plus ⅓ cup (82 grams) juice (2 lemons)
3 tablespoons (42 grams) sherry vinegar

2 garlic cloves (10 grams), minced
1 teaspoon (8 grams) sugar
   Salt and pepper
1 large orange (225 grams)
2 celery ribs (150 grams), sliced thin on bias
1 red bell pepper (150 grams), stemmed, seeded, and cut into 2-inch-long matchsticks
½ cup (80 grams) pitted brine-cured green olives, halved
2 tablespoons (6 grams) chopped fresh parsley

1 Using sous vide circulator, bring water to 175°F/79.5°C in 12-quart container.

2 Using sharp knife, separate octopus body (lower section with tentacles) from upper section (head, eyes, and mantle, or large upper sac); discard upper section. Cut body in half through core, leaving two pieces with four tentacles each. Transfer each piece to separate 1-gallon zipper-lock bag freezer bag. Add 2 tablespoons (28 grams) oil, ½ teaspoon (1 gram) smoked paprika, and 2 bay leaves to each bag and gently toss to coat. Seal bags, pressing out as much air as possible. Place each bag in second 1-gallon zipper-lock freezer bag and seal. Gently lower bags into prepared water bath until octopus is fully submerged, and then clip top corner of bag to side of water bath container, allowing remaining air bubbles to rise to top of bag. Reopen 1 corner of zipper, release remaining air bubbles, and reseal bag. Cover and cook octopus for 5 hours.

3 Transfer octopus to cutting board and let cool slightly; discard cooking liquid. Using fingers or paring knife, scrape skin from tentacles, being careful not to remove suction cups. Cut tentacles from around core of body; discard core.

4A For a charcoal grill Open bottom vent completely. Light large chimney starter filled with charcoal briquettes (6 quarts/2 kilograms). When top coals are partially covered with ash, pour evenly over half of grill. Set cooking grate in place, cover, and open lid vent completely. Heat grill until hot, about 5 minutes.

4B For a gas grill Turn all burners to high, cover, and heat grill until hot, about 15 minutes. Leave all burners on high.

5 Clean cooking grate, then repeatedly brush grate with well-oiled paper towels until black and glossy, 5 to 10 times. Brush tentacles with 1 tablespoon (14 grams) oil. Place octopus on grill (directly over coals if using charcoal). Cook (covered if using gas) until octopus is streaked with dark grill marks and lightly charred at tips of tentacles, 8 to 10 minutes, flipping halfway through grilling; transfer to cutting board.

6 Whisk remaining 6 tablespoons (84 grams) oil, remaining 2 teaspoons (4 grams) paprika, lemon zest and juice, vinegar, garlic, sugar, ¼ teaspoon (1.5 grams) salt, and ¼ teaspoon pepper (0.5 grams) together in large bowl. While octopus is still warm, slice ¼ inch thick on bias, then transfer to bowl with oil-lemon mixture and toss to coat.

7 Cut away peel and pith from orange. Holding fruit over bowl with octopus, use paring knife to slice between membranes to release segments. Add celery, bell pepper, olives, and parsley and gently toss to coat. Season with salt and pepper to taste. Serve.

Butter-Poached Lobster Tails

YIELD **SERVES 4**
Sous Vide Temperature 140°F/60°C
Sous Vide Time 45 minutes
Active Cooking Time 20 minutes

To Make Ahead We don't recommend making this recipe ahead of time, unless using for chilled lobster salad. In that case, lobster tails can be rapidly chilled in ice bath (see page 13) and then refrigerated for up to 24 hours.

Why This Recipe Works It's hard to believe that lobsters weren't always considered a delicacy. Until the mid-19th century, lobsters were so plentiful that they were held in particularly low regard. In fact, eating them was a sign of poverty. No longer. These days, when you want to cook a meal to impress—and we mean really impress—lobster is your friend. But cooking these crustaceans at home can be a daunting task. Traditional boiling and steaming techniques can lead to overcooked, rubbery lobster. But start with widely available frozen lobster tails and add sous vide? It's a breeze. With sous vide, we are able to cook lobster tails to exactly our preferred level of doneness—140°F/60°C—without having to worry about them going over. And by adding butter and fresh tarragon to the bag, we are able to impart even more flavor to our lobster. To thaw frozen lobster tails, either let them sit in the refrigerator for 24 hours or bag them up and submerge them in cold water for 30 minutes to 1 hour. Serve with lemon wedges and extra melted butter.

- 4 5- to 6-ounce (140 to 170 grams) lobster tails
- ¼ teaspoon (1.5 grams) salt
- 3 tablespoons (42 grams) unsalted butter, cut into 3 pieces
- 6 sprigs (6 grams) fresh tarragon

1 Using sous vide circulator, bring water to 140°F/60°C in 7-quart container.

2 Using kitchen shears, cut lengthwise through soft shell on underside of lobster tail. With lobster tail cut side up, grasp each side with hands and crack outer shell, opening cut side to expose meat. Lift meat from shell and remove; discard shells. Sprinkle lobster with salt on all sides. Transfer tails, butter, and tarragon sprigs to 1-gallon zipper-lock freezer bag. Arrange tails in single layer and seal bag, pressing out as much air as possible. Gently lower bag into prepared water bath until tails are fully submerged, and then clip top corner of bag to side of water bath container, allowing remaining air bubbles to rise to top of bag. Reopen 1 corner of zipper, release remaining air bubbles, and reseal bag. Cover and cook for 45 minutes.

3 Transfer lobster tails to plates; discard cooking liquid. Serve immediately.

Variation

Poached Lobster Tails with Beurre Monté
Bring ¼ cup (55 grams) water to gentle simmer in small saucepan over medium-low heat. While whisking constantly (or using immersion blender), slowly add 8 tablespoons (112 grams) unsalted butter, cut into ¼-inch pieces and chilled, one piece at a time, until butter is fully incorporated and emulsified. Stir in 1 teaspoon (5 grams) lemon juice and season with salt to taste. Substitute beurre monté for butter, salt, and tarragon. Spoon sauce over lobster tails before serving.

New England Lobster Roll

YIELD SERVES 6
Sous Vide Temperature 140°F/60°C
Sous Vide Time 45 minutes
Active Cooking Time 40 minutes

To Make Ahead Lobster tails can be rapidly chilled in ice bath (see page 13) and refrigerated for up to 24 hours. We don't recommend making lobster salad ahead of time.

Why This Recipe Works For our lobster roll, we mostly adhered to tradition—top-loading supermarket hot dog bun, mayonnaise, and lots of lobster—but we added a hint of crunch in the form of small amounts of lettuce and celery (a contentious addition), and we added complementary brightness with lemon juice, cayenne, and chives. Use a very small pinch of cayenne pepper, as it should not make the dressing spicy. We prefer New England–style top-loading hot dog buns because they provide maximum surface on the sides for toasting. If using another style of bun, butter, salt, and toast the interior of each bun instead of the exterior.

2 tablespoons (25 grams) mayonnaise
2 tablespoons (25 grams) minced celery
1½ teaspoons (8 grams) lemon juice
1 teaspoon (2 grams) minced fresh chives
  Salt
  Pinch cayenne pepper
1 recipe Butter-Poached Lobster Tails (page 125), chilled, cut into ½-inch pieces
6 New England–style hot dog buns
2 tablespoons (28 grams) unsalted butter, softened
6 leaves Boston lettuce

1 Whisk mayonnaise, celery, lemon juice, chives, ⅛ teaspoon (1 gram) salt, and cayenne together in large bowl. Add lobster and gently toss to combine.

2 Place 12-inch nonstick skillet over low heat. Butter both sides of buns and sprinkle lightly with salt. Place buns in skillet, 1 buttered side down. Increase heat to medium-low and cook until crisp and brown, 2 to 3 minutes. Flip and cook second side until crisp and brown, 2 to 3 minutes longer. Transfer buns to large platter.

3 Line each bun with lettuce leaf. Spoon lobster mixture into buns and serve immediately.

Brûléed Scallops with Dynamite Sauce

YIELD SERVES 4
Sous Vide Temperature 120°F/49°C
Sous Vide Time 30 minutes
Active Cooking Time 20 minutes

To Make Ahead We don't recommend making this recipe in advance.

Why This Recipe Works Scallops are tiny and delicate—which is what can make them great, but it is also why they can quickly overcook, turning dry and rubbery in a heartbeat. With sous vide, we are able to cook scallops at a very low temperature, cooking them through properly while retaining their light sweetness and tender texture. For this recipe, we wanted to re-create a version of seafood dynamite—a comforting and unique dish found in some sushi restaurants. It involves topping seafood with a spicy Sriracha-spiked mayonnaise before broiling to achieve a decadent, browned crust. Because broilers on home ovens can vary drastically in strength, we used a brûlée torch for the browning step, which ensured that our delicate scallops wouldn't overcook in the process. We recommend buying "dry" scallops, which don't have chemical additives and taste better than "wet." Dry scallops will look ivory or pinkish; wet scallops are bright white. For this recipe, we recommend using Kewpie brand mayonnaise, which has a very smooth texture. Serve over steamed white rice.

1½ pounds (675 grams) large sea scallops, tendons removed

1 teaspoon (6 grams) salt

1 tablespoon (14 grams) vegetable oil

½ cup (110 grams) mayonnaise

2 teaspoons (12 grams) Sriracha sauce

1 teaspoon (4 grams) sugar

4 scallions (60 grams), sliced thin

1 Line large plate with paper towels. Sprinkle scallops evenly on both sides with salt. Transfer scallops to prepared plate and place second layer of paper towels on top. Refrigerate scallops and allow moisture to release onto paper towels, at least 10 minutes or up to 30 minutes.

2 Using sous vide circulator, bring water to 120°F/49°C in 7-quart container.

3 Transfer scallops and vegetable oil to 1-gallon zipper-lock freezer bag and toss to coat. Arrange scallops in single layer and seal bag, pressing out as much air as possible. Gently lower bag into prepared water bath until scallops are fully submerged, and then clip top corner of bag to side of water bath container, allowing remaining air bubbles to rise to top of bag. Reopen 1 corner of zipper, release remaining air bubbles, and reseal bag. Cover and cook for 30 minutes.

4 Whisk mayonnaise, Sriracha, and sugar together in small bowl. Transfer scallops to cutting board and pat dry with paper towels. Arrange scallops, flat side up, on serving platter, spaced about ½-inch apart. Spread mayonnaise mixture evenly over scallops. Ignite torch and slowly sweep flame about 2 inches above scallops until mayonnaise mixture turns golden brown. Sprinkle with scallions and serve immediately.

Plastic Safety and Sous Vide

Key Points

- You don't need to vacuum seal in order to sous vide
- We believe it is safe to cook via sous vide in plastic bags
- Use high-quality bags, like Ziploc or Glad

The original concept of sous vide cooking entailed sealing cold food in thick plastic sheaths from which every bit of air was then electrically pumped, so the thin plastic clung to the contours of the food like a second skin. This approach of vacuum-sealing is still common, especially in restaurants. (See our winning vacuum sealer on page 7.) And being able to completely remove the air has advantages, but the home sous-vider can be perfectly content with our no-machine-needed method using zipper-lock bags.

When we started working with sous vide in the test kitchen, we had the same concern that those starting out at home sometimes do: We've heard about chemicals leaching from plastics. Isn't it potentially dangerous to seal food in a plastic bag and then heat it up?

COOKING IN PLASTIC IS SAFE

After reviewing the considerable amount of research that's been done, we believe the answer is: It's safe. Although some types of plastic have been found to release undesirable chemicals into food, especially under high heat or acidic conditions, the bags that we use for sous vide cooking are not among those plastics.

High-density polyethylene, low-density polyethylene, and polypropylene are considered the safest plastics. Many name-brand plastic bags are made with polyethylene and polypropylene. These types of plastic are resistant to the sub-boiling temperatures involved in sous vide cooking, and they are also considered safe in and of themselves: Even if you cut up and ate a polyethylene bag, there's no toxicity risk.

Even nontoxic plastics, though, are sometimes manufactured with additives to give them extra strength, flexibility, slipperiness, or other characteristics. There are legitimate concerns about health effects from overexposure to some of those plasticizing additives, of which phthalates and BPA are the most famous.

WHAT BAGS TO USE

So how do you choose? We always use name-brand bags from brands that have well-documented manufacturing details. The zipper-lock bags we use are made from polyethylene or polypropylene. Our top pick is Ziploc Brand Freezer Bag with Easy Open Tabs.

SC Johnson, the manufacturer of Ziploc bags, publishes the ingredients it uses in all of its products, and Ziploc bags are made using polyethylene without additives. Glad also publicizes the fact that there are no plasticizers in its bags.

The bags made by the manufacturer FoodSaver for use with its vacuum sealers use plasticizer-free polyethylene with a layer of nylon on the outside. (The plastic wraps sold in supermarkets, such as Saran, are also made of safe polyethylene—commercial plastic wraps used in restaurants, however, can use PVC, which is not recommended for heating.)

For sous vide cooks who are still hesitant, there are reusable bags made of food-safe silicone that are marketed specifically for sous vide cooking. Some foods can be cooked in glass Mason jars instead of bags, although the rigid jar means heat can't travel as well from the bath to the food (we account for this in our recipes that use Mason jars). These latter two options do have the added advantage of creating less waste.

Salmon

Even relatively fatty fish like salmon can go from tender and moist to chalky and dry in a flash. In the test kitchen, we prefer traditionally cooked salmon brought to 125°F/52°C for flesh that has the ideal balance of firm and silky. The majority of salmon we cook in the test kitchen is farmed Atlantic, but as we've cooked more wild varieties,

such as king, coho, sockeye, and chum, we began to wonder if this catchall temperature was appropriate across the board and would cooking the fish sous vide change it?

We tested cooking samples of wild salmon and farmed Atlantic salmon in a water bath heated from 115°F/46°C to 130°F/54°C. Tasters unanimously preferred the wild samples cooked to 120°F/49°C and the farmed cooked to 125°F/52°C.

Why? Farmed Atlantic salmon differs significantly from the half-dozen commercial wild varieties. Chief among the differences: The collagen protein in farmed Atlantic salmon contains fewer chemical cross-links than that in wild varieties, which translates into softer flesh; and farmed Atlantic salmon contains more fat than any wild varieties (up to four times as much fat as the leanest wild variety), proving the perception of juiciness when cooked.

With naturally firmer flesh, and less fat to provide lubrication, wild salmon can have the texture of overcooked fish even at 125°F/52°C. By cooking the wild varieties to just 120°F/49°C, their muscle fibers contract less and therefore retain more moisture.

Cooking Specifications for Salmon Fillet
(1 to 1.5 inches thick)

Temp	Time	Description
115°F (46°C)		*Farmed* Sashimi-like
		Wild Soft and buttery
120°F (49°C)	30 to 45 minutes	*Farmed* Soft and buttery
		Wild Silky and firm
125°F (52°C)		*Farmed* Silky and firm
		Wild Very firm and flaky
130°F (54°C)		*Farmed* Very firm and flaky
		Wild Chalky

VEGETABLES
AND GRAINS

You didn't think that sous vide was only about cooking proteins, did you? Well, sure, most of the hoopla about this cooking technique centers around the fancy stuff—the rib eye, the pork roast, the immaculately cooked soft-poached egg. But that's only part of the story.

Vegetables and grains are prime candidates for sous vide cookery. The precisely heated water bath allows you to cook green vegetables until they are crisp-tender but still a vibrant hue. It allows you to cook root vegetables to their tender ideal from end to end. Sealing vegetables in a plastic bag also ensures that there is no evaporation, which means that our sous vide potatoes taste more potato-y, our sous vide asparagus tastes more asparagus-y. As J. Kenji Lopez-Alt once wrote on Serious Eats, "It's one of the few cooking methods where the end result is a vegetable that tastes more like itself than when you started." The water bath also ensures that grains and beans are cooked to just the right amount of tender, with no blowouts, hotspots, or pots and pans to watch on the stove. What's not to love?

Start with our Perfect Asparagus (page 136), which cooks for just 20 minutes at 180 degrees Fahrenheit/82 degrees Celsius, and emerges bright green and fork tender. Move on to our Better-Than-Braised Beets (page 139). The beets' natural earthy, sweet flavor intensifies when cooked—sealed—in a water bath. The genius move? We cook these beets in what will become their vinaigrette—the beets enhance the dressing and vice versa during their 4-hour swim. Similarly, we dress our bright baby bok choy (page 142) in an addictive chile oil, our deeply flavored glazed carrots (page 145) in honey and thyme, and our corn on the cob (page 149) in butter.

Whatever you do, do not miss the Roasted Celery Root with Chimichurri (page 146). We know. It doesn't sound like it is one of the most interesting recipes in the book. But after cooking this bulby, jumbly looking root (cut in half but not peeled) in a water bath, you break it into jagged, asymmetrical pieces with your hands and then sear them in a hot skillet until they are browned and crispy. The result? A centerpiece side dish that's both creamy and crunchy, rustic and beautiful, topped with a refreshing green sauce.

Take your choice of potatoes: crisp and smashed (page 159) or in a warm salad (page 155). Meanwhile, our parsnips (page 152) get a final crisp in the oven before being tossed with a healthy amount of Pecorino Romano. Steel-Cut Oatmeal (page 162) and No-Fuss Polenta (page 165) embody the term "hands-off." The oatmeal cooks in a water bath overnight and is ready to go—already packaged in individual Mason jars—as soon as you wake up. The polenta? It just needs one little whisk before serving.

We will not lie, cooking beans sous vide is a time commitment. But we think the payoff is worth it: evenly cooked beans with zero blowouts. Our East African Black Lentil Stew (page 167) takes advantage of a homespun *berbere* spice blend. Spiced Red Lentils (page 168) need only a quick whisk out of the bag. Our Boston Not-Baked Beans (page 170) are just as smoky and satisfying as the traditional version but necessitate zero ovens, and therefore need zero babysitting. Our Cuban Black Beans (page 172) cook for an extended period of time in a solution of baking soda, salt, and water for a perfect batch of soft and creamy beans. We take advantage of the long cook time by throwing in a ham hock and letting it break down, which lends body to the cooking liquid and a delicious meaty flavor throughout. Our White Bean Hummus (page 175) again cooks with baking soda for ultimate creaminess, and then, after being buzzed with some tahini and lemon juice, is topped with a refreshing herb and olive salad.

While our vegetable and grain recipes may not have the pizzazz (or require the financial investment) of a thick-cut rib eye, they each come with the quiet triumph of being perfectly cooked, every time.

Perfect Asparagus with Tomato-Basil Vinaigrette

YIELD SERVES 4 TO 6	**To Make Ahead** We don't recommend making this
Sous Vide Temperature 180°F/82°C	recipe in advance.
Sous Vide Time 20 minutes	
Active Cooking Time 20 minutes	

Why This Recipe Works Properly cooking tender spring vegetables like asparagus is challenging. Divert your attention for just a few seconds and those babies go from perfectly green and snap-tender to Hulk-green and floppy. Cooking asparagus sous vide takes away the guesswork. At 180°F/82°C, we found that the spears softened just enough while still keeping their snap. They remained bright green, and, because the spears were sealed in a bag while cooking, they retained all of their delicate, vegetal flavor (no evaporation here!). We serve our asparagus with a simple tomato and basil vinaigrette, but feel free to pair your asparagus with any vinaigrette or bright sauce of your choosing. This recipe works best with thick asparagus spears that are between ½ and ¾ inch in diameter. Do not use pencil-thin asparagus; it overcooks too easily. Be sure to double bag the asparagus to protect against seam failure. Asparagus have a tendency to float when placed in a sous vide water bath, which can lead to uneven cooking. Use weights to make sure the asparagus are fully immersed during cooking (see page 14).

2 pounds (900 grams) thick asparagus, trimmed

1 tomato, cored, seeded, and chopped fine (about ½ cup/113 grams)

1 shallot (25 grams), minced

1½ tablespoons (22 grams) lemon juice

1 tablespoon (1 gram) chopped fresh basil

3 tablespoons (42 grams) extra-virgin olive oil

Salt and pepper

1 Using sous vide circulator, bring water to 180°F/82°C in 7-quart container.

2 Arrange asparagus in single layer in 1-gallon zipper-lock freezer bag and seal bag, pressing out as much air as possible. Place bag in second 1-gallon zipper-lock freezer bag and seal. Gently lower bag into prepared water bath, weight bag (see page 14) until asparagus is fully submerged, and then clip top corner of bag to side of water bath container, allowing remaining air bubbles to rise to top of bag. Reopen 1 corner of zipper, release remaining air bubbles, and reseal bag. Cover and cook for 20 minutes.

3 Whisk tomato, shallot, lemon juice, basil, oil, and ¼ teaspoon (1.5 grams) salt in bowl. Season with salt and pepper to taste. Transfer asparagus to serving platter and drizzle with vinaigrette. Serve.

Variations

Perfect Asparagus with Soy-Ginger Vinaigrette
Substitute 2 minced scallions (34 grams), ¼ cup (60 grams) lime juice, 3 tablespoons (42 grams) sesame oil, 3 tablespoons (45 grams) soy sauce, 1 tablespoon (5 grams) grated fresh ginger, 1 tablespoon (21 grams) honey, and 2 minced garlic cloves (10 grams) for tomato, shallot, lemon juice, basil, and olive oil.

Perfect Asparagus with Mustard-Thyme Vinaigrette
Substitute 1 tablespoon (2 grams) chopped fresh thyme and ¼ teaspoon (1.5 grams) Dijon mustard for tomato and basil.

Better-Than-Braised Beets

YIELD **SERVES 4**
Sous Vide Temperature 191°F/88°C
Sous Vide Time 4 to 6 hours
Active Cooking Time 30 minutes

To Make Ahead Beets can be rapidly chilled in ice bath (see page 13) and then refrigerated for up to 7 days. Bring to room temperature before serving.

Why This Recipe Works You can't go wrong with good old steamed or oven-roasted beets. But sous vide is a powerful tool: It can elevate the humble beet to a tastier, more intensely flavored vegetable. Cooking beets in a sealed bag helps with flavor penetration; we found that the aromatics and seasoning we put in the bag with the beets seeped to their core. Because there was no moisture loss due to evaporation, the beets also stayed juicy. Because we didn't have to cook the beets in water, all those natural juices that accumulated during cooking remained and concentrated in the bag. Throw in some oil and a little sherry vinegar? We effectively created a ready-to-go vinaigrette. Last but certainly not least, cooking beets sous vide produced perfectly uniform, perfectly cooked texture from end to end (no easy task!). With this dish, you're really getting the most bang for your beet. Look for beets that are roughly 2 to 3 inches in diameter. Be sure to double bag the beets to protect against seam failure. Beets have a tendency to float when placed in a sous vide water bath, which can lead to uneven cooking. Use weights to make sure the beets are fully immersed during cooking (see page 14).

2 pounds (907 grams) beets, trimmed

3 tablespoons (42 grams) extra-virgin olive oil

2 tablespoons (28 grams) sherry vinegar

8 sprigs (4 grams) fresh thyme

Salt and pepper

2 tablespoons (4 grams) minced fresh chives

1 Using sous vide circulator, bring water to 191°F/88°C in 7-quart container.

2 Toss beets, oil, vinegar, thyme, 1½ teaspoons (9 grams) salt, and ¾ teaspoon (2 grams) pepper in 1-gallon zipper-lock freezer bag. Seal bag, pressing out as much air as possible. Place bag in second 1-gallon zipper-lock freezer bag and seal bag. Gently lower bag into prepared water bath, weight bag (see page 14) until beets are fully submerged, and then clip top corner of bag to side of water bath container, allowing remaining air bubbles to rise to top of bag. Reopen 1 corner of zipper, release any remaining air bubbles, and reseal bag. Cover and cook for 4 to 6 hours.

3 Transfer beets to cutting board. Discard thyme sprigs and transfer cooking liquid to large bowl. When beets are cool enough to handle, rub off skins with paper towel and cut into ½-inch wedges. Add beets and chives to bowl with cooking liquid and toss to combine. Season with salt and pepper to taste. Serve.

Charred Beet Salad

YIELD SERVES 4
Sous Vide Temperature 191°F/88°C
Sous Vide Time 4 to 6 hours
Active Cooking Time 50 minutes

To Make Ahead Cooked beets can be chilled rapidly in ice bath (see page 13) and then refrigerated for up to 7 days. To serve, leave beets and their cooking liquid at room temperature for 30 minutes and then proceed with step 4.

Why This Recipe Works The ubiquitous combination of beets and goat cheese works because the tangy, creamy, salty goat cheese is a great foil for the beets' earthy sweetness. (Beets' sweetness is the result of a winter survival strategy. The sugars in beets act like antifreeze, keeping the fluid in their cells from freezing and forming destructive ice crystals.) But that doesn't mean the combination hasn't gotten tired. To reinvigorate this classic salad, we charred the beets, which we'd cooked using our foolproof sous vide method, to add some complementary bitterness. We amplified that bitterness with crisp radicchio and tossed it all with a dressing made from the beet cooking liquid. A simple spread of feta and Greek yogurt added plenty of creaminess instead of goat cheese. Tart pomegranate seeds provided pops of bright acidity, while fresh dill and tarragon rounded things out with some herbal notes. Be sure to double bag beets to protect against seam failure. Beets have a tendency to float when placed in a sous vide water bath, which can lead to uneven cooking. Use weights to make sure the beets are fully immersed during cooking (see page 14).

- 2 pounds (900 grams) beets, trimmed
- 3 tablespoons (42 grams) extra-virgin olive oil
- 2 tablespoons (28 grams) sherry vinegar
  Salt and pepper
- 4 ounces (105 grams) feta cheese, crumbled (1 cup)
- ½ cup (120 grams) plain Greek yogurt
- 1 tablespoon (14 grams) vegetable oil
- ½ head (142 grams) radicchio, cored and cut into 2-inch pieces
- ½ cup (75 grams) pomegranate seeds
- 1 tablespoon (1.5 grams) chopped fresh dill
- 1 tablespoon (1.5 grams) chopped fresh tarragon

1 Using sous vide circulator, bring water to 191°F/88°C in 7-quart container.

2 Toss beets, oil, vinegar, 1½ teaspoons (9 grams) salt, and ¾ teaspoon (2 grams) pepper in 1-gallon zipper-lock freezer bag. Seal bag, pressing out as much air as possible. Place bag in second 1-gallon zipper-lock freezer bag and seal. Gently lower bag into prepared water bath, weight bag (see page 14) until beets are fully submerged, and then clip top corner of bag to side of water bath container, allowing remaining air bubbles to rise to top of bag. Reopen 1 corner of zipper, release any remaining air bubbles, and reseal bag. Cover and cook for 4 to 6 hours.

3 Transfer beets to cutting board. Transfer cooking liquid to medium bowl. When beets are cool enough to handle, rub off skins with paper towel and cut into ½-inch wedges.

4 Using back of fork, mash feta and ¼ cup (60 grams) yogurt together in small bowl to form coarse spread; refrigerate until ready to serve. Whisk remaining ¼ cup (60 grams) yogurt into beet cooking liquid until combined.

5 Heat oil in 12-inch skillet over high heat until just smoking. Carefully place beets cut side down in skillet and cook until well charred on both sides, 5 to 7 minutes. Transfer beets to cutting board and cut into 1½-inch pieces.

6 Add beets and radicchio to bowl with dressing and gently toss to combine. Season with salt and pepper to taste. Spread feta mixture in even layer on large serving plate. Arrange beets and radicchio on top, then sprinkle with pomegranate seeds, dill, and tarragon, and serve.

Baby Bok Choy with Chile Vinaigrette

YIELD SERVES 4
Sous Vide Temperature 185°F/85°C
Sous Vide Time 12 minutes
Active Cooking Time 40 minutes

To Make Ahead Vinaigrette can be refrigerated for up to a week. We don't recommend making the bok choy in advance.

Why This Recipe Works Bok choy is often served as a side dish and can too easily take a back seat to the main meaty stir-fry. But this mild, quick-cooking vegetable is great in its own right. It has a nice peppery bite, and it doesn't need a lot of work to unlock its delicate, fresh flavor. A short, 12-minute swim at 185°F/85°C cooked the bok choy just long enough to render it tender and crisp, but not long enough to beat it into mushy, dull-green submission. After cooking, we tossed the bok choy in a generous amount of a Sichuan-style chile oil vinaigrette, which gets into all the little nooks and crannies of the layered vegetable. The dish is bright, savory, malty, spicy, and seriously addictive—plus, it's vegan! Black vinegar, an important ingredient and condiment in Chinese cuisine, is a dark vinegar made from glutinous rice or sorghum. It can be found at Asian markets or online. Bird chiles are a specific cultivar of *Capsicum annuum* commonly found in Southeast Asia and Ethiopia. (They get their name because when dried, the bright red, thin-skinned chiles take on a hooked appearance that resembles a bird's beak.) Be sure to double bag the bok choy to protect against seam failure. Bok choy have a tendency to float when placed in a sous vide water bath, which can lead to uneven cooking. Use weights to make sure the bok choy are fully immersed during cooking (see page 14).

Chile Vinaigrette

5–10	bird chiles (3–8 grams), finely ground
¼	cup (56 grams) vegetable oil
2	garlic cloves (10 grams), sliced thin
1	1-inch piece fresh ginger (12 grams), peeled and sliced thin
1	tablespoon (4 grams) Sichuan peppercorns
½	cinnamon stick (2 grams)
1	star anise pod (1 gram)
1	tablespoon (15 grams) soy sauce
1	tablespoon (15 grams) black vinegar
1½	teaspoons (7.5 grams) toasted sesame oil
½	teaspoon (2 grams) sugar

Bok Choy

8	small heads baby bok choy (2 ounces/57 grams each), halved, washed and dried thoroughly
	Salt

1 For the chile vinaigrette Place chiles in large heatproof bowl. Place fine-mesh strainer over bowl and set aside. Combine vegetable oil, garlic, ginger, peppercorns, cinnamon stick, and star anise pod in small saucepan and heat over medium-high heat until sizzling. Reduce heat to low and gently simmer until garlic and ginger are slightly browned, 10 to 12 minutes. Pour oil mixture through prepared strainer into bowl with chiles; discard solids in strainer. Stir chiles and oil to combine; let cool for 5 minutes. Stir in soy sauce, vinegar, sesame oil, and sugar until combined; set aside.

2 For the bok choy Using sous vide circulator, bring water to 185°F/ 85°C in 7-quart container.

3 Place bok choy in 1-gallon zipper-lock freezer bag. Seal bag, pressing out as much air as possible. Place bag in second 1-gallon zipper-lock freezer bag and seal. Gently lower bag into prepared water bath, weight bag (see page 14) until bok choy is fully submerged, and then clip top corner of bag to side of water bath container, allowing remaining air bubbles to rise to top of bag. Reopen 1 corner of zipper, release any remaining air bubbles, and reseal bag. Cover and cook for 12 minutes.

4 Transfer bok choy to bowl with vinaigrette and toss to coat. Season with salt to taste. Serve.

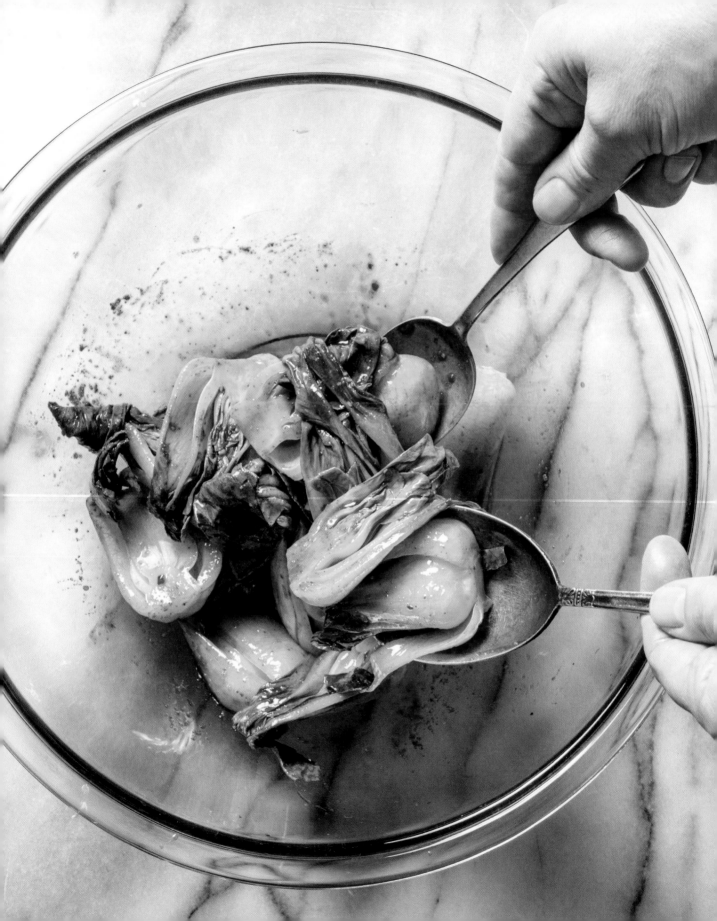

Honey-Glazed Carrots with Lemon and Thyme

YIELD SERVES 4
Sous Vide Temperature 190°F/88°C
Sous Vide Time 1 to 2 hours
Active Cooking Time 25 minutes

To Make Ahead We don't recommend making this recipe in advance.

Why This Recipe Works If you've never had sous vide carrots before, you're in for a treat. Traditional recipes for glazed carrots result in carrots that are unevenly cooked at best, or, in dire cases, supermushy. Either way, their flavor tends to be mild and watered down. But when cooked in a sealed environment, carrots become sweeter, more aromatic, and more intense versions of themselves. Gone is the evaporation of aromas that happens during braising or the dilution of flavor that occurs when carrots are blanched. And to (carrot) top it all off, when cooked sous vide, they come out perfectly even and just tender. To give our carrots a boost, we added butter, honey, lemon, thyme, and a little chicken broth to the bag. All those aromatics and liquids formed the base of a shiny, buttery glaze that coated each and every piece in more carroty goodness. Even for the glazed-carrot skeptics out there, it's hard to say no to this dish. Be sure to double bag the carrots to protect against seam failure. Carrots have a tendency to float when placed in a sous vide water bath, which can lead to uneven cooking. Use weights to make sure the carrots are fully immersed during cooking (see page 14).

1 pound (450 grams) carrots, peeled, halved lengthwise, and sliced ½ inch thick on bias

2 tablespoons (28 grams) unsalted butter, plus 2 tablespoons (28 grams) cut into 2 pieces and chilled

¼ cup (45 grams) chicken broth

2 tablespoons (42 grams) honey

4 teaspoons (20 grams) lemon juice

8 sprigs (4 grams) fresh thyme

Salt and pepper

2 tablespoons (4 grams) minced fresh chives

1 Using sous vide circulator, bring water to 190°F/88°C in 7-quart container.

2 Place carrots, 2 tablespoons (28 grams) butter, broth, honey, lemon juice, thyme sprigs, and ¼ teaspoon (1.5 grams) salt in 1-gallon zipper-lock freezer bag. Seal bag, pressing out as much air as possible. Place bag in second 1-gallon zipper-lock freezer bag and seal. Gently lower bag into prepared water bath, weight bag (see page 14) until carrots are fully submerged, and then clip top corner of bag to side of water bath container, allowing remaining air bubbles to rise to top of bag. Reopen 1 corner of zipper, release remaining air bubbles, and reseal bag. Cover and cook for 1 to 2 hours.

3 Drain carrots through fine-mesh strainer set over 12-inch skillet; transfer carrots to bowl and discard thyme sprigs. Bring cooking liquid to simmer over medium-high heat and cook until reduced to 2 tablespoons (40 grams), 5 to 7 minutes. Off heat, whisk in remaining 2 tablespoons chilled butter until mixture is smooth and glossy. Add carrots and chives and toss to combine. Season with salt and pepper to taste. Serve.

Variation
Honey-Ginger Glazed Carrots
Substitute 1 1-inch piece fresh ginger (12 grams), peeled and sliced thin, and ⅛ teaspoon cayenne pepper for thyme sprigs.

Roasted Celery Root with Chimichurri

YIELD **SERVES 4**
Sous Vide Temperature 185°F/85°C
Sous Vide Time 3 to 5 hours
Active Cooking Time 45 minutes

To Make Ahead Chimichurri can be refrigerated for up to 2 days. We don't recommend making celery root in advance.

Why This Recipe Works When you think about a vegetable side dish that is both innovative and tasty, we're guessing that roasted celery root isn't the first thing to jump into your mind. But it should. For starters, celery root is a versatile vegetable. It makes great soups, stews, and purees. It's great mashed and is delicious when baked whole. It just doesn't get the love it deserves. We decided to fix that by developing a rustic, satisfying roasted celery root dish that highlights the earthy, creamy qualities of this root vegetable. We started by scrubbing and halving the roots—yes, skin and all—and cooking them sous vide until they were tender throughout. That's right—no peeling required! With enough heat and time, the tough, hardy exterior of the vegetable broke down, turning completely edible. In fact, after a few hours, the entire root was rendered creamy, tender, and aromatic. Once out of the bag, we broke the celery root apart by hand into random, jagged chunks, providing greater surface area for crisping up during a final pan-roasting step. To finish the dish, we spooned a generous amount of chimichurri over the tops of the roasted root pieces. Be sure to double bag the celery root to protect against seam failure. Celery root has a tendency to float when placed in a sous vide water bath, which can lead to uneven cooking. Use weights to make sure the roots are fully immersed during cooking (see page 14).

- 2 pounds (900 grams) celery root, trimmed and halved
- 3 tablespoons (42 grams) unsalted butter
- ¼ cup (60 grams) hot tap water
- 2 teaspoons (2 grams) dried oregano
  Salt and pepper
- 1⅓ cups (18 grams) fresh parsley leaves
- ⅔ cup (9 grams) fresh cilantro leaves
- 6 garlic cloves (30 grams), minced
- ½ teaspoon (1 gram) red pepper flakes
- ¼ cup (60 grams) red wine vinegar
- ½ cup plus 3 tablespoons (42 grams) extra-virgin olive oil

1 Using sous vide circulator, bring water to 185°F/85°C in 7-quart container.

2 Place celery root and butter in 1-gallon zipper-lock freezer bag. Seal bag, pressing out as much air as possible. Place bag in second 1-gallon zipper-lock freezer bag and seal. Gently lower bag into prepared water bath, weight bag (see page 14) until celery root is fully submerged, and then clip top corner of bag to side of water bath container, allowing remaining air bubbles to rise to top of bag. Reopen 1 corner of zipper, release remaining air bubbles, and reseal bag. Cover and cook for 3 to 5 hours.

3 Meanwhile, combine hot water, oregano, and 1 teaspoon (6 grams) salt in small bowl and let sit for 5 minutes. Pulse parsley, cilantro, garlic, and pepper flakes in food processor until coarsely chopped, about 10 pulses. Add water mixture and vinegar to food processor and pulse briefly to combine. Transfer mixture to medium bowl and slowly whisk in ½ cup oil until incorporated. Cover and set aside.

4 Transfer celery root to cutting board and let sit until cool enough to touch. Using your hands, break celery root into rough 1-inch chunks. Heat remaining 3 tablespoons oil in 12-inch skillet over high heat until shimmering. Add half of celery root and cook, turning occasionally, until browned on all sides, 6 to 8 minutes. Transfer celery root to serving platter and tent with aluminum foil. Repeat with remaining celery root. Season with salt to taste, drizzle with chimichurri, and serve.

Butter-Poached Corn on the Cob

YIELD SERVES 4
Sous Vide Temperature 185°F/85°C
Sous Vide Time 40 minutes
Active Cooking Time 30 minutes

To Make Ahead We don't recommend making this recipe in advance.

Why This Recipe Works You wouldn't guess it, but corn goes on the list of vegetables (which also includes carrots, sweet potatoes, and parsnips) that benefit significantly from sous vide cooking. Its flavor intensifies when cooked sealed in a plastic bag. It comes out juicy, crunchy, and sweet—not waterlogged and anemic. To impart some subtle grassy notes, we cooked the corn in the husk, which also made peeling the corn far easier. Our base recipe contains just a little butter and salt, but this method lends itself to all kinds of variations and compound butters: chili-lime, cilantro, even *berbere* and *ras el hanout*. Feel free to go crazy. Be sure to double bag the corn to protect against seam failure. Corn has a tendency to float when placed in a sous vide water bath, which can lead to uneven cooking. Use weights to make sure the corn is fully immersed during cooking (see page 14). This recipe can easily be doubled by using a 12-quart container.

4 ears corn, husks and silk left intact, trimmed
2 tablespoons (28 grams) unsalted butter, plus 2 tablespoons (28 grams) softened
Salt and pepper

1 Using sous vide circulator, bring water to 185°F/85°C in 7-quart container.

2 Place corn, 2 tablespoons (28 grams) butter, and ½ teaspoon (3 grams) salt in even layer in 1-gallon zipper-lock freezer bag. Seal bag, pressing out as much air as possible. Place bag in second 1-gallon zipper-lock freezer bag and seal. Gently lower bag into prepared water bath, weight bag (see page 14) until corn is fully submerged, and then clip top corner of bag to side of water bath container, allowing remaining air bubbles to rise to top of bag. Reopen 1 corner of zipper, release any remaining air bubbles, and reseal bag. Cover and cook for 40 minutes.

3 Transfer corn to cutting board and let sit until cool enough to touch. Using your hands, remove husks and silk from corn. Brush corn with remaining 2 tablespoons (28 grams) softened butter, season with salt and pepper to taste, and serve.

Variation

Butter-Poached Corn on the Cob with Chili and Lime
Stir ½ teaspoon (1 gram) chili powder and 1 tablespoon (15 grams) lime juice into softened butter before brushing onto corn in step 3. Serve with lime wedges.

Vegetables and Grains

149

Mediterranean Braised Green Beans

YIELD SERVES 4 TO 6
Sous Vide Temperature 194°F/90°C
Sous Vide Time 2 to 3 hours
Active Cooking Time 40 minutes

To Make Ahead We don't recommend making this recipe in advance.

Why This Recipe Works Most of the time, when we talk about cooking spring vegetables sous vide, we envision properly cooked, al dente haricots verts or just-tender asparagus. But let's not sleep on those old-school army-green bean braises that may have defined our childhood. It's not that they were ever bad, per se, but they could use some improvement. Here we take advantage of the consistent and precise heat that sous vide cooking provides to make a fork-tender, super-savory green bean dish. To facilitate the breakdown of the tough pectin exterior of the beans, we add a little baking soda—which plays double duty by also neutralizing the acidic tomato base of the accompanying sauce we add to the bag, too. We cook this flavor base to a relatively dry paste before it goes in the bag, and as the beans cook, the juices released hydrate the paste, resulting in a rich, satisfying sauce that coats each bean. With some crusty bread and company, this dish is sure to take you back in time and warm up your soul. A dollop of yogurt spooned over the beans adds nice tang. Be sure to double bag the green beans to protect against seam failure. Green beans have a tendency to float when placed in a sous vide water bath, which can lead to uneven cooking. Use weights to make sure the beans are fully immersed during cooking (see page 14).

5   tablespoons (70 grams) extra-virgin olive oil
1   onion (140 grams), chopped fine
1   teaspoon (6 grams) salt
4   garlic cloves (20 grams), minced
1   tablespoon (16 grams) tomato paste
¼   teaspoon (1 gram) pepper
    Pinch cayenne pepper

1   14.5-ounce can (410 grams) diced tomatoes, drained with juice reserved, chopped
¼   teaspoon (1.5 grams) baking soda
1½ pounds (680 grams) green beans, trimmed and cut into 2-inch lengths
¼   cup (5 grams) chopped fresh parsley
    Red wine vinegar

1 Using sous vide circulator, bring water to 194°F/90°C in 7-quart container.

2 Heat 3 tablespoons (42 grams) oil in 12-inch skillet over medium-high heat until shimmering. Add onion and salt and cook until softened, about 5 minutes. Stir in garlic, tomato paste, pepper, and cayenne and cook until fragrant, about 1 minute. Stir in tomatoes and their juice and baking soda, scraping up any browned bits. Cook, stirring occasionally, until mixture is thickened and just beginning to brown, 8 to 10 minutes.

3 Transfer green beans and tomato mixture to 1-gallon zipper-lock freezer bag. Seal bag, pressing out as much air as possible. Place bag in second 1-gallon zipper-lock freezer bag and seal. Gently lower bag into prepared water bath, weight bag (see page 14) until beans are fully submerged, and then clip top corner of bag to side of water bath container, allowing remaining air bubbles to rise to top of bag. Reopen 1 corner of zipper, release remaining air bubbles, and reseal bag. Cover and cook for 2 to 3 hours.

4 Transfer beans to serving bowl. Stir in parsley and season with vinegar to taste. Drizzle with remaining 2 tablespoons (28 grams) oil. Serve warm or at room temperature.

Crispy Roasted Parsnips

YIELD **SERVES 6**
Sous Vide Temperature 200°F/90°C
Sous Vide Time 1 to 1 ½ hours
Active Cooking Time 1 hour

To Make Ahead We don't recommend making this recipe in advance.

Why This Recipe Works A popular misconception: Parsnips are just fancy carrots. That couldn't be further from the truth. Starchier, sweeter, and distinctly more aromatic than their orange cousins, parsnips take well to various cooking methods—everything from purees to roasts. We wanted to create a recipe for something akin to parsnip fries, because, well, nobody ever makes good parsnip fries. (Challenge accepted!) We discovered that a solution of baking soda roughed up the surface of the parsnips without breaking them down too much—just enough to create more surface area and miniature crags on their exteriors. Tossing the parsnips in salt roughed them up even more, and it created a bit of a starchy paste that led to a crisper exterior when, after an hour swim, they were given a final blast in a hot oven. We like to toss these crispy gems in a healthy amount of tangy Pecorino Romano, but the possibilities are endless. Be sure to double bag the parsnips to protect against seam failure. Parsnips have a tendency to float when placed in a sous vide water bath, which can lead to uneven cooking. Use weights to make sure the parsnips are fully immersed during cooking (see page 14).

2 cups (450 grams) water
Salt and pepper
½ teaspoon (3 grams) baking soda
2 pounds (900 grams) parsnips, peeled and sliced ½ inch thick on bias
2 tablespoons (28 grams) unsalted butter
½ cup vegetable oil
1 ounce (28 grams) Pecorino Romano cheese, grated fine (½ cup)

1 Using sous vide circulator, bring water bath to 200°F/90°C in 7-quart container.

2 Whisk water, 1 teaspoon (6 grams) salt, and baking soda in bowl until dissolved. Add parsnips, water mixture, and butter to 1-gallon zipper-lock freezer bag. Seal bag, pressing out as much air as possible. Place bag in second 1-gallon zipper-lock freezer bag and seal. Gently lower bag into prepared water bath, weight bag (see page 14) until parsnips are fully submerged, and then clip top corner of bag to side of water bath container, allowing remaining air bubbles to rise to top of bag. Reopen 1 corner of zipper, release any remaining air bubbles, and reseal bag. Cover and cook for 1 to 1½ hours.

3 Adjust oven rack to upper-middle position and heat oven to 450°F/232°C. Drain parsnips and transfer to bowl. Add oil and ½ teaspoon (3 grams) salt and toss to combine. Spread parsnips into even layer on rimmed baking sheet and roast until crisp and well browned, 40 to 50 minutes, flipping parsnips halfway through roasting. Parsnips will brown faster at edges of pan; transfer to bowl if browning too quickly. Transfer parsnips to bowl, add Pecorino Romano, and gently toss to combine. Season with salt and pepper to taste. Serve.

German Potato Salad

YIELD **SERVES 6 TO 8**
Sous Vide Temperature 194°F/90°C
Sous Vide Time 60 to 75 minutes
Active Cooking Time 40 minutes

To Make Ahead We don't recommend making this recipe in advance.

Why This Recipe Works Potato salad is an all-time classic. All you need to do is boil some potatoes and dress them. We decided to replace boiling with sous vide cookery and, happily, we found ourselves with the ultimate 21st-century potato salad. Why is sous vide better for this straight-forward application? The reason is simple: Sous vide potatoes taste more like potatoes than boiled potatoes. Why? When cooked in a sealed bag, there's no dilution and no evaporation. Instead, these potatoes are fork-tender but not mushy, creamy but not crumbly, and earthy in the most pleasant sense. Here we dress our potatoes with a tangy, mustard- and bacon-laden onion vinaigrette that cuts through all that heartiness. We prefer to serve this salad warm, but it's great hot, cold, or any temperature in between. Look for potatoes 1 to 2 inches in diameter. Be sure to double bag the potatoes to protect against seam failure. Potatoes have a tendency to float when placed in a sous vide water bath, which can lead to uneven cooking. Use weights to make sure the potatoes are fully immersed during cooking (see page 14).

2 pounds (900 grams) small red potatoes, unpeeled, halved

½ cup (118 grams) chicken broth

8 sprigs (4 grams) fresh thyme

Salt and pepper

8 slices (225 grams) bacon, cut into ½-inch pieces

1 onion (140 grams), chopped fine

½ teaspoon (2 grams) sugar

⅓ cup (80 grams) white wine vinegar

1 tablespoon (20 grams) whole-grain mustard

¼ cup (16 grams) chopped fresh parsley

1 Using sous vide circulator, bring water to 194°F/90°C in 7-quart container.

2 Place potatoes, broth, thyme sprigs, and ½ teaspoon (3 grams) salt in 1-gallon zipper-lock freezer bag. Seal bag, pressing out as much air as possible. Place bag in second 1-gallon zipper-lock freezer bag and seal. Gently lower bag into prepared water bath, weight bag (see page 14) until potatoes are fully submerged, and then clip top corner of bag to side of water bath container, allowing remaining air bubbles to rise to top of bag. Reopen 1 corner of zipper, release remaining air bubbles, and reseal bag. Cover and cook for 60 to 75 minutes.

3 Drain potatoes in fine-mesh strainer set over bowl; discard thyme sprigs. Measure out and reserve ½ cup cooking liquid; discard remaining liquid.

4 Cook bacon in 12-inch skillet over medium heat until crisp, about 5 minutes. Using slotted spoon, transfer bacon to paper towel–lined plate. Pour off all but ¼ cup fat. Add onion to fat left in skillet and cook over medium heat, stirring occasionally, until softened and beginning to brown, about 4 minutes. Stir in sugar until dissolved, about 30 seconds. Stir in vinegar and reserved cooking liquid, bring to simmer, and cook until mixture is reduced to about ¾ cup, about 3 minutes. Off heat, whisk in mustard and ¼ teaspoon (1 gram) pepper. Add potatoes, parsley, and bacon to skillet and toss to combine. Season with salt to taste. Serve.

Vegetables and Grains

155

French-Style Mashed Potatoes

YIELD SERVES 8
Sous Vide Temperature 194°F/90°C
Sous Vide Time 45 minutes
Active Cooking Time 35 minutes

To Make Ahead We don't recommend making this recipe in advance.

Why This Recipe Works Butter, milk, potatoes: You really can't go wrong. Especially when you treat them like the French do. *Pommes purées* is a rich, smooth, velvety, and supremely satisfying French side dish that pairs well with pretty much everything—mushrooms, steak, chicken, scallops, lamb, you name it. We found that cooking the potatoes directly in milk and butter in a bag in the water bath concentrated the potato flavor and helped cook the potatoes evenly. All that was left to do was run the contents through a food mill, whisk it all together, and boom: decadent pommes purées. You can omit the final straining step, but the potatoes will be slightly less smooth and velvety. Be sure to double bag the potatoes to protect against seam failure. Potatoes have a tendency to float when placed in a sous vide water bath, which can lead to uneven cooking. Use weights to make sure the potatoes are fully immersed during cooking (see page 14).

2 pounds (900 grams) Yukon Gold potatoes, peeled and sliced ¼ inch thick

20 tablespoons (2½ sticks/280 grams) unsalted butter

1⅓ cups (310 grams) whole milk

Salt and white pepper

1 Using sous vide circulator, bring water to 194°F/90°C in 7-quart container.

2 Rinse potatoes in fine-mesh strainer under cold running water until water runs clear. Drain potatoes well.

3 Place potatoes, butter, milk, and 1 teaspoon (6 grams) salt in 1-gallon zipper-lock freezer bag. Seal bag, pressing out as much air as possible. Place bag in second 1-gallon zipper-lock freezer bag and seal. Gently lower bag into prepared water bath, weight bag (see page 14) until potatoes are fully submerged, and then clip top corner of bag to side of water bath container, allowing remaining air bubbles to rise to top of bag. Reopen 1 corner of zipper, release remaining air bubbles, and reseal bag. Cover and cook for 45 minutes.

4 Drain potatoes in fine-mesh strainer set over large saucepan; place saucepan over low heat. Working in batches, transfer potatoes to hopper of food mill or potato ricer and process into saucepan. Using whisk, recombine potatoes and cooking liquid until smooth, 10 to 15 seconds (potatoes should almost be pourable). Strain potatoes through fine-mesh strainer into bowl, pressing on solids with ladle to extract as much as possible. Season with salt and pepper to taste. Serve immediately.

Crispy Smashed Potatoes

YIELD **SERVES 6 TO 8**

Sous Vide Temperature 194°F/90°C

Sous Vide Time 60 to 75 minutes

Active Cooking Time 75 minutes

To Make Ahead We don't recommend making this recipe in advance.

Why This Recipe Works Crispy potatoes will never go out of style. And on the crispiness-per-square-inch scale, smashed potatoes come in near the top. While most recipes call for boiling potatoes, we found that cooking ours sous vide gave them a uniform, creamy texture and amplified their potato-y flavor. To jazz up this dish, we tossed the potatoes in an intense garlic oil before roasting them. Look for potatoes 1 to 2 inches in diameter. Be sure to double bag the potatoes to protect against seam failure. Potatoes have a tendency to float when placed in a sous vide water bath, which can lead to uneven cooking. Use weights to make sure the potatoes are fully immersed during cooking (see page 14).

2 pounds (900 grams) small red potatoes, scrubbed

½ cup (118 grams) chicken broth

 Salt and pepper

6 tablespoons (84 grams) vegetable oil

1 tablespoon (5 grams) chopped rosemary

3 garlic cloves (15 grams), minced

1 Using sous vide circulator, bring water bath to 194°F/90°C in 7-quart container.

2 Place potatoes, broth, and ½ teaspoon (3 grams) salt in 1-gallon zipper-lock freezer bag. Seal bag, pressing out as much air as possible. Place bag in second 1-gallon zipper-lock freezer bag and seal. Gently lower bag into prepared water bath, weight bag (see page 14) until potatoes are fully submerged, and then clip top corner of bag to side of water bath container, allowing remaining air bubbles to rise to top of bag. Reopen 1 corner of zipper, release remaining air bubbles, and reseal bag. Cover and cook for 60 to 75 minutes.

3 Adjust oven rack to upper-middle position and heat oven to 450°F/232°C. Microwave oil, rosemary, and garlic in bowl, stirring occasionally, until garlic begins to brown, 2 to 4 minutes. Strain oil into large bowl, reserving garlic and rosemary.

4 Drain potatoes and let sit until surfaces are dry, about 10 minutes. Add potatoes and ½ teaspoon (3 grams) salt to bowl with herb oil and toss to combine. Arrange potatoes evenly on rimmed baking sheet and place second baking sheet on top. Press down firmly on top sheet, flattening potatoes until they are ⅓ to ½ inch thick; remove top sheet.

5 Roast potatoes until crisp and well browned, 40 to 50 minutes, flipping potatoes halfway through roasting. Transfer potatoes to serving bowl, add reserved garlic and rosemary, and gently toss to combine. Season with salt and pepper to taste. Serve.

Butternut Squash Puree

YIELD **SERVES 8 TO 10**
Sous Vide Temperature 200°F/93°C
Sous Vide Time 1 to 1 ½ hours
Active Cooking Time 20 minutes

To Make Ahead We don't recommend making this recipe in advance.

Why This Recipe Works Sometimes you just don't want to put another pot on your stove—especially for big-ticket dinners like Thanksgiving. By cooking winter squash sous vide, we eliminate the need for any stove space. We also found that by cooking the squash in a bag, we kept all that precious squash-y flavor, and we were able to cook the squash perfectly, to an even fork-tenderness. The result? Sweet, buttery, and vibrant orange goodness. Butternut squash is relatively low in overall fiber—most of which is soluble fiber as opposed to tough insoluble fiber—which made it easier to blend to a smooth consistency. To impart velvety richness to our puree, we threw in a little butter. If you're like us, you'll find yourself eating this stuff by the spoonful—straight out of the blender jar. Be sure to double bag the squash to protect against seam failure. Squash has a tendency to float when placed in a sous vide water bath, which can lead to uneven cooking. Use weights to make sure the squash is fully immersed during cooking (see page 14).

2 pounds (900 grams) butternut squash, peeled, seeded, and sliced ¼ inch thick
¼ cup (60 grams) water, plus extra as needed
3 tablespoons (42 grams) unsalted butter
Salt

1 Using sous vide circulator, bring water to 200°F/93°C in 7-quart container.

2 Place squash, water, butter, and ½ teaspoon (3 grams) salt in 1-gallon zipper-lock freezer bag. Seal bag, pressing out as much air as possible. Place bag in second 1-gallon zipper-lock freezer bag and seal. Gently lower bag into prepared water bath, weight bag (see page 14) until squash is fully submerged, and clip top corner of bag to side of water bath container, allowing remaining air bubbles to rise to top of bag. Reopen 1 corner of zipper, release remaining air bubbles, and reseal bag. Cover and cook for 1 hour to 1½ hours.

3 Transfer squash and cooking liquid to blender and process until smooth, about 2 minutes, scraping down sides of blender jar as needed. (If mixture is not blending easily, adjust consistency of puree with up to 2 tablespoons (30 grams) extra water.) Season with salt to taste. Serve.

Vegetables and Grains

Overnight Steel-Cut Oats

YIELD SERVES 4
Sous Vide Temperature 155°F/68°C
Sous Vide Time 12 to 16 hours
Active Cooking Time 15 minutes

To Make Ahead Cooked oats can be chilled rapidly in ice bath (see page 13) and then refrigerated for up to 5 days. To serve, microwave uncovered, stirring every 30 seconds, until oatmeal is warmed through and creamy, about 2 minutes.

Why This Recipe Works The traditional way of cooking steel-cut oats isn't hard, per se. But those hearty oats do need to simmer on the stove for some time, requiring a bit of babysitting. Even so-called overnight oats need 10 minutes of cooking in the morning. We decided to develop a hands-off method for steel-cut oats that would be ready to go right when you wake up. We knew we wanted to circulate the oats in individual 8-ounce wide-mouth Mason jars—because, hello, breakfast on the go! Circulating the oats with water alone in a moderate-temperature water bath sufficiently hydrated the grains, but we found these oats to be a little mushy. Why? Oats are abundant in pentosans, a group of naturally occurring gums that love water. These gums are responsible for the creaminess of hot cereal, but when overhydrated, the result is a mushy texture. Decreasing the amount of water helped. Adding a bit of salt resulted in oats with a pleasing bite. Like pentosans, salt loves water too. The salt competed with the gums for the water, and the result was a more toothsome cereal. In the end, all that science means you can have perfect oats, no mess and no babysitting required. Serve these oats with a little brown sugar and fresh fruit or some maple syrup and cinnamon. Do not substitute quick-cooking or rolled oats here. You will need four 8-ounce Mason jars for this recipe. Be careful not to overtighten the jars before placing them in the prepared water bath; that can cause the glass to crack.

Water
¾ cup (132 grams) steel-cut oats
Salt

1 Using sous vide circulator, bring water to 155°F/68°C in 7-quart container.

2 Fill four (8-ounce) wide-mouth Mason jars with following ingredients: 9 tablespoons (135 grams) water, 3 tablespoons (33 grams) oats, and pinch salt. Seal jars (do not overtighten lids) and gently lower into prepared water bath until fully submerged. Cover and cook for at least 12 hours or up to 16 hours.

3 Remove jars from water bath. Stir oats until smooth and serve.

No-Fuss Polenta

YIELD SERVES 6
Sous Vide Temperature 185°F/85°C
Sous Vide Time 1½ to 3 hours
Active Cooking Time 20 minutes

To Make Ahead Cooked polenta can be chilled rapidly in ice bath (see page 13) and then refrigerated for up to 3 days. To serve, heat polenta in microwave for 2 minutes, stirring halfway. Proceed with step 3.

Why This Recipe Works Making polenta the old-fashioned way is a commitment. To do it right, you need to watch those grits on the stove for up to 60 minutes, stirring or whisking and judging the consistency until it's just right. But if watching a pot for an hour isn't really your thing, then sous vide offers an easy, reliable way out. This recipe couldn't be simpler: Put water, cornmeal, and butter into a bag and cook it. We found that the gentle, consistent heat of the water bath cooked the polenta evenly—with no scorching at all. Because there's no evaporation, we didn't have to guess at the correct ratio of water to cornmeal, or give instructions dependent on the size of your pot—here, it's the same, every time. A simple whisk at the end brings everything together. Throw in some Parm and a healthy amount of salt and pepper, and you've got the easiest, most hands-off polenta recipe your *nonna* could only have dreamed about. Be sure to double bag the polenta to protect against seam failure. Polenta has a tendency to float when placed in a sous vide water bath, which can lead to uneven cooking. Use weights to make sure the polenta is fully immersed during cooking (see page 14). Do not substitute instant or quick-cooking cornmeal here.

3 cups (700 grams) water

1 cup (165 grams) coarse-ground cornmeal

3 tablespoons (42 grams) unsalted butter
  Salt and pepper

2 ounces (56 grams) Parmesan cheese, finely grated (1 cup)

1 Using sous vide circulator, bring water to 185°F/85°C in 7-quart container.

2 Place water, cornmeal, butter, and ¾ teaspoon (4.5 grams) salt in 1-gallon zipper-lock freezer bag. Seal bag, pressing out as much air as possible. Place bag in second 1-gallon zipper-lock freezer bag and seal. Gently lower bag into prepared water bath, weight bag (see page 14) until polenta is fully submerged, and then clip top corner of bag to side of water bath container, allowing remaining air bubbles to rise to top of bag. Reopen 1 corner of zipper, release remaining air bubbles, and reseal bag. Cover and cook for at least 1½ hours or up to 3 hours.

3 Transfer polenta to serving bowl and whisk vigorously to break apart any lumps. Whisk in Parmesan and season with salt and pepper to taste. Serve.

East African Black Lentil Stew

YIELD SERVES 4 TO 6
Sous Vide Temperature 194°F/90°C
Sous Vide Time 3 to 5 hours
Active Cooking Time 30 minutes

To Make Ahead Stew can be refrigerated for up to 3 days. To serve, bring to a simmer in medium saucepan or heat in microwave for 2 minutes. Proceed with step 4.

Why This Recipe Works Lentils are a staple of East African cuisine, particularly in the Horn of Africa. In Ethiopia, spicy vegetable or meat stews, known as *wat*, are common. These dishes rely heavily on *berbere*—a spice mixture of chile peppers, garlic, ginger, basil, fenugreek, and other lesser known spices native to Ethiopia and Eritrea. We wanted to come up with a dish of black lentils heavily inspired by those flavors. We started with a homespun berbere blend using common pantry spices. We bloomed the spices in oil before sweating the rest of the aromatics and adding a bit of tomato for brightness and acidity. We circulated black lentils in this intense, aromatic base until they were just tender but remained whole. The resulting lentils were creamy, with no blowouts. To give the stew a little body, we whisked the whole mixture at the end of the cooking process, which broke up some of the lentils' starch and thus thickened the stew. You can find berbere in specialty food stores and substitute 2–3 tablespoons of berbere in place of the spices in this recipe, though the resulting flavor may be slightly different. Be sure to double bag the lentils to protect against seam failure. This dish pairs perfectly with some fresh yogurt and crusty bread.

2 tablespoons (28 grams) vegetable oil

4 teaspoons (9 grams) paprika

1 teaspoon (2 grams) cayenne pepper

1 teaspoon (2 grams) ground coriander

¼ teaspoon (0.5 grams) ground allspice

¼ teaspoon (0.5 grams) ground cumin

¼ teaspoon (0.5 grams) ground cardamom

¼ teaspoon (1 gram) pepper

1 onion (140 grams), chopped fine

Salt

1 tablespoon (16 grams) grated fresh ginger

2½ cups (590 grams) vegetable broth

1 14.5-ounce can (411 grams) diced tomatoes, drained

1½ cups (10½ ounces/298 grams) black lentils

½ cup (10 grams) chopped fresh cilantro, plus extra for serving

½ cup (125 grams) plain yogurt

1 Using sous vide circulator, bring water to 194°F/90°C in 7-quart container.

2 Cook oil, paprika, cayenne, coriander, allspice, cumin, cardamom, and pepper in large saucepan over medium heat, stirring often, until fragrant, about 30 seconds. Stir in onion and ¾ teaspoon (4.5 grams) salt and cook until softened, about 5 minutes. Stir in ginger and cook for 30 seconds. Stir in broth and tomatoes and bring to simmer.

3 Place onion mixture and lentils in 1-gallon zipper-lock freezer bag. Seal bag, pressing out as much air as possible. Place bag in second 1-gallon zipper-lock freezer bag and seal. Gently lower bag into prepared water bath until lentils are fully submerged, and then clip top corner of bag to side of water bath container, allowing remaining air bubbles to rise to top of bag. Reopen 1 corner of zipper, release remaining air bubbles, and reseal bag. Cover and cook for at least 3 hours or up to 5 hours.

4 Transfer lentils to bowl. Using whisk, stir lentils vigorously until mixture thickens slightly. Stir in cilantro and season with salt to taste. Serve with yogurt and extra cilantro.

Spiced Red Lentils

YIELD SERVES 4
Sous Vide Temperature 194°F/90°C
Sous Vide Time 2 to 4 hours
Active Cooking Time 30 minutes

To Make Ahead Lentils can be refrigerated for up to 3 days. To serve, bring to a simmer in medium saucepan or heat in microwave for 2 minutes, stirring halfway. Proceed with step 4.

Why This Recipe Works Dal is a class of soups or stews native to the Indian subcontinent made from split beans, lentils, peas, and other legumes. Since red lentils break down relatively easily, we chose them for our take on sous vide dal. First, we tried cooking them for just a couple hours in a hot bath. This yielded evenly cooked and tender lentils—but when we poured them out of the bag, the overall texture wasn't quite right. These lentils were cooked, but still fully intact and the liquid was watery. Fortunately, we found a simple solution: whisking. Whisking the mixture briefly after cooking broke down the lentils, thickened the mixture, and resulted in the ideal consistency—porridge-like but still loose. After a bit more trial and error, we pared down the spice blend to a combination of coriander, cumin, cinnamon, turmeric, cardamom, and red pepper flakes. To brighten the dish, we added chopped fresh tomatoes and cilantro plus a little butter to replicate some of the flavors typically provided by ghee. Do not substitute other varieties of lentils here; red lentils have a much different cooking time and consistency. Be sure to double bag the lentils to protect against seam failure.

1 tablespoon (14 grams) vegetable oil
½ teaspoon (1 gram) ground coriander
½ teaspoon (1 gram) ground cumin
½ teaspoon (1 gram) ground cinnamon
½ teaspoon (1 gram) ground turmeric
⅛ teaspoon (0.5 grams) ground cardamom
⅛ teaspoon (0.5 grams) red pepper flakes
1 onion (140 grams), chopped fine
4 garlic cloves (20 grams), minced
  Salt and pepper
1½ teaspoons (8 grams) grated fresh ginger

2 cups (472 grams) water
1¼ cups (240 grams) red lentils, picked over and rinsed
2 tablespoons (28 grams) unsalted butter
1 pound (450 grams) plum tomatoes, cored, seeded, and chopped
½ cup (15 grams) chopped fresh cilantro, plus extra for serving
  Lemon wedges

1 Using sous vide circulator, bring water to 194°F/90°C in 7-quart container.

2 Cook oil, coriander, cumin, cinnamon, turmeric, cardamom, and pepper flakes in large saucepan over medium heat, stirring often, until fragrant, about 30 seconds. Stir in onion, garlic, and ¾ teaspoon (4.5 grams) salt and cook until onion is softened, about 5 minutes. Stir in ginger and cook for 30 seconds. Off heat, stir in water, scraping up any browned bits.

3 Place onion mixture and lentils in 1-gallon zipper-lock freezer bag. Seal bag, pressing out as much air as possible. Place bag in second 1-gallon zipper-lock freezer bag and seal. Gently lower bag into prepared water bath until lentils are submerged, and then clip top corner of bag to side of water bath container, allowing remaining air bubbles to rise to top of bag. Reopen 1 corner of zipper, release remaining air bubbles, and reseal bag. Cover and cook for at least 2 hours or up to 4 hours.

4 Transfer lentils to bowl and add butter. Whisk lentils vigorously until mixture reaches porridge-like consistency. Stir in tomatoes and cilantro and season with salt and pepper to taste. Serve with lemon wedges and extra cilantro.

Boston Not-Baked Beans

To Make Ahead Beans can be refrigerated for up to 3 days. To serve, bring to a simmer in medium saucepan or heat in microwave for 2 minutes, stirring halfway.

Why This Recipe Works If we had to pick one recipe in this book that surprised us by how well it adapted to sous vide, it might be this one. After all, they are "baked" beans. But moving beans from oven to water bath worked well. First, we didn't have to babysit the oven for hours. Second, cooking the beans sous vide ensured no blowouts and creamy, tender beans. To neutralize the acidic molasses-laden cooking liquid, we added a bit of baking soda to the bag and cooked the beans in this intense mixture for a full day. Yes, a full day! But it's worth it given the hands-off process and the perfectly cooked legumes that result. Out of the bath, a final simmer thickened up the sauce so that it coated the beans evenly. This dish is just as smoky and just as satisfying as the real deal, and it might even make a believer out of the staunchest baked bean traditionalists. Note that the beans need to brine overnight before they are cooked sous vide. Be sure to double bag the beans to protect against seam failure.

Salt and pepper

1 pound (2½ cups /450 grams) dried navy beans, picked over and rinsed

½ cup (175 grams) molasses

2 tablespoons packed (12.5 grams) dark brown sugar

1 tablespoon (15 grams) soy sauce

2 teaspoons (4 grams) dry mustard

6 ounces (170 grams) salt pork, rinsed, cut into ½-inch pieces

1 onion (140 grams), chopped

½ teaspoon (3 grams) baking soda

1 bay leaf (0.5 grams)

1 Dissolve 1½ tablespoons (27 grams) salt in 2 quarts cold water in large container. Add beans and let soak at room temperature for at least 8 hours or up to 24 hours. Drain and rinse well.

2 Using sous vide circulator, bring water to 194°F/90°C in 7-quart container.

3 Whisk 1½ cups (354 grams) water, molasses, sugar, soy sauce, mustard, and ½ teaspoon (1.5 grams) pepper in bowl. Cook salt pork in Dutch oven over medium heat until rendered and beginning to crisp, 4 to 8 minutes. Stir in onion and cook until softened, about 5 minutes. Stir in molasses mixture and bring to simmer. Stir in baking soda and cook until foaming subsides, about 30 seconds. Place salt pork mixture, beans, and bay leaf in 1-gallon zipper-lock freezer bag. Seal bag, pressing out as much air as possible. Place bag in second 1-gallon zipper-lock freezer bag and seal. Gently lower bag into prepared water bath until beans are fully submerged, and then clip top corner of bag to side of water bath container, allowing remaining air bubbles to rise to top of bag. Reopen 1 corner of zipper, release remaining air bubbles, and reseal bags. Cover and cook for at least 18 hours or up to 24 hours.

4 Transfer beans to Dutch oven; discard bay leaf. Cook beans over medium-high heat, stirring occasionally, until liquid has thickened slightly and clings to beans, 8 to 12 minutes. Season with salt and pepper to taste. Serve.

Cuban Black Beans

YIELD SERVES 6
Sous Vide Temperature 194°F/90°C
Sous Vide Time 20 to 24 hours
Active Cooking Time 35 minutes

To Make Ahead Beans can be refrigerated for up to 3 days. To serve, bring to a simmer in medium saucepan or heat in microwave for 2 minutes, stirring halfway.

Why This Recipe Works Sous vide cooking provides a foolproof method for creamy, evenly cooked beans with virtually no messy bean blowouts. For our take on Cuban black beans, we cooked the beans for an extended period of time in a solution of baking soda, salt, and water. This moderately alkaline environment sped up the deterioration of each bean's pectin-rich exterior, leading to softer, creamier beans more quickly. Taking advantage of the extended cooking time, we decided to throw in a ham hock, which broke down beautifully over the 20-plus hours of cooking. The rendered fat gave body to the cooking liquid and smokiness and shine to the beans. To finish the dish, we mashed some of the beans with bean cooking liquid and a *sofrito* of onion and bell pepper. We then stirred this in with the rest of the beans, plenty of lime juice, and the shredded ham hock. These beans are hearty and satisfying and sure to get you through the tough winter months. Be sure to double bag the beans to protect against seam failure.

- 1 pound (2½ cups/454 grams) dried black beans, picked over and rinsed
- 1 smoked ham hock (12 ounces/340 grams), rinsed
  Salt and pepper
- 2 bay leaves (0.5 grams)
- ¼ teaspoon (1.5 grams) baking soda
- 2 tablespoons (28 grams) extra-virgin olive oil
- 1 onion (140 grams), chopped fine
- 1 green bell pepper (227 grams), stemmed, seeded, and chopped fine
- 6 garlic cloves (30 grams), minced
- 2 tablespoons (6 grams) minced fresh oregano or 2 teaspoons (2 grams) dried
- 1½ teaspoons (3 grams) ground cumin
- ½ cup (10 grams) minced fresh cilantro
- 1 tablespoon (15 grams) lime juice, plus extra for seasoning

1 Using sous vide circulator, bring water to 194°F/90°C in 7-quart container.

2 Combine 5 cups (1.2 kilograms) water, beans, ham hock, 1 teaspoon (6 grams) salt, bay leaves, and baking soda in 1-gallon zipper-lock freezer bag. Seal bag, pressing out as much air as possible. Place bag in second 1-gallon zipper-lock freezer bag and seal. Gently lower bag into prepared water bath until beans are fully submerged, and then clip top corner of bag to side of water bath container, allowing remaining air bubbles to rise to top of bag. Reopen 1 corner of zipper, release remaining air bubbles, and reseal bag. Cover and cook for at least 20 hours or up to 24 hours.

3 Drain beans, reserving 1½ cups (350 grams) cooking liquid; discard bay leaves. Transfer ham hock to cutting board, let cool slightly, then shred into bite-size pieces using 2 forks; discard fat, skin, and bones.

4 Heat oil in Dutch oven over medium heat until shimmering. Add onion, bell pepper, and ¼ teaspoon (1.5 grams) salt and cook, stirring occasionally, until softened, about 5 minutes. Stir in garlic, oregano, and cumin and cook until fragrant, about 1 minute. Reduce heat to low, add reserved cooking liquid and one-third of beans, and mash with potato masher until mostly smooth. Stir in remaining beans, shredded ham hock, cilantro, and lime juice. Season with salt, pepper, and extra lime juice to taste. Serve.

White Bean Hummus

YIELD SERVES 6
Sous Vide Temperature 194°F/90°C
Sous Vide Time 3 to 5 hours
Active Cooking Time 40 minutes

To Make Ahead Hummus can be refrigerated for up to 3 days. Let sit at room temperature for 30 minutes and then proceed with step 4.

Why This Recipe Works Short of pressure cooking, there are few methods out there for cooking beans that can produce consistently creamy and evenly cooked beans. Those two qualities are essential if you want to make hummus. Fortunately, sous vide is a simple, foolproof way to get there. Here we wanted to make an easy white bean hummus with the familiar garlic and lemon flavors. A simple solution of baking soda and salt went a long way toward speeding the deterioration of the tough pectin exterior and softening the beans. Since there was little to no agitation from a vigorous boil or simmer, there were virtually no blowouts, and the beans cooked at relatively the same rate, which translated to a smoother puree with a uniform texture. To lend some complexity, we buzzed in some tahini and fancied it up with a simple herb salad on top. This hummus keeps surprisingly well in the fridge, but after one bite, storage won't be necessary. Be sure to double bag the beans to protect against seam failure.

Salt

¼ teaspoon (1 gram) baking soda

8 ounces (225 grams) dried navy beans, picked over and rinsed

½ cup (120 grams) plus 2 teaspoons (10 grams) lemon juice

4 cloves garlic (20 grams), unpeeled

⅔ cup (165 grams) tahini

¼ teaspoon (1 gram) ground cumin

¾ cup (10 grams) coarsely chopped fresh parsley

½ cup (5 grams) coarsely chopped fresh dill

½ cup (80 grams) pitted kalamata olives, sliced thin

¼ cup (56 grams) extra-virgin olive oil

2 tablespoons (20 grams) pepitas, toasted

2 tablespoons (20 grams) sunflower seeds, toasted

2 tablespoons (20 grams) white sesame seeds, toasted

1 Using sous vide circulator, bring water to 194°F/90°C in 7-quart container.

2 Dissolve ½ teaspoon (3 grams) salt and baking soda in 5 cups (1180 grams) water in 1-gallon zipper-lock freezer bag. Add beans and seal bag. Place bag in second 1-gallon zipper-lock freezer bag and seal. Gently lower bag into prepared water bath until beans are fully submerged, and then clip top corner of bag to side of water bath container, allowing remaining air bubbles to rise to top of bag. Reopen 1 corner of zipper, release remaining air bubbles, and reseal bag. Cover and cook for at least 3 hours or up to 5 hours.

3 Drain beans and set aside. Pulse ½ cup (125 grams) lemon juice, ⅓ cup (79 grams) water, garlic, and 1 teaspoon (6 grams) salt in food processor until coarse puree forms, about 20 pulses. Transfer to small bowl and let steep for 10 minutes. Strain lemon juice mixture through fine-mesh strainer back into processor; discard solids. Add tahini and process until mixture is smooth and well combined, about 1 minute, scraping down sides of bowl as needed. Add beans and cumin and process until mixture is very smooth, about 4 minutes. Adjust consistency with up to 2 tablespoons (30 grams) water and season with salt to taste.

4 Toss parsley, dill, and olives with 2 tablespoons (28 grams) oil, remaining 2 teaspoons (10 grams) lemon juice, and ⅛ teaspoon (1 gram) salt in small bowl. Transfer hummus to large bowl and use back of large spoon to spread hummus up sides of bowl, leaving well at center. Place herb salad in center of well. Sprinkle pepitas, sunflower seeds, and sesame seeds over top. Drizzle with remaining 2 tablespoons (28 grams) oil and serve.

Vegetables and Grains

Plant Cookery and Sous Vide

Key Points

- Plants are made up of microscopic cells
- The cell walls break down with heat
- We cook most sous vide vegetables at 185°F/85°C or higher to ensure tenderness

Just like animals (including us), plants are made of microscopic cells. These cells contain, among other important ingredients, starches, sugars, and water, which are all held in place by sturdy cell walls. In a crisp fresh fruit or vegetable, the cells are full of water, which causes them to inflate like a balloon. As the fruit or vegetable ages, some of that water leaves the cells, causing them to deflate, and thus the plant becomes progressively more limp over time.

When a plant is ready to eat, it shouldn't be too hard to bite into or unpleasantly bland or starchy. It should have an appealing aroma and flavor and maybe some sweetness. Some plants (or plant parts) get there on their own: A ripening fruit gets soft, sweet, and fragrant as its own enzymes convert tasteless starch to sugar and break down the pectin that strengthens its cell walls.

Other plants, however, we need to cook before they can reach that point. Specifically, vegetables don't ripen the way fruits do, but we can use heat to soften those cell walls and transform a tough and dense artichoke or potato into dinner. Even ripe fruits can benefit from the softening force of heat.

HEAT CAUSES STRUCTURAL CHANGES

Sous vide has advantages when it comes to fruit and vegetable cookery. While roasting does a good job of softening vegetables, it causes significant water loss in the process—hello, leathery roasted carrots. Sous vide also has advantages over boiling or steaming these plants; the sealed bag means you're not washing away delicate vegetable flavor. In addition, the precision of sous vide cooking allows us to easily home in on the ideal texture for cooked vegetables, cooking them until appropriately softened but before they turn to mush.

When plant cells are heated to about 140°F/60°C, a series of structural transformations starts to occur. The hotter the temperature, the faster they happen.

First, the balloon-like membranes inside the cells that hold onto water rupture. The vegetable starts to release some moisture and its cells start to deflate, making the vegetable limper, though its structure is still intact.

With continued cooking, the cell walls start to break down. Cell walls are rigid enclosures made up of three different types of structural molecules that have different properties: cellulose, hemicellulose, and pectin. Cellulose—think of the strings in a celery stalk—doesn't break down readily in cooking, but the other two do. Gradually, hemicellulose and pectin begin to dissolve in the surrounding liquid, which lets the cells separate from each other and collapse. With continued cooking, the plant becomes softer and softer until it is mush.

Almost all of our vegetable recipes call for a water bath temperature of at least 180°F/82°C. This is the temperature at which cell walls begin to weaken significantly, which translates to tender but still toothsome vegetables. We like this temperature for more delicate and quick-cooking produce like asparagus (page 136), fresh corn (page 149), and bok choy (page 142). For sturdier, starchier vegetables, we had success raising the sous vide temperature further. Pectin and hemicellulose start to dissolve between 190°F/88°C and 198°F/92°C. In this range, a carrot softens from snappy to bendy, the perfect texture for our Honey-Glazed Carrots (page 145).

LET'S TALK ABOUT STARCH

All plants have cell walls, but some plants have a significant amount of starch as well, which they store inside their cells as a source of energy. Cooking transforms these starchy plants (think potatoes and winter squash) too. In the raw plant, starch is stored in the form of microscopic, tightly clumped starch molecules.

Two ingredients are needed to soften starch molecules: heat and water. If you soak potatoes in cool water, nothing dramatic happens, but as soon as they heat up, the granules start to absorb water. They swell and soften as the water penetrates, and ultimately the granules burst apart. When they do, the starch molecules stretch out and tangle up with each other to create a mesh that holds onto water: the result is a starch gel. Starch in this form is tender and edible.

The starches in different plants have different characteristics, and they burst at different temperatures. Fluffy baking potatoes have starch that bursts and gels around 136°F/57°C, while waxier boiling potatoes don't unclump their starch until they reach 158°F/70°C. We found that cooking starchy vegetables at relatively high sous vide temperatures rendered them fork-tender, but not mushy. Small red potatoes cooked at 194°F/90°C along with broth or water for 60 to 75 minutes exited the bath tender from end to end, perfect for German Potato Salad (page 155) or for smashing and crisping up in the oven (page 159). Butternut squash cooked at 200°F/93°C for 1½ to 2 hours came out sweet and soft and easily pureed into a silky-smooth side dish (page 161).

Whether you're cooking bok choy, potato puree, or butternut squash, just remember: It all comes down to the cells walls.

SAUCES AND
INFUSIONS

If you've gotten this far in the book, you're probably not surprised to discover that eggs, dairy, poultry, meat, seafood, grains, and vegetables are not the only things you can sous vide. (Have you read the column on Lifehacker.com called "Will It Sous Vide?" If not, we give it a hearty recommend.) Behold: the sauces and infusions chapter.

To infuse means "to steep in liquid (such as water) without boiling so as to extract the soluble constituents or principles," according to *Merriam-Webster's Collegiate Dictionary, Eleventh Edition*. Sous vide allows us to steep ingredients like herbs, spices, fruits, vegetables, meat, and poultry in liquid at a constant temperature in order to create flavorful broths, oils, and syrups.

The flavor of many of these steepable ingredients comes mainly from their aroma, which we detect from the volatile molecules they release into the air. Spices have a high proportion of these flavor molecules, which is why they are incredibly potent.

These flavor compounds generally fall into three categories: those that are water soluble, those that are fat soluble, and those that form new flavor molecules when exposed to dry heat alone. In this chapter, for obvious reasons, we're sticking with the liquid applications. Like most substances, these flavor molecules dissolve faster and to a greater extent in a hot solvent (such as fat or oil) than a cold one.

Our Chicken Broth (page 181), All-Purpose Beef Broth (page 183), and Vegetable Broth (page 184) all cook in a water bath set to 185 degrees Fahrenheit/85 degrees Celsius for around 4 hours—the ideal combination for maximum extraction of water-soluble flavor molecules. Plus, no babysitting a simmering pot on the stove required. For the chicken broth, we use wings to create a clear broth with intense chicken flavor. We use ground beef for our beef broth, as the increased surface area of the ground meat creates the beefiest broth possible. We again take advantage of surface area in our vegetable broth, maximizing it (and therefore flavor) by cutting our classic broth-base vegetables—onion, carrot, and celery—plus mushrooms, tomatoes, and scallions, thin and on the bias.

When we bloom spices in oil, the fat-soluble flavor molecules are released from a solid state into solution form, where they mix and interact, thereby producing even more complex flavors. We take advantage of this in our Spicy Rosemary-Chile Oil (page 187), grabbing herbal flavor from the fresh rosemary and subtle heat from red pepper flakes and smoked paprika. (Bonus: Because there is no evaporation from the sealed bag, we retain the volatile aroma compounds from the extra-virgin olive oil, too.)

Take your pick of sweet syrups: raspberry, grapefruit, pomegranate, or spicy ginger (page 188). Cooked in a moderate water bath of 140°F/60°C, these delicate berries and citrus fruits retain their fresh flavor, and they don't end up tasting overmanipulated or cooked. Just combine water, sugar, and raspberries (we actually prefer frozen to fresh for this application), and you'll have a bright red, subtle syrup that tastes of fresh fruit and is perfect in our nonalcoholic Raspberry Lime Rickey (page 193). Want a little buzz? Our Grapefruit Paloma (page 190) combines tequila, grapefruit syrup, grapefruit juice, lime juice, seltzer—and, of course, a little salt. Really want to impress your brunch guests? Try our Sichuan Bloody Mary (page 194) for a mouth-tingling infusion experience.

And now you know: Sous vide can be used as a tool for everything from soup making to cocktail-party throwing.

Chicken Broth

YIELD MAKES ABOUT 2 QUARTS (1.8 KILOGRAMS)
Sous Vide Temperature 185°F/85°C
Sous Vide Time 4 to 5 hours
Active Cooking Time 30 minutes

To Make Ahead Broth can be refrigerated for up to 4 days or frozen for up to 2 months.

Why This Recipe Works Chicken broth is an essential ingredient in the kitchen, acting as a building block of flavor for soups, stews, sauces, and more. Making broth from scratch is a simple process of gently cooking bones and aromatics in water, but doing it on the stovetop can be a tedious task that requires constant monitoring. With sous vide, there is no need for broth vigilance, as cooking in a precise, temperature-controlled environment ensures flavor extraction from the chicken bones without evaporation. We found that chicken wings worked best to produce a remarkably clear broth with unadulterated chicken flavor. The simple additions of onion, bay leaves, and a little salt complemented the chicken flavor without overpowering it. If you want more roasted chicken flavor, try our Rich Brown Chicken Stock variation. To fit all of the ingredients in one bag, this recipe calls for 2-gallon zipper-lock freezer bags. If you do not have 2-gallon bags, simply divide the ingredients between two 1-gallon bags. Be sure to double bag the mixture to protect against seam failure. Note that this recipe requires a 12-quart container.

2½ pounds (1.1 kilograms) chicken wings, cut into 2-inch pieces
1 large onion (450 grams), chopped
8 cups (1.8 kilograms) water
3 bay leaves (0.5 grams)
1 teaspoon (6 grams) salt

1 Using sous vide circulator, bring water to 185°F/85°C in 12-quart container.

2 Place all ingredients in 2-gallon zipper-lock freezer bag and seal bag, pressing out as much air as possible. Place bag in second 2-gallon zipper-lock freezer bag and seal. Gently lower bag into prepared water bath until chicken is fully submerged, and then clip top corner of bag to side of water bath container, allowing remaining air bubbles to rise to top of bag. Reopen 1 corner of zipper, release remaining air bubbles, and reseal bag. Cover and cook for at least 4 hours or up to 5 hours.

3 Strain broth through fine-mesh strainer into large container; discard solids. Let broth settle for 5 to 10 minutes, then skim excess fat from surface using wide, shallow spoon or fat separator. Let cool, then transfer to airtight container and refrigerate or freeze until ready to use.

Variation

Rich Brown Chicken Stock
Heat 1 tablespoon (14 grams) vegetable oil in Dutch oven over medium-high heat until just smoking. Pat chicken dry with paper towels. Brown half of chicken, about 5 minutes; transfer to bowl. Repeat with remaining chicken; transfer to bowl. Add onion to fat left in pot and cook over medium heat until softened, about 5 minutes. Stir in 1 cup (225 grams) water, scraping up any browned bits; transfer to bowl with chicken. Proceed with step 2 as directed.

All-Purpose Beef Broth

YIELD MAKES ABOUT 3 QUARTS (2.7 KILOGRAMS)

Sous Vide Temperature 185°F/85°C

Sous Vide Time 4 to 5 hours

Active Cooking Time 45 minutes

To Make Ahead Broth can be refrigerated for up to 4 days or frozen for up to 2 months.

Why This Recipe Works Making beef broth at home can feel like a chore reserved for overachievers, often requiring roasted bones and hours of watching a simmering pot on the stovetop. Even though homemade broth tastes better than the store-bought boxed version, it rarely seems worth the effort. However, with sous vide cooking, broth is a set-it-and-forget-it breeze. To make life even easier, we ditched beef bones and turned to ground beef—its increased surface area enables more beef flavor to be absorbed by the liquid. We bumped up the meaty under-tones in the broth further by cooking earthy mushrooms with the traditional *mirepoix* ingredients, along with tomato paste, red wine, and a little soy sauce for background umami notes. We bagged up the beef and aromatics with water and cooked the mixture sous vide for 4 hours, giving us a well-rounded, no-fuss broth. To fit all of the ingredients in one bag, this recipe calls for 2-gallon zipper-lock freezer bags. If you do not have 2-gallon bags, simply divide the ingredients between two 1-gallon bags. Be sure to double bag the mixture to protect against seam failure. Note that this recipe requires a 12-quart container.

1 tablespoon (14 grams) vegetable oil

1 pound (450 grams) white mushrooms, trimmed and halved

1 onion (227 grams), chopped

1 carrot (75 grams), peeled and chopped

1 celery rib (70 grams), chopped

3 tablespoons (45 grams) tomato paste

1½ pounds (680 grams) 85 percent lean ground beef

¾ cup (170 grams) dry red wine

3 quarts (2.7 kilograms) water

2 tablespoons (30 grams) soy sauce

3 bay leaves (0.5 grams)

1 Using sous vide circulator, bring water to 185°F/85°C in 12-quart container.

2 Heat oil in 12-inch skillet over medium heat until shimmering. Add mushrooms, onion, carrot, and celery, and cook until softened, 5 to 10 minutes. Add tomato paste and continue to cook until mixture is dry, about 5 minutes.

3 Stir in ground beef and cook, breaking up any large pieces with wooden spoon, until no longer pink, about 5 minutes. Stir in wine, scraping up any browned bits, and cook until nearly evaporated, 5 to 7 minutes. Transfer to 2-gallon zipper-lock freezer bag. Add water, soy sauce, and bay leaves to bag and stir to combine. Seal bag, pressing out as much air as possible. Place bag in second 2-gallon zipper-lock freezer bag and seal. Gently lower bag into prepared water bath until broth mixture is fully submerged, and then clip top corner of bag to side of water bath container, allowing remaining air bubbles to rise to top of bag. Reopen 1 corner of zipper, release remaining air bubbles, and reseal bag. Cover and cook for at least 4 hours or up to 5 hours.

4 Strain broth through fine-mesh strainer into large container; discard solids. Let broth settle for 5 to 10 minutes, then skim excess fat from surface using wide, shallow spoon or fat separator. Let cool, then transfer to airtight container and refrigerate or freeze until ready to use.

Vegetable Broth

YIELD **MAKES ABOUT 3 QUARTS (2.7 KILOGRAMS)**
Sous Vide Temperature 185°F/85°C
Sous Vide Time 3 to 4 hours
Active Cooking Time 25 minutes

To Make Ahead Broth can be refrigerated for up to 4 days or frozen for up to 2 months.

Why This Recipe Works Vegetable broth needs to be cooked gently to bring out the subtle flavors of its ingredients, and sous vide is a perfect method for the task. For this recipe, we combined classic broth-base vegetables—onion, carrot, and celery—with mushrooms (for earthiness), tomato (for acidity), and scallions (for an allium boost). Thyme, bay leaves, and peppercorns provided herbal background notes. By slicing the vegetables thin we were able to maximize the amount of surface area for flavor extraction, which also cut down our cooking time. The resulting broth is full of clean, vegetal flavor. To avoid a cloudy broth, do not press on solids when straining. To fit all of the ingredients in one bag, this recipe calls for 2-gallon zipper-lock freezer bags. If you do not have 2-gallon bags, simply divide the ingredients between two 1-gallon bags. Be sure to double bag the mixture to protect against seam failure. Note that this recipe requires a 12-quart container.

7 cups (1.6 kilograms) water

2 pounds onions (900 grams), halved and sliced thin

3 carrots (225 grams), peeled and sliced thin

2 celery ribs (120 grams), sliced thin

1 tomato (175 grams), cored and chopped

5 ounces (145 grams) white mushrooms, trimmed and sliced thin

4 scallions (50 grams), sliced thin

8 sprigs (2 grams) fresh thyme

1 teaspoon (3 grams) black peppercorns

½ teaspoon (3 grams) salt

3 bay leaves (0.5 grams)

1 Using sous vide circulator, bring water to 185°F/85°C in 12-quart container.

2 Combine all ingredients in 2-gallon zipper-lock freezer bag and seal bag, pressing out as much air as possible. Place bag in second 2-gallon zipper-lock freezer bag and seal. Gently lower bag into prepared water bath until vegetables are fully submerged, and then clip top corner of bag to side of water bath container, allowing remaining air bubbles to rise to top of bag. Reopen 1 corner of zipper, release remaining air bubbles, and reseal bag. Cover and cook for at least 3 hours or up to 4 hours.

3 Strain broth through fine-mesh strainer into large container; discard solids. Let cool, then transfer to airtight containers and refrigerate or freeze until ready to use.

Spicy Rosemary-Chile Oil

YIELD 1 CUP (225 GRAMS)
Sous Vide Temperature 150°F/65.5°C
Sous Vide Time 2 to 3 hours
Active Cooking Time 20 minutes

To Make Ahead Oil can be refrigerated for up to 1 week. Bring to room temperature before serving.

Why This Recipe Works Many of the grassy, fruity, nutty, spicy, and funky aromas in food—aromas that are responsible for much deliciousness, we must say— dissolve much more readily in oil than in water. For this recipe, we took advantage of the aroma-grabbing qualities of olive oil and created a sous vide infusion. The moderate heat of the water bath helps to quickly extract a ton of herbal flavor from fresh rosemary and subtle heat from red pepper flakes and smoked paprika. Plus, by containing the infusion in a sous vide bag, there is no risk of losing the volatile aroma compounds found in the extra-virgin olive oil either, which lends its characteristic fruity flavor to the infusion. This is a great item to keep on hand for spicing up hummus, bruschetta, or pasta—or drizzling over roasted meats, fish, or poultry. To prevent any risk of bacterial growth, store this oil in the refrigerator.

1 cup (225 grams) extra-virgin olive oil
⅓ cup (12 grams) fresh rosemary leaves
1 tablespoon (6 grams) red pepper flakes
1 teaspoon (2 grams) smoked paprika

1 Using sous vide circulator, bring water to 150°F/65.5°C in 7-quart container.

2 Combine all ingredients in 1-gallon zipper-lock freezer bag. Seal bag, pressing out as much air as possible. Gently lower bag into prepared water bath, and then clip top corner of bag to side of water bath container, allowing remaining air bubbles to rise to top of bag. Reopen 1 corner of zipper, release remaining air bubbles, and reseal bag. Cover and cook for at least 2 hours or up to 3 hours.

3 Strain oil through fine-mesh strainer into airtight container; discard solids. Let cool slightly, then refrigerate until ready to use.

Variation

Thyme–Black Pepper Oil
Substitute ⅓ cup (10 grams) fresh thyme leaves and 1 tablespoon (10 grams) toasted and cracked black peppercorns for rosemary, red pepper flakes, and smoked paprika.

Raspberry Syrup

YIELD 1 CUP (225 GRAMS)
Sous Vide Temperature 140°F/60°C
Sous Vide Time 2 to 3 hours
Active Cooking Time 25 minutes

To Make Ahead Syrup can be refrigerated for up to 1 week.

Why This Recipe Works Extracting flavor from ingredients with the help of heat is an integral part of cooking. High-temperature cooking methods are ideal for coaxing the maximum amount of flavor from meat and bones and vegetables for making broth (see pages 181, 183, and 184), but it can be problematic when working with delicate ingredients. Berries and citrus fruits, for example, quickly lose their vibrant, fresh flavor when cooked with high heat. With sous vide, we were able to treat these ingredients very gently, extracting their flavor at a much lower temperature and without evaporation, which in turn delivered a more natural-tasting result. This is particularly useful for making flavored syrups for mixing into cocktails as well as nonalcoholic beverages. For this recipe, we used raspberries, sugar, and water to produce a syrup that tasted of incredibly fresh raspberries, with no hint of artificial raspberry candy lurking in the background. Use this syrup in our Raspberry Lime Rickey (page 193) and use the grapefruit variation in our Grapefruit Paloma (page 190). Try the ginger syrup in cocktails such as a Moscow Mule or Dark and Stormy, or use it to spice up traditional lemonade. And you have probably had pomegranate syrup in drinks before but know it by its other name: grenadine. Unfortunately, nowadays most commercially produced grenadine is just simple syrup with added food coloring. We definitely recommend making the real deal for a better Shirley Temple. Either fresh or frozen raspberries can be used in this recipe; however, we prefer frozen raspberries since they produce a more vibrantly colored syrup.

½ cup (113 grams) sugar
½ cup (113 grams) warm tap water
8 ounces (225 grams) frozen raspberries

1 Using sous vide circulator, bring water to 140°F/60°C in 7-quart container.

2 Whisk sugar and warm water together in bowl until sugar has dissolved. Combine sugar mixture and raspberries in 1-gallon zipper-lock freezer bag. Seal bag, pressing out as much air as possible. Gently lower bag into prepared water bath until raspberries are fully submerged, and then clip top corner of bag to side of water bath container, allowing remaining air bubbles to rise to top of bag. Reopen 1 corner of zipper, release remaining air bubbles, and reseal bag. Cover and cook raspberries for at least 2 hours or up to 3 hours.

3 Set fine-mesh strainer over large bowl and line with double layer of cheesecloth. Pour raspberry mixture into prepared strainer and let sit, without pressing on solids, until all liquid has passed through cheesecloth, about 5 minutes; discard solids. Transfer syrup to airtight container, let cool slightly, then refrigerate until ready to use.

Variations
Grapefruit Syrup
Substitute ½ cup (120 grams) grapefruit juice for water and 8 to 10 2-inch strips (13 grams) grapefruit zest for raspberries.

Pomegranate Syrup
Substitute pomegranate seeds for raspberries.

Spicy Ginger Syrup
Increase sugar to 1 cup (226 grams). Substitute ¼ cup (64 grams) grated fresh ginger and ½ teaspoon (1 gram) ground ginger for raspberries.

Grapefruit Paloma

YIELD **MAKES 4 COCKTAILS**
Sous Vide Temperature 140°F/60°C
Sous Vide Time 2 to 3 hours
Active Cooking Time 30 minutes

To Make Ahead Tequila mixture can be refrigerated for up to 4 hours.

Why This Recipe Works In the world of Mexican mixology, the margarita casts a pretty big shadow. But there are plenty of cocktails that are worthy of their own time in the lime (and tequila) light, and the paloma is at the top of that list. Traditionally, the paloma is a simple drink prepared by mixing tequila, fresh lime juice, and grapefruit-flavored soda. It is served on the rocks, and like a margarita, often comes with a salted rim and a lime wedge. For our own version, we wanted to amp up the natural flavor of grapefruit by ditching the artificial-tasting soda and replacing it with a combination of tart fresh grapefruit juice and our sous vide Grapefruit Syrup (page 188). The syrup, made with both grapefruit juice and zest, provided sweetness with subtle background floral notes. A little lime juice, a healthy amount of tequila, and a pinch of salt balanced out the base for our paloma. Top it off with a splash of seltzer for a refreshing drink that will put you in a summer state of mind, no matter what time of year it is.

1 cup (240 grams) blanco tequila

½ cup (136 grams) Grapefruit Syrup (page 188)

½ cup (120 grams) grapefruit juice, plus grapefruit slices for serving

¼ cup (60 grams) lime juice

⅛ teaspoon salt

1 cup (225 grams) seltzer or club soda

1 Stir tequila, grapefruit syrup, grapefruit juice, lime juice, and salt in 4-cup liquid measuring cup until salt has dissolved.

2 For each cocktail: Fill 10-ounce glass with ice. Add ½ cup plus 1 tablespoon (135 grams) tequila mixture and ¼ cup (56 grams) seltzer and gently stir to combine. Garnish with grapefruit slices before serving.

Raspberry Lime Rickey

YIELD **MAKES 4 DRINKS**
Sous Vide Temperature 140°F/60°C
Sous Vide Time 2 to 3 hours
Active Cooking Time 30 minutes

To Make Ahead Raspberry mixture can be refrigerated for up to 4 hours.

Why This Recipe Works The raspberry lime rickey is a classic holdover from the soda fountains of the Prohibition era, and it stands as one of the OG "mocktails." Taking inspiration from its boozy antecedent, the gin rickey, the original nonalcoholic version was a tart mixture of lime juice, simple syrup, and seltzer. In New England, raspberry flavor became a common addition. The result: the bright red raspberry lime rickey. Unfortunately, old-school soda-jerk techniques for from-scratch fruit syrups went out of fashion, due in part to the proliferation of mass-produced bottled soda. These days it can be hard to find a raspberry lime rickey that actually tastes of raspberries; most are made with the artificial red flavoring associated with commercial frozen treats and lollipops. We decided to change that by making our own version using our sous vide Raspberry Syrup (page 188). The result is bright and refreshing; the acidity of fresh lime juice pairs well with the sweet, real, botanical raspberry flavor.

¾ cup (200 grams) Raspberry Syrup (page 188)
¼ cup (60 grams) lime juice (2 limes), plus lime slices for serving
3 cups (675 grams) seltzer or club soda

1 Combine raspberry syrup and lime juice in 2-cup liquid measuring cup.

2 For each drink: Fill 12-ounce glass with ice. Add ¼ cup (60 grams) raspberry mixture and ¾ cup (170 grams) seltzer and gently stir to combine. Garnish with lime slice and serve.

Sichuan Bloody Mary

YIELD MAKES 6 COCKTAILS
Sous Vide Temperature 149°F/65°C
Sous Vide Time 30 to 40 minutes
Active Time 1 hour

To Make Ahead Vodka mixture can be refrigerated for up to 1 week. Tomato juice mixture can be refrigerated for up to 4 hours.

Why This Recipe Works Sichuan cuisine may be famous for its use of fiery chili oil, but the ingredient that makes Sichuan dishes unique isn't a spicy chile. And despite their name, Sichuan peppercorns aren't even peppercorns. They're actually the dried seed husks from a small Chinese citrus tree called the prickly ash. Instead of the burn experienced from the capsaicin compound found in chiles, Sichuan peppercorns contribute a unique tingling or buzzing sensation in the mouth, not unlike how it feels to sip a carbonated beverage. The tingling is caused by a pungent compound called sanshool, which acts on receptors in the mouth that usually respond to touch. Spicy and numbing Sichuan chili oil is known as *má là*, as it combines Sichuan peppercorns (*má*) and chiles (*là*). We wanted to bring that numbing heat to a brunch cocktail, the Bloody Mary. A good Bloody Mary is all about balancing sweet, spicy, and savory elements in a drink that keeps you coming back for more. The classic source of umami in a Bloody Mary is Worcestershire sauce, which gets its savoriness from anchovies. Here we replaced it with two potent sources of meatiness: oyster sauce and broad bean chili paste. And to deliver the mouth-numbing effects of Sichuan peppercorns, we infused just enough of them into the vodka to create a slow-building mouth buzz. Campbell's makes our favorite tomato juice. If your chili paste is particularly chunky, you may need to strain the tomato juice mixture in step 4 before proceeding with the recipe. For an even more impressive cocktail, garnish with skewered Chinese sausage (*lop cheong*), water chestnuts, pickled vegetables, and/or the sous vide shrimp from our Shrimp Cocktail (page 119).

1 cup plus 2 tablespoons (250 grams) vodka
1½ teaspoons (2 grams) Sichuan peppercorns
3¾ cups (930 grams) tomato juice, chilled
¼ cup (60 grams) Asian broad bean chili paste
3 tablespoons (54 grams) oyster sauce
2 tablespoons (30 grams) lemon juice
1 tablespoon (18 grams) rice vinegar
½ teaspoon (3 grams) salt
Celery ribs
Lemon wedges

1 Using sous vide circulator, bring water to 149°F/65°C in 7-quart container.

2 Combine vodka and peppercorns in 1-quart zipper-lock freezer bag and seal bag, pressing out as much air as possible. Gently lower bag into prepared water bath until vodka is fully submerged, and then clip top corner of bag to side of water bath container, allowing remaining air bubbles to rise to top of bag. Reopen 1 corner of zipper, release remaining air bubbles, and reseal bag. Cover and cook for 30 minutes. Taste vodka. It should be assertively mouth-numbing. If it is not, return bag to water bath and cook for up to 10 minutes longer.

3 Strain vodka through fine-mesh strainer into airtight container; discard peppercorns. Let cool slightly, then refrigerate until completely chilled, about 30 minutes.

4 Whisk tomato juice, chili paste, oyster sauce, lemon juice, vinegar, and salt in 8-cup liquid measuring cup until chili paste and salt have dissolved.

5 For each cocktail: Fill 10-ounce glass with ice. Combine ¾ cup (180 grams) tomato juice mixture, 3 tablespoons (42 grams) peppercorn-infused vodka, and ¼ cup (36 grams) ice in cocktail shaker and vigorously shake for 30 seconds. Strain into prepared glass, garnish with celery rib and lemon wedge, and serve.

DESSERTS

Sous vide . . . desserts? Yes, you read that correctly. You can sous vide dessert. Not all dessert. You cannot sous vide cake or pie or cookies. As baking expert Stella Parks wrote on Serious Eats: "Desserts need to expand, rise, evaporate, reduce, brown, crisp, and so many other things that just aren't going to happen in a steamy bag." But you can sous vide *some* desserts—and they're worth it.

What it comes down to is choice. Choose the correct dessert, and you get to make something delicious that comes with the guarantee of the sous vide technique. Through our testing, we found that sous vide is most effective with creamy, custardy desserts—from pudding to ice cream—and fruit-based desserts.

Speaking of creamy custards: They're a good place to start (page 200).

Custards excel in a sous vide environment. Why? The key to creamy, tender custards is to cook them gently and precisely. This way the egg proteins, interacting with the milk and sugar, unfurl and set *just so*—not grainy and not too firm. On the stovetop, heat comes from the bottom of the pan, so you're pretty much guaranteed to have uneven cooking when making custard. Constant whisking or stirring is required to ameliorate this problem. Plus, if the heat is too high, there is the risk of scorching, evaporation throwing off the ratio of the recipe, or curdling the custard. Sous vide is a hands-free solution. We found that the ideal temperature for light and creamy custards is 180 degrees Fahrenheit/82 degrees Celsius. We use this to great effect in our Vanilla Bean Ice Cream (page 200) and Crème Brûlée (page 203).

Puddings and cheesecake bites (you know, the kind without the crust) also do well sous vide. While chocolate pots de crème are traditionally cooked in ramekins arranged in a water bath in the oven, ours (page 204) just go straight in to swim (in Mason jars, of course). After chilling in the refrigerator, we like to serve them with just a bit of flaked sea salt on top. Our Upside-Down Cheesecake Cups (page 207) are also cooked in Mason jars in a water bath—and then topped with a crunchy graham cracker crumble for a little twist on the traditional approach. The starch in the rice for our Coconut Rice Pudding with Mango and Basil (page 209) breaks down slowly and steadily with the gentle heat of sous vide, resulting in a supercreamy pudding.

Like vegetables, firm fruits benefit from the low, slow cooking of sous vide. In our Miso-Caramel Apple Crunch (page 210), we set about trying to create a warm apple dessert with firm but tender fruit, awash in the flavors of apple cider, brown sugar, warm spices, and miso (which adds a bit of umami nuttiness). Cooking the apples at 180°F/82°C allows us to keep them just below the temperature in which they completely break down. A peanut-oat topping adds a sophisticated crunch.

Most traditional recipes for poached pears call for simmering the fruit in a loose and syrupy base on the stovetop. We cook our Red Wine–Poached Pears (page 212) sealed in a bag with a thick, reduced sauce—perfectly calibrated for the flavorful liquid released by the pears during cooking. For a little texture, we serve them with whipped sour cream and candied pistachios.

Our advice? When you invite people over for dinner and you tell them that you made sous vide cheesecake for dessert, savor the dubious expression on their faces. You are about to prove them so, so wrong.

Dulce de Leche

YIELD 14 OUNCES (400 GRAMS)
Sous Vide Temperature 185°F/85°C
Sous Vide Time 12 to 16 hours
Active Cooking Time 20 minutes

To Make Ahead Dulce de leche can be refrigerated for up to 7 days.

Why This Recipe Works *Dulce de leche* translates to "sweet milk." A staple of the Latin American pantry, it is used as a sweetener for candies, cakes, ice creams, cookies, churros, and as a topping for waffles and pancakes—even stirred straight into coffee. Traditionally, it is made by slowly cooking milk and sugar together for hours, until the mixture is light brown and possesses a caramel-like flavor. These days, most dulce de leche is made by cooking unopened cans of sweetened condensed milk in a pot of boiling water or even in a pressure cooker. Textures vary from thick and fudgy to runny and smooth, but the principle remains the same: Heat accelerates the Maillard reaction, a chemical reaction between amino acids and reducing sugars, that gives many foods their distinctive browned, cooked flavor. This reaction happens quickly at high temperatures (as with searing a steak) but also occurs at lower temperatures— as low as 150°F/65.5°C. At these lower temperatures, it just takes more time. We decided to take advantage of this low, slow reaction by cooking our dulce de leche sous vide. Our version cooks for 12 hours at 185°F/85°C. The benefit? You don't have to worry about cooking a can lined with BPA, or, worse, risk having the can explode due to heat. And because we cook our dulce de leche in Mason jars, you can stir in whatever flavorings (vanilla, salt, cinnamon, just for starters) that you want before cooking. The seeds from a vanilla bean give the dulce de leche the deepest flavor, but 1 teaspoon (5 grams) vanilla extract can be substituted. You will need one 16-ounce Mason jar for this recipe. Be careful not to overtighten the jar before placing it in the water bath; it can cause the glass to crack.

1 vanilla bean (2 grams)
1 14-ounce can (397 grams) sweetened condensed milk
¼ teaspoon (1.5 grams) salt

1 Using sous vide circulator, bring water to 185°F/85°C in 7-quart container.

2 Cut vanilla bean in half lengthwise. Using tip of paring knife, scrape out seeds; reserve vanilla bean for another use. Combine vanilla seeds, condensed milk, and salt in 16-ounce Mason jar and seal; do not overtighten lid. Gently lower jar into water bath until fully submerged. Cover and cook for at least 12 hours or up to 16 hours. Serve warm or at room temperature.

Vanilla Bean Ice Cream

YIELD MAKES ABOUT 1 QUART (900 GRAMS)
Sous Vide Temperature 180°F/82°C
Sous Vide Time 1 to 1½ hours
Active Cooking Time 50 minutes, plus chilling and churning time

To Make Ahead Ice cream can be frozen for up to 2 weeks.

Why This Recipe Works When you think of sous vide cooking, ice cream is probably not the first thing that comes to mind. What does a hot water bath have to do with a frozen dessert? Well, before the freezing happens, an ice cream base often needs to be cooked. This cooking process denatures dairy proteins, which then capture free-roaming water in the base, resulting in smoother and less icy ice cream. Precise temperature control is important when cooking the base, especially with custard-based ice creams that include egg yolks. If the heat is too high, there is the risk of curdling the yolks. With sous vide, we eliminated potential problems and simplified the process. We just combined the ingredients and circulated them for an hour. We further combated iciness by incorporating nonfat milk powder and corn syrup, which help by trapping water in the base, thus preventing the formation of large ice crystals. The base is "cured" overnight in the refrigerator to give the dairy proteins more opportunities to capture water. A vanilla bean gives the ice cream the deepest flavor, but 2 teaspoons (10 grams) vanilla extract can be substituted. Be sure to double bag ice cream base to protect against seam failure. If using a canister-style ice cream maker, be sure to freeze the empty canister for at least 24 hours and preferably 48 hours before churning. For self-refrigerating ice cream makers, prechill the canister by running the machine for 10 minutes before pouring in the custard.

1 vanilla bean (2 grams)
1½ cups (375 grams) whole milk
1½ cups (375 grams) heavy cream
¾ cup (75 grams) nonfat dry milk powder
½ cup (100 grams) sugar
¼ cup (85 grams) light corn syrup
6 large egg yolks (90 grams)
¼ teaspoon (1.5 grams) salt

1 Using sous vide circulator, bring water to 180°F/82°C in 7-quart container.

2 Cut vanilla bean in half lengthwise. Using tip of paring knife, scrape out seeds. Whisk vanilla bean and seeds, milk, cream, milk powder, sugar, corn syrup, egg yolks, and salt in large bowl until sugar has dissolved. Transfer mixture to 1-gallon zipper-lock freezer bag. Seal bag, pressing out as much air as possible. Place bag in second 1-gallon freezer bag and seal. Gently lower bag into prepared water bath until ice cream base is fully submerged, and then clip top corner of bag to side of water bath container, allowing remaining air bubbles to rise to top of bag. Reopen 1 corner of zipper, release remaining air bubbles, and reseal bag. Cover and cook for at least 1 hour or up to 1½ hours.

3 Fill large bowl halfway with ice and water. Transfer zipper-lock bag to ice bath and let sit until chilled, about 30 minutes. Strain custard through fine-mesh strainer into airtight container; discard solids. Refrigerate for at least 12 hours or up to 24 hours.

4 Churn custard in ice cream maker until mixture resembles thick soft serve ice cream and registers 21°F/–6°C. Transfer to clean airtight container and freeze until hard, at least 2 hours, before serving.

Variations

Chocolate Ice Cream
Substitute ¼ cup (20 grams) cocoa powder and 1 teaspoon (1 gram) instant espresso powder for vanilla bean.

Thai Iced Tea Ice Cream
Substitute 2 tablespoons (10 grams) Thai iced tea mix for vanilla bean.

Crème Brûlée

YIELD **SERVES 4**
Sous Vide Temperature 180°F/82°C
Sous Vide Time 60 to 75 minutes
Active Cooking Time 40 minutes, plus resting and chilling time

Make Ahead Strategy Crème brûlée can be refrigerated for up to 3 days.

Why This Recipe Works While sous vide is not the answer for most baked desserts, it most definitely is when it comes to custard. Conventional custard recipes require care and attention with temperature-sensitive steps like tempering eggs with the hot dairy to avoid curdling and arranging a water bath in the oven. The precise temperature control of sous vide cooking makes custardy desserts like crème brûlée easier to execute. We whisked the base together, portioned it into Mason jars, and circulated for one hour. It was that easy. Once the custards finished cooking, we chilled them before the finale of a torched sugar topping. We found that crunchy turbinado sugar made for a satisfyingly crackly crust. A vanilla bean gives the crème brûlée the deepest flavor, but 1 teaspoon (5 grams) vanilla extract can be substituted. For the caramelized sugar crust, we recommend turbinado or Demerara sugar; regular granulated sugar will work, but use only 1 scant teaspoon (4 grams) for each Mason jar portion. You will need four 8-ounce widemouthed Mason jars and a kitchen torch for this recipe. Be careful not to overtighten the jars before placing them in the water bath; it can cause the glass to crack.

½ vanilla bean (1 gram)
2 cups (500 grams) heavy cream
5 large egg yolks (75 grams)
⅓ cup (65 grams) granulated sugar
  Pinch salt
4 teaspoons (20 grams) turbinado or Demerara sugar

1 Using sous vide circulator, bring water to 180°F/82°C in 7-quart container.

2 Cut vanilla bean in half lengthwise. Using tip of paring knife, scrape out seeds. Whisk vanilla bean and seeds, cream, egg yolks, granulated sugar, and salt in bowl until sugar has dissolved. Strain custard through fine-mesh strainer into 4-cup liquid measuring cup, then divide evenly among four 8-ounce widemouthed Mason jars. Gently tap jars on counter to remove any air bubbles, then seal; do not overtighten lids.

3 Gently lower jars into water bath until fully submerged. Cover and cook for at least 60 minutes or up to 75 minutes.

4 Transfer jars to wire rack and let cool to room temperature, about 1 hour. Refrigerate until chilled, at least 4 hours.

5 Gently blot away condensation on top of custards using paper towels. Sprinkle each custard with 1 teaspoon (5 grams) turbinado sugar. Tilt and tap each jar to distribute sugar evenly, then wipe rims of jars clean. Ignite torch and caramelize sugar by sweeping flame of torch from perimeter of custard toward middle, keeping flame about 2 inches above jar, until sugar is bubbling and deep golden brown. Let sit for 5 minutes to allow sugar crust to harden, then serve.

Desserts

Chocolate Pots de Crème

YIELD **SERVES 6**
Sous Vide Temperature 167°F/75°C
Sous Vide Time 60 to 75 minutes
Active Cooking Time 25 minutes, plus resting and chilling time

Make Ahead Strategy Pots de crème can be refrigerated for up to 3 days.

Why This Recipe Works We like to think of pots de crème as chocolate pudding that has studied abroad in France. It's rich, decadent, and with the help of sous vide, super-simple to make. Traditional cooking methods call for managing ramekins in a water bath in the oven or carefully monitoring the temperature of a pot on the stovetop. With sous vide, all we needed to do was whip up our chocolate custard base (a small amount of instant espresso powder ensured deep chocolate flavor), divide it among Mason jars, and leave the jars in the water bath for one hour. Once they finished cooking, we chilled the pots de crème in the refrigerator, and then they were ready to go. We prefer pots de crème made with 60 percent cacao bittersweet chocolate (our favorite brands are Ghirardelli and Callebaut). You will need six 4-ounce widemouthed Mason jars for this recipe. Be careful not to overtighten the jars before placing them in the water bath; it can cause the glass to crack. Serve with lightly sweetened whipped cream, chocolate shavings, and/or flake sea salt.

6 ounces (170 grams) bittersweet chocolate, chopped
1¼ cups (310 grams) heavy cream
3 tablespoons (38 grams) sugar
¼ teaspoon (0.5 grams) instant espresso powder
⅛ teaspoon (1 gram) salt
3 large egg yolks (45 grams)
1½ teaspoons (8 grams) vanilla extract

1 Using sous vide circulator, bring water to 167°F/75°C in 7-quart container.

2 Microwave chocolate, cream, sugar, espresso powder, and salt in bowl at 50 percent power, stirring occasionally, until chocolate is melted and mixture is thoroughly combined, 2 to 4 minutes. Whisk in egg yolks and vanilla until combined.

3 Strain chocolate mixture through fine-mesh strainer into 4-cup liquid measuring cup, then divide evenly among six 4-ounce widemouthed Mason jars. Gently tap jars on counter to remove any air bubbles, then seal; do not overtighten lids.

4 Gently lower jars into water bath until fully submerged. Cover and cook for at least 60 minutes or up to 75 minutes.

5 Transfer jars to wire rack and let cool to room temperature, about 1 hour. Refrigerate until chilled, at least 4 hours. Let pots de crème sit at room temperature for 20 minutes and serve.

Upside-Down Cheesecake Cups

YIELD SERVES 8
Sous Vide Temperature 176°F/80°C
Sous Vide Time 60 to 75 minutes
Active Cooking Time 30 minutes, plus resting and chilling time

To Make Ahead Cheesecake cups can be refrigerated for up to 3 days. Graham cracker crumble can be stored at room temperature for up to 3 days.

Why This Recipe Works Cheesecake is often a baking project reserved for special occasions. But we found that using sous vide (and Mason jars) turned this decadent cake into a streamlined dessert. Our upside-down cheesecake cups are everything we love about cheesecake without the hassle (plus cute little jars). The cheesecake base came together in a snap in the food processor; sour cream provided a little tang to balance out the sweetness of cream cheese, sugar, and vanilla. We transformed the traditional graham cracker crust into a quick stovetop crumble topping. Sharing is optional. You will need eight 4-ounce widemouthed Mason jars for this recipe. Be careful not to overtighten the jars before placing them in the water bath; it can cause the glass to crack. Serve with fresh berries if desired.

- 3 whole graham crackers (45 grams), broken into 1-inch pieces
- 1 tablespoon (14 grams) unsalted butter
- 1½ teaspoons (5 grams) plus ⅔ cup (140 grams) sugar
- ¼ teaspoon (1 gram) ground cinnamon
  Salt
- 16 ounces (450 grams) cream cheese, softened
- 1 teaspoon (5 grams) vanilla extract
- ¼ cup (60 grams) sour cream
- 2 large eggs (110 grams), room temperature

1 Using sous vide circulator, bring water to 176°F/80°C in 7-quart container.

2 Pulse graham crackers in food processor to fine crumbs, about 15 pulses. Melt butter in 10-inch nonstick skillet over medium-low heat. Stir in graham cracker crumbs, 1½ teaspoons (5 grams) sugar, cinnamon, and pinch salt. Cook, stirring frequently, until fragrant, about 1 minute; transfer graham cracker topping to small bowl and set aside for serving.

3 Wipe food processor bowl clean. Process cream cheese, vanilla, ¼ teaspoon (1.5 grams) salt, and remaining ⅔ cup (140 grams) sugar until combined, about 15 seconds, scraping down sides of bowl as needed. Add sour cream and eggs and process until just incorporated, about 15 seconds; do not overprocess. Strain mixture through fine-mesh strainer into 4-cup liquid measuring cup, then divide evenly among eight 4-ounce widemouthed Mason jars. Gently tap jars on counter to remove any air bubbles, then seal; do not overtighten lids.

4 Gently lower jars into water bath until fully submerged. Cover and cook for at least 60 minutes or up to 75 minutes.

5 Transfer jars to wire rack and let cool to room temperature, about 1 hour. Refrigerate until chilled, at least 4 hours. Let cheesecake cups sit at room temperature for 20 minutes, then sprinkle with graham cracker topping and serve.

Coconut Rice Pudding with Mango and Basil

YIELD **SERVES 6**
Sous Vide Temperature 200°F/93°C
Sous Vide Time 1½ hours to 2 hours
Active Cooking Time 25 minutes

To Make Ahead Pudding can be refrigerated for up to 5 days.

Why This Recipe Works Rice pudding is a classic dessert. Versions of this dish exist in nearly every part of the world—probably because it's so easy to make. All you need to do is cook rice, liquid, and sugar until the mixture is nice and soft and you're good to go. Rice is rich in starch that, when broken down, forms a gel in solution—and that translates to a creamy pudding. But since most rice puddings get cooked on the stovetop, there is a fair bit of intuition involved in nailing the perfect consistency. Stir too little and your pudding ends up lumpy. Use too much heat and you risk overreducing your pudding and scorching your saucepan. The amount of evaporation varies depending on the size of your pot, meaning the finished texture can vary. Making rice pudding sous vide removes all of the guesswork. There's no evaporation, resulting in a consistent texture every time. And because we were not cooking on the stovetop, there was no need to stir nonstop until the very end. We went with a Thai-inspired flavor profile that's heavy on coconut with a touch of ginger and cardamom. To give this dessert some crunch and variety, we topped our pudding with plenty of toasted coconut flakes, mango, and some fresh basil. Be sure to double bag the rice mixture to protect against seam failure.

2 cups (500 grams) whole milk
1 14-ounce can (400 grams) coconut milk
½ cup (100 grams) sugar
2 teaspoons (10 grams) vanilla extract
¼ teaspoon (1.5 grams) salt
¼ teaspoon (0.5 grams) ground cardamom
¼ teaspoon (0.5 grams) ground ginger
½ cup (100 grams) long-grain white rice
1 mango (284 grams), peeled, pitted, and cut into ¼-inch pieces
¾ cup (60 grams) sweetened flaked coconut, toasted
¼ cup (2 grams) shredded fresh basil

1 Using sous vide circulator, bring water to 200°F/93°C in 7-quart container.

2 Whisk milk, coconut milk, sugar, vanilla, salt, cardamom, and ginger in bowl until sugar has dissolved. Transfer milk mixture and rice to 1-gallon zipper-lock freezer bag. Seal bag, pressing out as much air as possible. Place bag in second 1-gallon zipper-lock freezer bag and seal. Gently lower bag into prepared water bath until rice is fully submerged, and then clip top corner of bag to side of water bath container, allowing remaining air bubbles to rise to top of bag. Reopen 1 corner of zipper, release remaining air bubbles, and reseal bag. Cover and cook for at least 1½ hours or up to 2 hours.

3 Transfer rice mixture to bowl and stir vigorously to break up any lumps of rice; discard any lumps that remain. Cover surface of pudding with plastic wrap and refrigerate until chilled, about 4 hours.

4 Stir pudding to recombine. Sprinkle individual portions with mango, coconut, and basil and serve.

Miso-Caramel Apple Crunch

YIELD SERVES 4 TO 6
Sous Vide Temperature 180°F/82°C
Sous Vide Time 30 to 45 minutes
Active Cooking Time 40 minutes

To Make Ahead Topping can be stored for up to 2 days. Apples can be rapidly chilled in ice bath (see page 13) and then refrigerated after step 4 for up to 2 days. To reheat, return zipper-lock bag to water bath set to 180°F/82°C for 15 minutes; proceed with step 5.

Why This Recipe Works Baked apples often end up mushy and overly sweet. We wanted to create a warm apple dessert with fruit that retained some of its texture and savory notes that balanced the sweetness. The strength and structure of pectin is the chief factor contributing to apple texture. As a general rule, the firmer the raw apple, the better it will retain its texture during cooking. We decided to use Granny Smith apples because along with their firm texture, they are high in calcium and acidity, which both reinforce pectin and allow the apples to hold up to cooking. Pectin begins to rapidly break down at 183°F/84°C, so we decided to cook our apples at 180°F/82°C, which allowed them to soften slightly without turning them to mush. Adding a mixture of apple cider, brown sugar, warm spices, and miso to the bag provided a bit of background umami notes. After cooking the apples, we emulsified butter into the cooking liquid to create a rich sauce. A simple peanut-oat topping provided a crunchy contrast to the apples. Serve with vanilla ice cream or whipped cream. Be sure to double bag the apples to protect against seam failure. Apples have a tendency to float when placed in a sous vide water bath, which can lead to uneven cooking. Use weights to make sure the apples are fully immersed during cooking (see page 14).

Topping

½ cup (80 grams) unsalted dry-roasted peanuts
½ cup (60 grams) all-purpose flour
¼ cup packed (50 grams) light brown sugar
¼ teaspoon (0.5 grams) ground cinnamon
¼ teaspoon (1.5 grams) salt
⅛ teaspoon (0.5 grams) ground nutmeg
5 tablespoons (70 grams) unsalted butter, melted and cooled
¾ cup (80 grams) old-fashioned rolled oats
2 tablespoons (28 grams) honey

Apples

½ cup (112 grams) apple cider
¼ cup packed (50 grams) light brown sugar
3 tablespoons (50 grams) white miso
¼ teaspoon (0.5 grams) ground cinnamon
⅛ teaspoon ground nutmeg
4 Granny Smith apples (200 grams each), peeled, cored, and halved
4 tablespoons (56 grams) unsalted butter, cut into 4 pieces

1 For the topping Adjust oven rack to upper-middle position and heat oven to 375°F/190°C. Pulse peanuts, flour, sugar, cinnamon, salt, and nutmeg in food processor until peanuts are finely chopped, about 10 pulses. Drizzle melted butter over top and pulse until mixture resembles crumbly wet sand, about 5 pulses. Add oats and honey and pulse until evenly incorporated, about 3 pulses.

2 Spread oat mixture evenly over parchment paper–lined rimmed baking sheet. Pinch mixture between your fingers into small pea-size pieces (some small loose bits are okay). Bake until golden brown, 8 to 12 minutes, rotating sheet halfway through baking; set aside for serving.

3 For the apples Using sous vide circulator, bring water to 180°F/82°C in 7-quart container.

4 Whisk cider, sugar, miso, cinnamon, and nutmeg together in small bowl. Transfer mixture and apples to 1-gallon zipper-lock freezer bag. Seal bag, pressing out as much air as possible. Place bag in second 1-gallon freezer bag and seal. Gently lower bag into prepared water bath, weight bag (page 14) until apples are fully submerged, and then clip top corner of bag to side of water bath container, allowing remaining air bubbles to rise to top of bag. Reopen 1 corner of zipper, release remaining air bubbles, and reseal bag. Cover and cook for at least 30 minutes or up to 45 minutes.

5 Using tongs, transfer apples to plate and tent with aluminum foil. Transfer cooking liquid to small saucepan, bring to simmer over medium heat, and cook until reduced to ½ cup, about 1 minute. Off heat, whisk in butter, one piece at a time, until fully incorporated. Transfer apples to individual serving bowls, spoon sauce over top, and sprinkle with peanut-oat topping. Serve.

Desserts

Red Wine–Poached Pears with Whipped Sour Cream and Candied Pistachios

YIELD SERVES 6
Sous Vide Temperature 176°F/80°C
Sous Vide Time 30 to 60 minutes
Active Cooking Time 30 minutes, plus resting and chilling time

To Make Ahead Pears can be refrigerated for up to 2 days.

Why This Recipe Works Old school is still cool. And when it comes to desserts, there are few dishes more retro than poached pears. This French dessert features just-ripe pears poached gently in an intensely sweet, boozy syrup. Served hot or cold, the fruit practically melts in your mouth, perfect with ice cream or crème fraîche. Typically, most recipes call for simmering pears in a loose, syrupy base. But stovetop simmering often results in mushy, overcooked fruit. Instead we started with a spicy red-wine sauce, which we add to the bag to cook with the pears sous vide. At 176°F/80°C, pectin breaks down at a moderate rate, which guarantees just-tender pears that aren't mushy. But cooking pears sous vide releases a lot of water, and because there was no evaporation in our cooking method, the syrup ended up watery and diluted. To compensate, we reduced our cooking liquid significantly at the beginning, so that the liquid released from the pears rehydrated the syrup to the perfect consistency. Since everything is in a bag already, it's easy to chill everything down. All you have to do is open the bag and serve. To give this dessert some textural contrast, we made a simple pistachio brittle. Some whipped sour cream added a bit of tang. Use a good-quality medium-bodied wine, such as a Côtes du Rhône or Pinot Noir, for this recipe. Be sure to double bag the pears to protect against seam failure. Pears have a tendency to float when placed in a sous vide water bath, which can lead to uneven cooking. Use weights to make sure the pears are fully immersed during cooking (see page 14).

Pears

- 1 vanilla bean (2 grams)
- 1 bottle (750 milliliters/750 grams) dry red wine
- ¾ cup (149 grams) sugar
- ½ teaspoon (2 grams) black peppercorns, cracked
- 6 whole cloves (1 gram)
- 1 cinnamon stick (3 grams)
- ⅛ teaspoon (1 gram) salt
- 6 ripe but firm Bosc or Bartlett pears (about 113 grams each), peeled, halved, and cored

Candied Pistachios

- ½ cup (65 grams) pistachios, chopped coarse
- 3 tablespoons (38 grams) sugar
- 1 tablespoon (18 grams) honey

Whipped Sour Cream

- ¼ cup (56 grams) heavy cream
- 1 tablespoon (12 grams) sugar
- ¼ cup (60 grams) sour cream

1 For the pears Using sous vide circulator, bring water to 176°F/80°C in 7-quart container.

2 Cut vanilla bean in half lengthwise. Using tip of paring knife, scrape out seeds. Bring vanilla bean and seeds, wine, sugar, peppercorns, cloves, cinnamon, and salt to simmer in 12-inch skillet over medium-high heat.

Cook, stirring occasionally, until mixture is reduced to ⅔ cup (180 grams), about 20 minutes. Strain mixture through fine-mesh strainer into bowl; discard solids. Let mixture cool slightly, about 2 minutes.

3 Place pears and wine mixture in 1-gallon zipper-lock freezer bag and seal, pressing out as much air as possible. Place bag in second 1-gallon zipper-lock freezer bag and seal. Gently lower bag into prepared water bath, weight bag (page 14) until pears are fully submerged, and then clip top corner of bag to side of water bath container, allowing remaining air bubbles to rise to top of bag. Reopen 1 corner of zipper, release remaining air bubbles, and reseal bag. Cover and cook for at least 30 minutes or up to 1 hour.

4 Transfer bag with pears to plate and let cool to room temperature, about 30 minutes. Refrigerate until chilled, about 4 hours.

5 For the candied pistachios Lightly grease rimmed baking sheet. Combine pistachios, sugar, and honey in 8-inch nonstick skillet. Cook over medium heat, stirring constantly, until pistachios are fragrant and sugar has melted and is light golden brown, 2 to 4 minutes. Off heat, stir mixture until pistachios are evenly coated with caramel, then quickly transfer to prepared sheet. Spread into thin, even layer and let cool completely, about 10 minutes. Break pistachios into bite-size pieces.

6 For the whipped sour cream Combine cream, sugar, and pinch (0.5 grams) salt in bowl. Using whisk, whip cream mixture to stiff peaks, 3 to 4 minutes. Whisk in sour cream until just combined.

7 Divide pears and syrup among individual serving bowls. Dollop whipped sour cream over top and sprinkle with candied pistachios.

Desserts

213

Conversions and Equivalents

Some say cooking is a science and an art. We would say that geography has a hand in it, too. Flours and sugars manufactured in the United Kingdom and elsewhere will feel and taste different from those manufactured in the United States. So we cannot promise that the loaf of bread you bake in Canada or England will taste the same as a loaf baked in the States, but we can offer guidelines for converting weights and measures. We also recommend that you rely on your instincts when making our recipes. Refer to the visual cues provided. If the dough hasn't "come together in a ball" as described, you may need to add more flour—even if the recipe doesn't tell you to. You be the judge.

The recipes in this book were developed using standard U.S. measures following U.S. government guidelines. For this book, we also developed using grams. The charts below offer equivalents for U.S. and metric measures. All conversions are approximate and have been rounded up or down to a whole number.

Example

1 teaspoon	=	4.9292 milliliters, rounded up to 5 milliliters
1 ounce	=	28.3495 grams, rounded down to 28 grams

Volume Conversions

U.S.	METRIC
1 teaspoon	5 milliliters
2 teaspoons	10 milliliters
1 tablespoon	15 milliliters
2 tablespoons	30 milliliters
¼ cup	59 milliliters
⅓ cup	79 milliliters
½ cup	118 milliliters
¾ cup	177 milliliters
1 cup	237 milliliters
1¼ cups	296 milliliters
1½ cups	355 milliliters
2 cups (1 pint)	473 milliliters
2½ cups	591 milliliters
3 cups	710 milliliters
4 cups (1 quart)	0.946 liter
1.06 quarts	1 liter
4 quarts (1 gallon)	3.8 liters

Weight Conversions

OUNCES	GRAMS
½	14
¾	21
1	28
1½	43
2	57
2½	71
3	85
3½	99
4	113
4½	128
5	142
6	170
7	198
8	225
9	255
10	283
12	340
16 (1 pound)	450

Conversions for Common Baking Ingredients

Baking is an exacting science. Because measuring by weight is far more accurate than measuring by volume, and thus more likely to produce reliable results, in our recipes we provide ounce measures in addition to cup measures for many ingredients. Refer to the chart below to convert these measures into grams.

INGREDIENT	OUNCES	GRAMS
Flour		
1 cup all-purpose flour*	5	142
1 cup cake flour	4	113
1 cup whole-wheat flour	5½	156
Sugar		
1 cup granulated (white) sugar	7	198
1 cup packed brown sugar (light or dark)	7	198
1 cup confectioners' sugar	4	113
Cocoa Powder		
1 cup cocoa powder	3	85
Butter†		
4 tablespoons (½ stick or ¼ cup)	2	57
8 tablespoons (1 stick or ½ cup)	4	113
16 tablespoons (2 sticks or 1 cup)	8	227

* U.S. all-purpose flour, the most frequently used flour in this book, does not contain leaveners, as some European flours do. These leavened flours are called self-rising or self-raising. If you are using self-rising flour, take this into consideration before adding leaveners to a recipe.

† In the United States, butter is sold both salted and unsalted. We generally recommend unsalted butter. If you are using salted butter, take this into consideration before adding salt to a recipe.

Oven Temperatures

FAHRENHEIT	CELSIUS	GAS MARK
225	105	¼
250	120	½
275	135	1
300	150	2
325	165	3
350	180	4
375	190	5
400	200	6
425	220	7
450	230	8
475	245	9

Converting Temperatures from an Instant-Read Thermometer

We include doneness temperatures in many of the recipes in this book. We recommend an instant-read thermometer for the job. Refer to the table above to convert Fahrenheit degrees to Celsius. Or, for temperatures not represented in the chart, use this simple formula:

Subtract 32 degrees from the Fahrenheit reading, then divide the result by 1.8 to find the Celsius reading.

Example:
"Roast chicken until thighs register 175 degrees."
To convert:
$$175°F - 32 = 143°$$
$$143° \div 1.8 = 79.44°C, \text{ rounded down to } 79°C$$

Index

Note: Page references in *italics* indicate photographs.